Korrika

Books in the Basque Series

TERESA DEL VALLE

Korrika

Basque Ritual for Ethnic Identity

TRANSLATED BY LINDA WHITE

University of Nevada Press   Reno   Las Vegas   London

Basque Series
Editor: William A. Douglass
A list of books in the series
follows the index.

University of Nevada Press
Reno, Nevada 89557 USA
Copyright © 1994 by the
University of Nevada Press
All rights reserved
Cover design by Kristina E. Kachele
Cover art by Begoña del Valle
Printed in the United States of America

The paper used in this book meets the
requirements of American National
Standard for Information Sciences—
Permanence of Paper for Printed Library
Materials, ANSI Z39.48-1984. Binding
materials were selected for strength and
durability.

9 8 7 6 5 4 3 2 1

This book was published with the
support of The Program for Cultural
Cooperation Between Spain's Ministry
of Culture and United States'
Universities.

Library of Congress
Cataloging-in-Publication Data
Valle, Teresa del.
  [Korrika. English]
  Korrika : Basque ritual for ethnic
identity / Teresa del Valle : translated by
Linda White.
      p.   cm. — (Basque series)
  Includes bibliographical references
and index.
    ISBN 0-87417-215-2 (alk. paper)
  1. Basques—Rites and ceremonies.
2. Basques—Games.   3. Basques—
Ethnic identity.   4. Relay racing—
Spain—País Vasco.   5. Relay racing—
France—Pays Basque.   6. Games—
Spain—País Vasco—Symbolic aspects.
7. Games—France—Pays Basque—
Symbolic aspects.   I. Title.   II. Series.
GN549.B3V3413   1993
796.42'7'09466—dc20   93-19034
                                         CIP

In memory of Begoña Landaburu, proof of the power of action

Contents

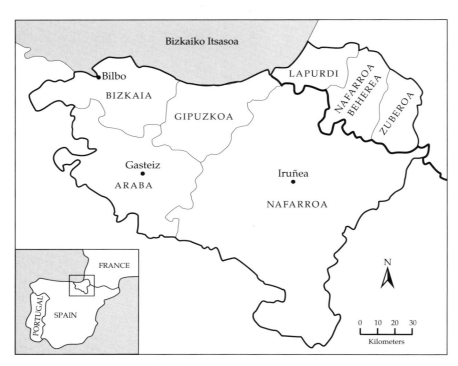

Euskalerria (The Basque Country)

Preface

My interest in Korrika was born during its first celebration in 1980. As I followed its development through the media, from its departure from the University of Oñati on November 29 amidst the ringing of the bells to its end in Bilbo, where I ran the last kilometer, and the final fiesta in the Feria de Muestras, my initial interest and curiosity were transformed into intellectual challenge. I became aware of the relevance of the event and was convinced that its impact would transcend the week dedicated to the race. Later, when I began to relate Korrika to Basque ethnicity, it was transformed for me into a theme of anthropological interest, and my study began.

Evidence of interest in the theme was made clear in the response to the paper I presented entitled "Korrika: una acción simbólica vasca" during the Segundos Cursos de Verano.[1] The more general interest it might arouse outside the academic environment was demonstrated during Korrika 3 when its organizers asked me to give my view of the event and later published it in the newspaper *Egin* (December 9, 1983, p. 17). Nevertheless, I was aware from the beginning of the possible interpretations the work could give rise to depending on different political positions, an aspect that had been made clear during the celebration of Korrika 2, as I will show. From that I deduced the anthropological value of the study, the widespread interest, and the advantage of the proximity of the sources and the event itself, without underestimating the need to establish distance as a person interested in the goals and objectives of Korrika. Thus I continued a systematic study of Korrika, participating directly in the race from the third running and broadening the study to a team effort for the fourth (see Methodology).

The study was first published in Spanish under the title *Korrika. Rituales de la lengua en el espacio*. Some changes have been made for the English edition. A much more extensive introduction has been provided, and a section on methodology that was previously in an appendix has been added. Maps have been added, and changes have been made in the narrative for the purpose of clarifying the theme, thus incorporating suggestions made by anonymous readers and adding the data gathered during the sixth and seventh Korrikas, since the Spanish version ended with the fifth Korrika.

With regard to Basque names, whether of people or places, I have followed modern spellings. The Appendix lists Basque place-names and their Spanish equivalents, and the Glossary defines Basque terms and provides information on some of the people mentioned in the text. I have used Euskara terms in the text because they are used even when a speaker is speaking in Spanish, evidence of loanwords that occur in languages that are in contact.

Beyond Korrika

This book and the study it represents contribute to ethnography in eight distinct and important ways.

1. The study of a ritual or other event that is realized through continuous movement requires differentiated methodological strategies. What we did during the Korrikas can serve in studies of other events in motion—the carrying of the Olympic torch, or a bicycle race (the circuit around Spain, the Giro de Italia, the Tour de France, to cite the most relevant European races that usually take place in June and July)—as well as secular rituals that involve mobilization. In the case of Korrika, of course, there is movement from beginning to end.

2. In spite of the fact that the unifying element of the study of Korrika was the ritual, my real objectives were to understand the motivations behind its organization, to see the impact of the people's participation, and to establish the relationship between the race and the local populations, always from a symbiotic focus. Taking an event that transcends geographic, political, economic, and linguistic divisions is relevant to our ability to break away from the limiting effects such divisions usually have in such a way that elements of continuity and contrast can be seen, elements that may or may not correspond to those that have been established a priori. This is valid in cases where borders exist that are not in harmony with the divisions assumed by the populations. At the current time the theme of borders in Europe demands innovative studies. Europe can be viewed as a laboratory where the dividing lines that have been emerging and changing down through the centuries seem to be undergoing a process of accelerated evolution. The study of different levels of meaning makes necessary historical contextualizations that allow the emergence of a variety of meanings they may have for the different populations. In this sense, terms such as *the united market* and *a Europe of twelve,* to cite two, derive from political constructions that sometimes overlap and at other times conceal very disparate realities, and they can act as a barrier to understanding. Peter Sahlins's book *Boundaries: The Making of France and Spain in the Pyrenees* (1989) describes the construction of

the border between Spain and France since the seventeenth century and the effect that has had on the Catalan people situated in a valley divided by that frontier. Although I became aware of that work after the Spanish version of this book had already been published, I call the reader's attention to possible comparisons with the subject matter of chapter 3.

3. The relationship between the process of ethnicity and nationalism is a current theme. The emergence of old and new social causes is of concern to European historians, students of literature, anthropologists, and sociologists. Some interpret what they call the "return to a tribal existence" in a regressive way (Dahrendorf 1991:3–4). In his historical analysis, Gabriel Jackson considers nationalism to be "the strongest political sentiment in Europe since 1789" (1991:4–5). Regis Debray links the emergence of nationalism to instinct and innate qualities (1991:4–5); Ernest Gellner sees the different nationalisms as forms of self-identification for industrial society (1991:7); and Eric Hobsbawm offers four reasons to explain the broad support that separatist movements receive. In the midst of the veil of concern that seems to surround modern nationalism, Josep Llobera, who is familiar with the Catalan situation, stands firm in the face of the variety and complexity presented by the various nationalisms (1991:6). In the light of these varied contributions, my interpretation of Korrika is located within the creative aspects of the processes of identity. Korrika is a clear example of how social and cultural processes are created and re-created, within a given historical period and without having to resort to biological or immanentist explanations.

4. One of the concerns I have maintained throughout this book, and which may be useful in the study of other rituals, is that of delving into the reasons why some elements in a ritual are selected and others are not. In addition to stopping and letting oneself be captured by the power of the ritual, by strategies of communication, and by its transforming force, one must delve into the information being collected in order to understand the cultural mechanisms that are at work, even though at times the explanation issues from the investigator. I would dare to say that at those times the nearness of the sources and the degree of identification can act as detectors since one must have sufficient knowledge to evaluate what has been selected on the basis of other possible choices. In my concluding chapter I establish some of the reasons that appear to be functioning in Korrika.

5. The investigation of Korrika contributes to the study of the creation of traditions with a modern case in the manner suggested by Hobsbawm, through the detailed study of how a tradition has been created in a period of eleven years (1980–91). The weight of tradition and the ways in which it is incorporated into the personal experience of the ritual all appear in Korrika.

One can follow the genesis of traditions in Korrika to understand how an event so recent can refer to its own short history in order to institutionalize moments, symbols, and actions.

6. This book contributes to the study of secular rituals, particularly political rituals. Korrika is a case that is both broad and specific at the same time, a case in which many of the aspects treated by other authors can be viewed in microcosm: the power of symbols, the recurrence of symbols in a united effort and a fight for power, the elaboration of tradition, or the power of the alteration of ordinary time and space. The value and strength of metaphor appear full force in Korrika, as does the social dimension proposed by James W. Fernandez. Korrika can be seen as a metaphor of Basque unity, and it contains metaphorical nuclei associated with territory and movement that are in turn the source of an identifying dynamic of what is Basque for people and groups.

7. This book contributes to the debate about the difficulties of explaining a phenomenon when the actors and the researcher can present a variety of interpretations for the same action. The position defended here is that including the richly different perceptions of people who participate in the action is more important than reaching a single interpretation, an only truth. Also, I emphasize repeatedly that the consideration of the context within which the action takes place is central to the analysis.

8. Finally, the analysis of Korrika presented in these pages demonstrates the interrelationship between the symbolic and the social, historical, and political context, especially when phenomena are studied in industrialized societies.

Methodology

This book has as its point of departure an investigation entitled "Identidad étnica y procesos migratorios en Euskadi," which analyzed Basque ethnicity at three levels: historical, interactional, and symbolic.[1] The study of Korrika began in the back room of symbolic actions, where it appeared as a secular ritual in which the interactional was contextualized in the historical, political, and linguistic moment in which it emerged and developed. From the methodological approach, placing this analysis on a symbolic level allows us to perceive, interpret, and give meaning to ethnic relationships and demonstrations through a series of ritual actions. By focusing on interactions both of individuals and groups and within groups, I propose to analyze aspects of the process of elaboration of identity. By setting it within the context of the historical moment, I hope to establish an interpretive symbiosis through which questions will be generated in both directions that increase the richness of the analysis. Moreover, given that the research described here has to do with different conceptions and manifestations of Basque nationalism, creating such a symbiosis constitutes a personal imperative, not just an option.[2]

I collected graphic material from the first and second Korrikas and interviewed the main organizers, carriers of the testigo, runners, and local organizers. The most intensive research was carried out during the third and fourth Korrikas, and complementary research was carried out during the fifth. I participated in the running of the third from Donostia to Larrabetzu—three days and nights—and later in the arrival in Bilbo and in the final party in the Feria de Muestras. At the time of the fourth running I organized a team whose purpose was to collect data.[3] The methodologies for gathering data and analyzing it were designed by myself and two other members of the study team. Complementary data gathered during the sixth and seventh Korrikas have been introduced in this English edition.

Researching an event with mobile characteristics that takes place in a limited time requires a specific methodology because it is necessary to capture the intensity of the moment, both with regard to the action itself and in relation to the interpretations offered by the organizers and participants. This transitory quality must differentiate itself from narrative and afterthought, for the latter may contain more general evaluations on the development of the event that can be discordant with first impressions. This is important in a ritual where politics plays either a direct or an indirect role.

The exact date of the Korrika is usually known only a few months beforehand. The dates for the fourth running were initially set for December 1984, but they were changed shortly afterward. The fifth running depended on the celebration of the anticipated general elections, and when these were held in November Korrika was forced to move to April because the organizers had to make sure that it did not coincide with any other important cultural or linguistic event that would detract from its leading role. The route is not fixed until the last minute, and thus everything is subject to change during the race.

At all times the focus of my study has been the celebration of Korrika: the planning and preparation done by the organizing committee, the celebration of the precampaign, and the race itself. The study team's participation in Korrika 4 was made possible by the organizing committee, which gave us permission to follow the race with the organizers. The team also participated in various moments of the precampaign such as Korrika's presentation to the press. The limits of the geographical territory for the intensive participation-observation were based on the route established for each Korrika, and this had to be kept in mind for the definition and placement of observation and data-collecting units.

In order to be able to visualize the total race, two perspectives had to be kept in mind: the general and the specific. The general view was obtained from participation in the race itself—that is, from the experience of following it step by step as the members of the organizing body do. Thus the geographic and ecological differences in the route were captured, as well as the degrees of people's participation, support, and rejection, and all this served to delineate comparisons and contrasts. The general view is thus the view from within influenced by the vision of the organizers and by constant physical movement through very different localities. Capturing this transitory quality is key to studying an event of this type.

This general perspective was gathered by the mobile team, which included three persons who followed the race as part of the organizing body. As we followed the daily changes in the relays, one or two members of the team were always in the race. We ran at intervals. During the race we gathered data in field journals and by taking photographs, although this turned out to be secondary since the two photographers from the organizing body later put all their photographic material at our disposal.

Our specific perspective was acquired through living the race in the localities through which Korrika passed, with the goal of capturing the context in which the action within each community developed through the personal experiences of the actors (the *korrikalariak,* or runners in general, and the carriers of the *testigo*), the active spectators, and the organizers. To this end, the "fixed team," composed of nineteen people, was organized, and we carefully selected communities in which to carry out observations and hold interviews before and after the passing of Korrika.

Criteria for the Selection of Communities

In order for the different members of the team to gather data as the Korrika passed through, we had to consider how the selected populations would contribute examples of the variety that exists in Euskalerria with regard to degrees of linguistic diversity, the continuum between the rural and the urban, population densities, the presence or absence of a nationalist consciousness, and a population mix of the autochthonous and the emigrant. The impact of Korrika on each variable was measured. Thus in Hegoalde (the four territories of the southern Basque Country) eighteen communities were selected (see map 1), and in the larger ones observations were made in different neighborhoods as explained below.

GIPUZKOA: HERNANI, RENTERIA, AND ORDIZIA
Hernani presents the characteristics of an urban zone in which a strong development of nationalist consciousness is evident along with the advance of modernization. Different neighborhoods show apparently contradictory attitudes. The activity of cultural groups whose social ideologies have been evolving is important. Rentería offers a variation that is the result of strong, rapid migratory currents in its population. In comparison with Hernani, a major radicalization of its nationalist movement is evident, and the contradictions that appear in other areas of Gipuzkoa in a more scattered form become clear. Ordizia represents the center of social and political life for the towns in the area of Goiherri. It played a central political role during Franco's regime.

NAFARROA: ISABA, ETXARRI-ARANAZ, IRUÑEA, AND TUTERA
Nafarroa shows a wide range of linguistic and economic differences and variations in population density. Thus Isaba was chosen for the northwest zone, and Etxarri-Aranaz and Iruñea were selected for the middle zone (and because the latter is the capital). Tutera was chosen to represent Erribera.

ARABA: ZALDUONDO, AGURAIN, KANPEZU, AND GASTEIZ

Zalduondo and Agurain were chosen because they are going through a nationalist phase, and a strong differentiation is emerging between inside and outside. Zalduondo has given rise to a cultural movement, significant in a population of 136 inhabitants (Apaolaza 1985–87:157), that is expressed through a tendency to reaffirm Basque roots. Agurain plays a central role with regard to the importance of Euskara in the process of ethnic reaffirmation, for it has the only ikastola in the area that children from several surrounding towns attend. Kanpezu represents the classic Araban town, having less contact with the more generally Basque-speaking zones and an isolated dynamic of its own. Gasteiz was chosen because it is a capital city and because it is the seat of the Basque government.

BIZKAIA: SANTURTZI, PORTUGALETE, BILBO (NEIGHBORHOODS OF DEUSTO AND THE OLD QUARTER), AND ONDARRU

In general, areas were classified according to indices of emigration, economic activity, population density, and language. As in other areas, especially Gipuzkoa, the existence of strong contradictions within the same community was kept in mind.

Santurtzi presents characteristics similar in some aspects to those of Rentería, such as the increase in nationalist sentiment and the growing radicalization of certain sectors, especially among the younger population. Portugalete shares some characteristics with Santurtzi, but it differs in showing less radicalization.

In Bilbo the two selected neighborhoods are notably different. A deeply rooted population either because of generations of residence there or long-time business associations exists in the Old Quarter. It is the meeting place and point of reference for other sectors of the city that go there for commercial activity (shops and the market), relaxation (restaurants and bars), festivals (the principal fiestas of the city center in this location), and politics (demonstrations end in Arenal, and it is a place with a tradition of active confrontations with the police). Moreover, there are streets that constitute significant gathering places for both leftist political groups and for others identified with drugs and the drug culture.

Deusto, on the contrary, has changed enormously in the last few years since it went from being a rural area on the periphery of the city to a center of strong commercial activity with a youthful student population (some colleges of the public university and the private Jesuit university are located there). Deusto features many bars and pubs that attract people mainly on the weekends. Along with this recent activity Deusto continues to preserve its festive traditions, and within these there have been moments of strong political expression.

Ondarru represents a population that preserves Euskara, although there has been a lot of immigration. It is an important business and fishing center, and in the last few years movements for social change related to the problems of the fishing industry have centered there.

IPARRALDE

In Iparralde specific data were gathered in Atharratze, where the fourth Korrika began, and in Bayonne and Hendaye as well, since they were principal urban nuclei along the route.

A team seminar was held to organize and orient the mobile team so that the participants would know how their work fit into the larger picture. Once the data gathering was finished, another seminar was held in which the methodology was evaluated and personal impressions of the experience were shared by each member of the fixed teams. These experiences in turn constituted additional data that were incorporated into the data set. Gathering the data was an intense experience. In spite of the many changes of locale and the fact that at many times the study was done literally "on the run," it was also a positive experience.

In a study of this type it is important to keep in mind the type of material that is produced and how it is reflected in the press. One must be familiar with the different leanings of the newspapers, because a notice about Korrika that comes out on the first page of a newspaper like *Egin* may occupy a peripheral page in *Diario Vasco*. Without this sort of knowledge it would be difficult to interpret these variations.

The people of the central office of Alfabetatze Euskalduntze Koordinakundea (AEK) in Bilbo put all their archives at our disposal and let us make photocopies, and this was very useful in analyzing press coverage of the race. Likewise AEK made available to us copies of the Korrika posters, stickers, insignias, and other publicity material. "Radio popular" in Donostia gave us copies of programs that were broadcast during Korrika's precampaign. Moreover, additional interviews were carried out with the organizers of Korrika and with people knowledgeable about the linguistic situation of Euskara.

In each of the selected locations, members of the fixed team had a dual task to perform. The atmosphere before, during, and after the passing of Korrika was recorded in field journals. During this time the team members also interviewed people from the organizing body, the carriers of the testigo, people opposed to Korrika, and famous individuals, and those interviews contributed data from an ETIC-EMIC perspective.

The data from Iparralde were the responsibility of the mobile team, as was the gathering of intensive data in Atharratze, where the fourth Korrika began. The mobile team members continued their observations all along the route of the race.

In this way two perspectives on Korrika were gathered through the work of the two teams: a general perspective and a specific one, as well as the different nuances contained in the concept of inside-outside or us-them.

I analyzed the data during my stay at the Basque Studies Program at the University of Nevada, Reno (1985–86), where I consulted magazines, newspapers, and the bibliographic material necessary for completing the analysis and for documenting the linguistic, political, and cultural context within which Korrika emerged and developed.

Acknowledgments

First of all, I thank Txemi Apaolaza and Begoña Aretxaga, my fellow team members. The people of AEK supported my work and allowed me to follow part of the race during the third running and allowed the other two members of the team to follow in the fourth. Likewise, I thank AEK for the access I have had to all their archival material.

More directly, my thanks go to those who participated in the organization and observation of the third and fourth Korrikas. With regard to the latter, I thank Mari Carmen Diez and Carmen Larrañaga, with whom I shared the emotions and vicissitudes of the race. My thanks to Carmen Pérez, who coordinated one phase of data gathering, as well as to all the people who participated in that phase. My thanks to the editorial staff of the newspaper *Egin* for putting their photographic archive at my disposal, and especially to photographers Mikel Alonso and Roberto Zarraonaindia. Thanks to Enrique Ibabe and Joxe Egiluz for their support from the moment they learned of my interest in studying Korrika. Thanks to the collective Bai Euskarari for the use of their archive. Thanks to Enrique Cifuentes for drawing the maps. Isabel Espeja, from Donostia on, was receiving and passing indecipherable notes gathered "on the run," a task she carried out punctually from day to day during Korrika 4.

I owe the Sanfermin experiences reflected in the writing to Isabel Ciriza, Txus Elizondo, Txema Esparza, Paco López, Lolinche Rojo, and Vicente Vitoria.

My thanks also go to the Basque Studies Program at the University of Nevada, Reno, which offered me the opportunity to spend a year as a visiting scholar. Particular thanks go to anthropologist William A. Douglass, coordinator of the program and a specialist in Basque studies. With him, I critiqued the different chapters step by step, and his suggestions and criticisms have been invaluable. At the beginning of the creation of the manuscript the comments of Baleren Bakaikoa were valuable to me. I received support from other members of the program as well who demonstrated interest in my work.

In Reno the Department of Anthropology provided me with an office where I was able to organize my voluminous data and write while contemplating the seasons of the Reno countryside. The work atmosphere provided by the professors, students, and staff made my stay productive and pleasant. With Carter G. Bentley I discussed different parts of my work, and his suggestions served me well in solving theoretical problems.

During my stay at the Department of Anthropology at Princeton University in February 1986 I enjoyed the hospitality of anthropologists James W. Fernandez and Renate Lellep Fernandez, and I received intellectual reinforcement from them as well. I presented a part of the work at a seminar in that department, and the questions and answers that resulted served as a stimulus for me.

Carmelo Urza and Marian Zarraonaindia also read parts of the manuscript with a critical eye. The latter was a great help in the revision and translation of texts from Euskara. At other times I received help from Jone Aldave. I thank Javier Lezana for his detailed reading of the final manuscript and his observations. The collection of data was made possible by a grant from the Comisión Asesora of the Ministerio de Educación y Ciencia.

I am also grateful for the suggestions of the anonymous readers who read the manuscript, and I hope they see many of their suggestions incorporated here, as well as those of my editors, Melinda Conner and Sara Vélez Mallea. Finally, a direct acknowledgment of my translator, Linda White.

Introduction

The Power and Richness of Ritual

Korrika already has its own brief history. Technically Korrika is a colossal footrace run in relays of 1 kilometer in which thousands of runners, men and women of all ages, pass through the seven Basque territories carrying a symbol identified as the *testigo*, or "witness." The principal objective of the race is to generate popular support for Euskara, the Basque language. Along a route of more than 2,080 kilometers, economic contributions are collected and mass support is offered to the effort to reeducate the populace in Euskara. The Alfabetatze Euskalduntze Koordinakundea (AEK; Coordination of Education and Literacy in the Basque Language), a popular organization that has dedicated more than twenty years to promulgating Euskara, is in charge of the race.

The protagonist of Korrika is the testigo, a hollow wooden cylinder carved by Basque sculptor Remigio Mendiburu that symbolizes Euskara. The message carried inside the testigo is read at the beginning and end of each Korrika. The race is not competitive. Rather, the principal interest lies in passing the testigo from hand to hand until it arrives at the finish line.

Prior to beginning my study of Korrika I did a great deal of reading, including works by Victor Turner, Clifford Geertz, and James W. Fernandez. However, I did not establish my study within the theoretical limits of rituals; rather, I saw Korrika as a symbolic act loaded with cultural and political contexts that could illuminate my larger study of the formation and development of ethnic identities, specifically the Basque identity. In this sense, the works of Fredrik Barth, Anthony Cohen, and Gregory Bateson were inspiring.

In this analysis, different readings sometimes illuminated and sometimes framed the ethnographic richness of Korrika. Two works stand out: *The Invention of Tradition*, by Eric Hobsbawm (1986), unleashed my interest in the elaboration of tradition in Korrika. Reading *La Terra in Piazza*, by Alan Dundes and Alessandro Falassi, inspired me to maintain the link between the global event and the detailed analysis of its components; and it guided me in my reflections on the total metaphor of the Korrika. In focusing on the dual significance of the border, the personal contributions of W. A. Douglass from his studies of the frontier population of Etxalar were stimulating and elucidating.

It was during my experience of Korrika as both participant and investigator that I began identifying characteristics that, by their intrinsic power, clamored for my attention. Its evocative capacity, the recurrence of traditional and ancestral elements, its ties with deep levels of feeling, and its symbolic richness led me to consider the Korrika as an act with characteristics similar to those described in monographs on ritual. Nevertheless, I did not at first consider it necessary to outline the theoretical aspects of ritual because it seemed to me that the reader would be deprived of the possibility of discovering these through personal interpretation. Thus Ubaldo Martínez Veiga captured the theoretical contributions in the prologue of the Spanish edition of this book (1988:9). I found that understanding in one of the anonymous readers who evaluated the manuscript for publication, and in James W. Fernandez's commentaries on parts of the text during a doctoral course on metaphor that he taught at the University of the Basque Country in 1990.

Upon confirming their interpretations, I felt that the manuscript as it was had something of the power that I had captured through living the Korrika. It gave rise to the discovery of what I considered to be fundamentals of ritual, even though those theoretical fundamentals were not specified. Korrika is itself both theory and praxis. Other readers, however, have suggested that I place more emphasis on the theoretical aspects of my study and its contribution to the discipline of anthropology by including general information on Euskalerria at the beginning of the study to help readers who are not familiar with its geographic, political, and cultural complexity.

Frankly, it has been difficult to respond to these editorial suggestions— not because of the requests themselves but because they represent a type of subtle imposition that deserves comment. Originally, when anthropology surfaced at a distance from what was being studied and the anthropologists edited their investigations with the public in mind, this conflict did not appear. Verification was left for later, in the rather improbable case that a member of the researched population would read the already published study. The work was judged according to academically rigorous criteria that were configured in turn by a system of thought generated in distant workings. In the last few decades studies have been carried out by investigators who live within the same culture being studied, and questions have arisen regarding the objectivity of these studies. Can an investigator who is part of a culture look at that culture objectively? How objectivity is worked out and measured is a methodological theme that has yet to be developed. In the act of writing, the author is addressing a public. If he or she addresses the public of the studied culture itself, the form of writing will be a vehicle of communication about that culture, and it is important to keep that in mind as an ethnographic reference. Some things will be more or less explicit. Some examples will be selected because they have a greater chance of establishing a bond with the reader. Selection in writing, its style, and its structure are a communicative expression of the culture. The academic standard invoked to measure objectivity-subjectivity is in turn tied to cultural forms. I believe that it is important to keep in mind that Anglo-Saxon forms of scientific writing—the criteria of how a book should be structured, of what we assume the reader knows from the beginning—are imposed indiscriminately, without trying to separate the cultural formulas from what is applicable to a broader audience. In the cases of anthropology and literature, insisting on uniform structures can limit or obscure cultural analyses that might result through other forms of narration.

The effort to combine objectivity and subjectivity—being faithful to my concept of Korrika not only in my interpretation but also in my communication of it, and needing to keep in mind the American public's lack of knowledge with regard to Euskalerria's linguistic, economic, cultural, historical, and geographic realities—has been difficult. My view is that the challenge generated by the encounter with the unknown as a point of departure would be beneficial for the American public. Europeans make this effort to approach the unknown from other contexts when something written arrives from North American culture, resulting in stimulation and the generation of debate. I want to point out that the subject matter of this book is the analysis of a ritual, and the complex contextualization that it requires makes evident the need to read other studies in order to comprehend a situation of this depth and difficulty.[1] When one writes about an area where local anthropological production already exists, the study is considered incomplete if references to those works are not incorporated. This information should always be included.[2] However, because of the exigencies of publication, I have sought an intermediate formula. This introduction includes general knowledge for those who wish to have it before reading the study and explains my position and specifies my reasons for writing about the Korrika as I have done. Nevertheless, I still think it is better for the reader to move on at this point to the first chapter. If you are still curious, you may continue with this introduction after finishing the narrative.

General Information about Euskalerria

Situated on both sides of the western Pyrenees and administratively divided between France and Spain, Euskalerria is a nation without a state (see map 2). It has a total surface area of 20,750 square kilometers, and its

population stood at about three million in 1986. The western Pyrenees and
a mountain chain of lesser altitude that runs inland 50 kilometers from the
coast of the Gulf of Bizkaia divide the country from east to west into two
different parts. In the north, agriculture is well adapted to the moderate
climate and the humidity caused by the Atlantic Ocean. To the south, the
territories of Araba and Nafarroa experience a Mediterranean climate on the
banks of the Ebro River, and these zones have witnessed accelerated urban
and industrial development since the end of the 1950s.

At least since the end of the Middle Ages, Euskalerria has not developed
a joint political entity, and there exist seven territories known as "historical
territories." Three of these—Lapurdi, Nafarroa Beherea, and Zuberoa—belong to France, and they lost their individual political institutions during the
French Revolution. Today they lie within France's Department of the Atlantic Pyrenees and represent a small part of Euskalerria, both in territory and
in population (less than 15 percent of its territory and fewer than 250,000
inhabitants). The four historical territories within Spain are Araba, Bizkaia,
Gipuzkoa, and Nafarroa, and they are in turn divided into two autonomous
communities as outlined in the Spanish Constitution of 1978. The first three
are grouped together and constitute 35 percent of the territory and 75 percent of the population of Euskalerria. Nafarroa, with more than 500,000
inhabitants and 50 percent of Basque territory, has maintained at least some
political autonomy since its conquest by the king of Castille and subsequent
partitioning with France at the beginning of the sixteenth century.[3]

The continuous struggle between the absolutist and liberal factions during most of the nineteenth century had its influence on Euskadi. The de-
fenders of the Ancien Régime had strong popular support that stemmed
from the liberals' threat to traditional Basque autonomy, an autonomy contained in the ancient laws known as *fueros* and in the political institutions
themselves. After two civil wars (1832–39 and 1872–76) the urban bourgeoisie
concentrated in the coastal towns of Bilbo (Bizkaia) and Donostia (Gipuzkoa)
entered a period of industrial development based on the benefits derived
from the rich iron mines of Bizkaia. At the end of the nineteenth century
and during the first decades of the twentieth there was a consolidation of
this process of industrialization through the growth of powerful institutions
that were tightly linked to industrial interests and controlled by the families
of the Bilbo oligarchy (Arregui 1989:1–2).

Industrialization led to accelerated urban growth through immigration
from rural areas both within and outside Euskadi. The social change caused
by industrialization in Basque culture and the narrow limits that centraliza-
tion left to local political power influenced, among other things, the development of an acknowledged nationalistic consciousness. From the beginning

of the twentieth century Basque political life has been defined by a strong nationalist movement that has resisted the tendencies of socialist, liberal, and conservative (principally Carlist) parties.

Franco's victory in the Spanish Civil War (1936–39) substantially modi-fied the political panorama, but after the hard years of the 1940s Euskadi experienced another period of rapid growth with concomitant important social changes. Between 1950 and 1975 the population of Euskadi grew by almost 80 percent (as contrasted with the 58 percent growth during the fifty years before that), due principally to the immigration of almost half a million persons from different areas in Spain (ibid.:2–3).

This accelerated growth affected both the social structure and cultural pat-terns. Among other effects it resulted in the weakening of Euskara (in the coastal areas the Basque-speaking population fell from 90 percent in the middle of the nineteenth century to 35 percent in the 1980s), the expan-sion of modernization, and the birth of radical nationalism. The decade from 1975 to 1985 was dominated by instability in an economy traditionally based on heavy industry and mechanical production. The combination of acceler-ated growth and acute unemployment (unemployment affected 22 percent of the active population in 1985 and 50 percent of the active population under the age of twenty-five), a very young population (Euskadi has one of the youngest populations in the European Community), social and political radicalism stemming from Euskalerria's specific problems, and an uncertain institutional setting are some of the characteristics of modern Basque society.

In spite of the fact that the administrative capital and seat of the Basque government is Gasteiz (200,000 inhabitants), the economic and social cen-ter is Bilbo, the capital of Bizkaia. The Bilbo metropolitan area comprises around 1 million inhabitants, or 38 percent of the total population of Euskadi. The second center is Donostia, capital of Gipuzkoa with a population of some 200,000, or 12 percent of the population of Gipuzkoa. There also exists a nucleus of urban centers with 10,000–50,000 inhabitants located within a perimeter of 4,000 square kilometers outside the capital cities, and this nucleus has generated a mixture of modern and traditional ways of life that intermix within today's Basque society (Ibid.:3–4).

Structure, Action, and Meaning

The structure of this book is closely related to its subject matter. I made a conscious decision to begin with the action so that the reader could enter Korrika as a participant and experience, kilometer by kilometer, what the passage of a group with the testigo is like, while contemplating the variety of the countryside and the contrasts between plains and mountains, between villages lost among the mountains and the sprawling, crowded cities. At certain moments the reader is invited to take up the testigo and witness its passing from hand to hand, from village to village, with no thought to age, social class, or whether meters or kilometers have been run. The power of action can ignite an interest in or a curiosity about the motivation of the protagonists in the ritual, and thus the reader will progressively become a part of the geographic space and historical time of the culture that creates and re-creates Korrika. Instead of creating a setting for the reader where geographical, historical, and political information appears as it does in a traditional monograph, information is presented as Korrika unfolds. Keep in mind that any person may incorporate himself or herself into Korrika and participate, even though he or she knows nothing of the motive behind it. Those who spend time in the event begin to grasp the reasons for participating as they see symbols, slogans, and groups communicating with placards. For that reason it is not important if the reader does not know at the beginning what or where or why something happens. I am more interested in letting the event provoke curiosity and, perhaps, surprise. Let it incite commentary or even confusion, and let the reader formulate questions. Let him or her be surprised by the existence of a ritual that sets a varied population in motion.

The longitudinal and circular structures of the ritual are reflected in the structure of this narrative, and different rhythms appear through different grammatical models and the use of vital words, much as it happens in Korrika: the race accelerates at times and slows when night falls and the crowds from the cities or villages most committed to Korrika's cause dissipate. Such is the development and expansion of Euskara. The geographic, ecological, economic, and linguistic variety to which I allude in this introduction are described in detail in chapter 4, and I will also emphasize how unity arises through the force and power of ritual. The reader may be surprised and at times disturbed by the inclusion of texts in Basque and in Spanish. They have ethnographic meaning because they demonstrate several things, especially when the reader reflects on the context in which they appear. Although Korrika is a symbol of Euskara, there are persons and groups who support the presence and development of Euskara while expressing themselves in Spanish. It so happens that in Spanish-speaking populations minority groups fighting for Euskara gain courage because it is spoken in the street. This is most evident when Korrika crosses the territories of Nafarroa and Araba, where Euskara has disappeared in many places. Within the dynamics of Korrika, there is a place for these different versions of the importance of the language as a distinguishing element, and also for emphasizing the integrating power of ritual. Likewise, the order of information and the extensiveness with which some themes are treated are not by chance. A E K organizes Korrika and thus is presented and discussed before Helduen Alfabetatzen eta Berreuskalduntzen Erakunde (H A B E) enters the picture. According to the interpretation of the organizers and a good portion of the people who participate and support Korrika, H A B E is a usurper of A E K's protagonistic role as a popular organ.

From the methodological point of view, the presentation of the theme is a clear example of the relationship between the general and the specific, and especially of the importance of context. Korrika is tiring, and the text emphasizes this when it deals with the expansion or decline of Euskara in relation to political and historical events, not at the beginning but after the reader has taken the testigo. If one speaks of the regression of languages, the reasons why Euskara has been disappearing down through the centuries stand out, and, leaving the time frame of the ritual, we enter historical time, the game itself being a theoretical affirmation of one of the most powerful mechanisms of Korrika: atemporality. I do not start with a detailed description of geography that would set the reader to thinking of Euskalerria as a unity; that would prevent the gradual accumulation of a sense of the ritual. Instead the information appears at various moments, as it happens in chapter 4 when I wish to reflect on what Korrika's purpose is: to place us in a continuous global vision because in reality there is diversity and continuity-discontinuity. At that moment the reader will understand what occurred at the beginning of chapter 1 in the Atharratze plaza, but at the end of the study it will have a different power than it did at the beginning.

Keys to the Study

The interpretation of Korrika is full of details that are intertwined in various events with participation by people who are identified as if they were part of a historical narrative. In order to understand Korrika it is important to have some knowledge of the context in which it unfolds, and of the existence within that context of an important nucleus of people whose frame of reference is Euskara. Within this nucleus, the relationship with the language is active, militant, understood not as an archaic heritage but as a pertinent fact that must develop and be transmitted to others. The nucleus possesses some of the characteristics that Turner attributes to the ideological *communitas* (1988:137–57) and allows for the understanding of the different levels it plays within the binomial: inside-outside.

This nucleus is not a closed circle, it is more; it can be entered—independently of other factors—through the language by using it or learning it. For those who do not know Euskara, immersion in the process of learning through the *ikastola, euskaltegi,* or *barnategi*[4] is an efficient way of learning it. Informal methods of learning through immersion in groups of casual association, such as *cuadrillas* (groups of friends) and different organizations, form another route.

There enters into the identity of the nucleus a concept of that which is Basque that possesses specific characteristics: forms of relationship, concepts of what is festive, relative importance given to informal association, acceptance of certain symbols, generalized recognition of heroes, and valuation of specific qualities. On the other hand, the opposite—that is, that which would be contrary to the ideology of the nucleus—is itself delimited, and its definition and rejection reinforce the weight and dynamism of the nucleus, acting in turn as elements of social control.

This nucleus contains a series of references and establishes values that combine elements of the traditional Basque world with other elements present in modern industrialized society. The characters mentioned, the symbolic places, and the actions all form part of the cultural heritage, and their messages are easily grasped. However, by their very multivocality the symbols can give rise to many interpretations. The interpretations I have made here have a cultural foundation that in many cases supports a line of continuity toward the past. In other interpretations, that same past is introduced to revitalize a context that otherwise has no relationship with the one that gave rise to the creation of the symbol within a traditional framework. These are clear examples of the revitalizing power of ritual through appeal to different strategies.

Within the nucleus there are nuances that allow us to identify various sectors, for it is not a homogeneous group. One sector has its departure point in the experience and importance of the assumed language within the family milieu. This group's commitment to the external projection of Euskara is guided by the necessity of giving it social continuity beyond the domestic ambience. Thus, many of their activities run toward the support and development of schooling in Euskara in primary and secondary education. Their most direct action on behalf of the language is centered on the ikastolak and their slogans. Another broad sector comprises people who have learned Euskara outside the family, and many of this group's activities are oriented toward literacy and the broad politics of the language. Within the different sectors of the nucleus, interest in the language and its coupling with cultural elements can give rise to a common effort on behalf of Euskara without the need for the individuals of each sector to agree with regard to their other political and social positions. People of different political ideologies, but principally those identified with the so-called Basque cultural Left and with the *abertzale* Left,[5] can be included within the nationalist sector.

Centering myself in the analysis of Korrika with all its linguistic and political contexts, I argue that all the dynamics of the nucleus and many of the conflicts—some generated and some reflected—of the broader situation of Basque society appear in this event. The contradictions principally affect the language, the territory, and the existence of different cultural projects. Moreover, when the Korrika is analyzed diachronically (1980–91), the changes that have taken place can be appreciated, including a reduction in the number of people within the nucleus that identify with its objectives and participate actively in Korrika. I propose that those changes are related to the major differences that have been developing among the different sectors of the nucleus, and those major differences are related in turn to linguistic politics and to Basque politics in general.

Also, and this is the crucial point of this book, each time discontinuities and conflicts appear, an attempt is made to resolve some of them on a symbolic level through Korrika, by producing at different moments of the race and through different mechanisms a liminal situation and a realization of the metaphor of Basque unity, especially as far as the language, the territory, and the acceptance or rejection of a specific cultural project are concerned.

Part of the power of Korrika stems from the utilization of elements, symbols, and mechanisms solidly based in cultural tradition, although they are presented in a modern context appropriate to an industrialized society. Authors who falsely project a lack of ritual in industrialized societies, as David I. Kertzer (1988) says, base their statements on categories used to classify societies rather than on how societies really are. My knowledge of different metropolises on three continents—Europe, America, and Oceania—and what I have learned through studies of urban populations advocate the presence of ritual, and this ritual holds even more importance when the dimensions of time and space are more diversified. Moreover, following Turner's line of thinking, conflicts lead to the birth of rituals, but sometimes it is difficult for us to describe new elaborations of ritual or the forms rituals take. Many times the same conflict that reveals a secular, especially political, ritual obscures its own identification, and more so when the conflict occurs nearby in time and space. Kertzer explains how easy it is to discover a ritual in a distant place and how difficult it is to identify and study a ritual when it takes place nearby.

Korrika is a powerful example of a secular ritual in which the multivocality of the symbols and their evocative capacity (such as the power for revelation; Turner 1988:37, 52–53) have a metapolitical orientation in the final analysis.

Finally, bearing in mind that I belong to the culture being studied and am communicating an identification with the thematic material that in turn awakens diametrically opposed opinions, I ask the reader not to demand greater objectivity than that found in many anthropological monographs where the author belongs to the same religion he or she is describing or in studies of political or colonial situations carried out by anthropologists of the colonizing country. I ask, on the contrary, that the reader think critically about those studies of tribal societies carried out by people familiar only with the nuclear monogamous domestic unit or studies of peasant societies by people who live isolated in big city apartments and have seen domestic animals only in books or on television. It is true that some studies surprise us because their distance from the forest allows them to perceive what lies hidden to those under the trees. But there are also reflections that can arise only through profound interior closeness, the beat of the pulse, the familiarity from within. All these visions are necessary because they constitute different pieces of knowledge.

Organization of This Book

The first chapter introduces the action of Korrika and deals with the contradictions inherent in the situations through which it passes and in which Euskara is found. Thus are demonstrated the shrinking of the geographical boundaries of Euskara, the discontinuity in the generational transmission, and, on the other hand, Euskara's survival in spite of political oppression and its minority status. The internal divisions that separate the different nationalistic currents are revealed in the question of the leading role of teaching, preservation, and diffusion of Euskara as well as in the attitude they demonstrate toward the celebration of Korrika, a theme that is treated in chapter 2.

   In chapter 3 I describe how territorial boundaries in traditional Basque culture were established and ritualized, along with the associations that can be established with word and action. How the ritual is carried out in Korrika is the theme of chapter 4, and I follow in chapters 5 and 6 with the elements that allow the action to be carried out, a means of capturing the present, the assumption of the great variety of social causes that exist in Basque society, and the incorporation of groups considered peripheral to the system. It is in the comprehension of the dual dynamic of support in the past and its powerful invocation, and in the capture and integration of modern demonstrations and social causes, where Korrika attains the objective of presenting a singular concept of Basque society with strong support. For a period of time the metaphor of unity is realized, and this is the theme of chapter 7.

Presenting the results of my investigation in a meaningful and coherent form to a broad audience that includes people who have not had direct personal experience with the event is a difficult task. Combining the different dimensions and levels Korrika encompasses is even more complex, even for those who have followed it closely. In this study the thread that ties the framework of the narrative together is the running of Korrika. Just as the person carrying the testigo in the first kilometer initiates the fourth Korrika, so do we begin our story in the plaza of Atharratze on May 31, 1985, at 8:00 P.M.

In this way we will follow, or better, live the Korrika, traveling along 2,080 zigzagging kilometers through the seven territories that make up Euskalerria. Under the most significant themes and taking the territories as more general units of analysis, we will be recognizing places along the way, living events, identifying people, deciphering symbols, and letting ourselves be carried away by "the magic of Korrika."

Through the data collected from the seven Korrikas we will effect a chronological analysis of its evolution from 1980 to 1991—a limited period, yes, but a broad and complex period nevertheless—when it is placed within the context of the linguistic situation and political events beyond the specific act of the race. However, the principal focus will be on the different interpretations and levels of meaning that both the researcher-protagonist and the participants and spectators attribute to Korrika.

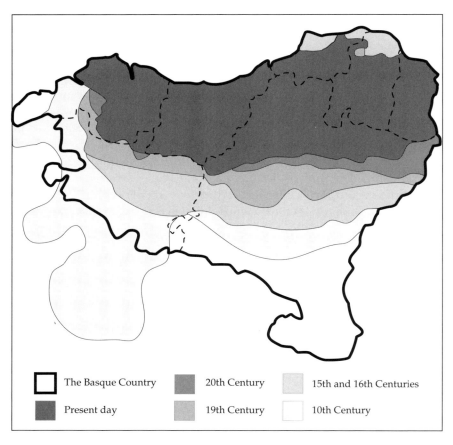

The Basque Country	20th Century	15th and 16th Centuries	
Present day	19th Century	10th Century	

Historical Development of Euskara

Chapter One

The Importance of Continuity

and Its Different Interpretations

The Past Becomes the Present in the Plaza

A sunny day in Euskalerria is considered a good omen and is interpreted as nature's own participation in a specific event. People comment that it is "about time nature is on our side." And that is what happened on the day the fourth Korrika began. All the elements of a fiesta were present in the small plaza of Atharratze:[1] the sun, music, and people of all ages. There was atmosphere.

The design of the plaza, with its empty central space and the porticoes that surround it, facilitated the interaction between the people who had arrived from the other side of the *muga* (border) to participate in the beginning of the race and those from different parts of Iparralde who were in some way linked to the people of Atharratze. The plaza was both an open and a closed space at the same time. The city hall, the businesses, and the dwellings were evidence of the different functions that the place serves in ordinary life and alluded to the centrality of its function in the town. In contrast, the yellow metal barricades indicated the transformation that had taken place in one part of the plaza; the tables where people signed up to run, the placards, and the musical instruments revealed a new temporary designation of the space. From the businesses, buyers and sellers could follow the action on the opposite side of the plaza and continue their everyday activities at the same time, thus showing the relationship between the activities of the open and the closed spaces.

As the appointed hour approached, the excitement mounted until music announced the first measures of the dance. The dancers were caught almost by surprise in the area staked out for them, where they were commemorating the tradition of the Xiberuko maskaradak (Zuberoan masked dancers; see photo 1). The high point, and the best expression of the masked dancers' festive, burlesque, and popular spirit, occurred when the group erupted

1

1. The **gatuzaina** *(cat) rhythmically opens and closes the wooden scissors he carries in his hands; he is followed by the* **kantineira** *(barmaid) and the rest of the group. On this occasion, the kantineira is a woman, although traditionally her role was played by a man.*

into the plaza, a moment known as the "arrival" (Garmendia 1973:68–88). The arrival of the five characters with their festive representations contributed an element evocative of the local fiestas celebrated annually from New Year's until the Tuesday of Carnaval. The five characters—Txerrena, Gatuzaina, Banderaia, Kantineira, and Zamalzaina—were performing the *baile jaustia*, a dance that combines rhythm, skill, and dexterity in such a way that the group's combined maneuvers are suddenly individualized when each performs a series of steps around a glass of wine.

The people followed the dancers, applauding the skill of each, until they disappeared single file at the same place they had entered, leaving behind rhythm in the air and the impression that they were going to continue dancing through the streets of the small town.

But the key moment in the preparation for the Korrika occurred when a strange person appeared unexpectedly in one corner of the plaza. At first the people heard only his cries. At last, near the stores, a prehistoric character emerged from behind a car. Dressed in skins, with long, uncombed hair and a wooden lance in his right hand, he maneuvered about with feline grace until he had become the central character in the closed space. His pantomime, his shouts, and the movements of his spear led observers to imagine his enemy, the animal he was trying to approach. The distant past, scenes from the hunt, and life in the caves evoked through his comic mime were not foreign creations to the people in the plaza at that moment. The long history of the occupation of the territory is present in the multiple prehistoric monuments shared throughout Euskalerria, and the scenes from the hunt are still outlined on the rough walls of the prehistoric caves of Santimamiñe and Arenaza in Bizkaia, and Ekain in Gipuzkoa.[2]

The maneuvers of the prehistoric character were followed by another character, to the delight and surprise of the crowd. By his stylized black suit and his mysterious leather attaché case, the people identified him as the stereotype of the wise man in search of the origins of the mysterious language Euskara. He responded to the cries of the prehistoric man with the emotion of one who had found the solution to a problem that had occupied him for years. Thus, triumphant, he announced to all those gathered in the plaza that he had found the first man who spoke Euskara. For the wise man, the people's applause constituted the greatest recognition possible for achieving this scientific feat. Next, the prehistoric man's gesture of taking the bone amulet—a reminder, perhaps, of a hunting exploit—from around his neck and putting it on the young man who would start the Korrika by being the first to carry the testigo was met with applause and great rejoicing. The symbolic relationship of the present to the past seemed obvious to the audience. Thus, his mission accomplished, the provocative cave man disappeared from current time and space, initiating once more his pursuit of an imaginary animal.

This incident is full of meaning, and in it we can find elements of the "reflexive humor" to which James W. Fernandez alludes (1983:199–299) in his analysis of the annual parade that marks the beginning of the international descent of the River Sella in canoes every summer in Arriondas (Asturias). In the Asturian case, the figures that appear in the parade help transcend the conflictive situation of the race—the contradictions of the political system and localism—and help the people internationalize and universalize their values. In the Basque case, the comic version of the past is proposed as a way of transcending the minority situation of Euskara—a situation full of conflict—by projecting its universal value as one of the most ancient languages of Europe and at the same time proclaiming the local context where it was developed and preserved.

Let us examine the state of Euskara and the process it has followed through time. Later, this will help us understand the way the solutions to the contradictions, which have already been outlined in the plaza of Atharratze, are demonstrated in Korrika.

Euskara Today and Its Historical Development

Euskara is a minority language within a territory that at one time was considered predominantly Basque speaking. Today, the population of Basques over the age of eighteen who know how to speak the language comprises approximately 325,788 persons in the historical territories of Araba, Bizkaia, and Gipuzkoa, and 30,067 persons in Nafarroa, for a total of 355,855 Basque-speaking adults in a population of more than 2 million inhabitants (Ruiz Olabuenaga 1984:1a). Euskara remains a minority language within the Basque Autonomous Community, although areas exist in Bizkaia and Gipuzkoa where its predominance over Spanish, the dominant language, is clear. If we examine the data regarding different levels of knowledge of the language presented in table 1, we see that the highest percentage corresponds to Gipuzkoa. Moreover, a global analysis points to a decline in Euskara in spite of the fact that the number of Basque speakers is increasing, since this increment does not overcome the demographic imbalance that exists between Spanish speakers and Basque speakers.

The situation of Euskara is similar in Iparralde. Data from 1975 indicate 78,453 Basque speakers in a population of 227,280 (Villán and Población 1980:43). Euskara's minority status is likewise clear, although the 1970 data show that in Zuberoa (Soule) and Nafarroa Beherea (Low Navarre)

TABLE 1

Euskara Literacy in Gipuzkoa, Bizkaia, and Araba
(percentage of the population)

	Comprehension	Speaker	Somewhat literate	Fully literate
Gipuzkoa	40.89	38.55	24.79	19.06
Bizkaia	15.97	14.54	8.76	6.63
Araba	4.48	3.80	3.33	2.60

Source: J. I. Ruiz Olabuenaga, *Atlas lingüístico vasco* (Gasteiz: Servicio Central de Publicaciones del Gobierno Vasco, 1984), pp. 21–22.

Euskara was the dominant language in relation to the total population, as table 2 shows.

If we keep in mind the spatial distribution of the language, which was identified with all Euskalerria in the activities at Atharratze, it is obvious that the percentage of Basque speakers varies by area and territory. In Nafarroa Beherea, Zuberoa, and Lapurdi, Euskara predominates in the rural areas but not in the coastal and urban areas. Of the eighty-six municipalities included in the category of 81–100 percent Basque-speaking population, only thirteen are in the coastal area. In the same category, the highest percentages correspond to seventy-four populations of between 92 and 3,000 inhabitants, all but seven of which are rural, and to those municipalities belong 74 percent of the total population of the three historical territories with the highest index of dominance of Euskara.

The language-territory association is an especially meaningful theme when applied to the study of Euskara. The contemplation of a map of Euskalerria indicating Basque-speaking nuclei (along with the experience of traveling the territory with attention to linguistic variations) makes obvious the fragmentation of Euskara, as José Ignacio Ruiz Olabuenaga points out: "Its space is not configured as a continuous stronghold, but rather as a species of archipelago in which a series of islets, more or less discontinuous, make up its geographical social space" (1984:17).

The fragmented situation of Euskara is the result of a historical process in which the borders have been changing and shrinking although there are no lineal explanations and the shrinkage has not been the result of a steady process of diminution. This is very different from the union of past and present presented in the plaza at Atharratze that introduced us to a nonhistorical time. Reality speaks of a process of contacts between populations and of

TABLE 2

Number and Ratio of Basque Speakers by Territory in Iparralde in 1970

	A Number of Basque speakers	Percentage of the total	B Number of inhabitants	Ratio A:B
Nafarroa Beherea	27,016	4	32,199	0.84
Lapurdi	39,530	7	166,870	0.24
Zuberoa	11,302	2	18,819	0.60
Totals	77,848	100	217,887	

Source: Adapted from L. C-Núñez, *Opresión y defensa del Euskara* (San Sebastián: Editorial Txertoa, 1977), p. 28.

linguistic influences that have affected the structure of the language and its spatial placement. It has nothing to do with an isolated population that lost its language in its first contacts with other differentiated linguistic populations, but rather its periods of recession can occur suddenly after epochs of reinforcement of the language and of the influence of Euskara on other languages (Ruiz Olabuenaga 1984:10–11).

Thus the geographic boundaries of Euskara in the pre-Roman epoch are difficult to establish because several languages existed on the peninsula before the implantation of Latin. It is possible that within the modern territory of Euskara the language has competed with others since ancient times. It seems certain that Euskara once occupied a more extensive territory than can be demonstrated with historical documents, and the documentation shows that there has been a shrinking of its borders.

Romanization and the spread of Christianity influenced the Latinization of the Basque population and its language, principally in Araba and Nafarroa. The choice of Huesca as a cultural capital and the establishment of Iruñea were significant events with regard to the retrogression of Euskara in the central Pyrenees and in the flatlands of Nafarroa. Communications and business resulted in the introduction of numerous words of Latin origin and in changes in the phonetic structure of Euskara. Christianity introduced ecclesiastical terms, although different authors vary in the weight they attribute to its impact on supplanting the native language (Echenique 1984:40–41, 46–57).

The impact of Latin, especially its relevance to commerce, certainly influenced a sector of the Basque-speaking population, giving rise to a Basque-

Latin bilingualism that at one time derived principally from the Romance language spoken in the modern territories of Gipuzkoa and Bizkaia. The characteristics this language presents "cannot be attributed to Basque-Romanic linguistic interference in an individual, but rather in a community, and perhaps they reveal to us the profile of the autochthonous Romance language" (ibid.:63).

As I have indicated, one cannot speak of the retrogression of Euskara without mentioning its simultaneous expansion. Throughout history a nucleus of Euskara-speaking territory has been maintained, and it is possible that the language reached other even more peripheral areas as a result of a period of medieval expansion. Opinions vary in this respect.

The shrinking of borders is especially evident in Araba, where by the sixteenth century a distinction was made between the capital, Gasteiz, where Spanish was spoken and people understood Euskara, and the towns, where Euskara was dominant. In Nafarroa, 58 Spanish-speaking towns and 451 Euskara-speaking towns were known. The geographical boundaries of Euskara remained rather stable in that area until the seventeenth century, with Tafalla and Estella as the southernmost limits, although there was a marked reduction in the general use of the language. The two centuries that followed exhibited two contiguous periods of great regression in Araba, Bizkaia, and Nafarroa. The result of this linguistic regression will be evident throughout this story of Korrika, especially in chapter 4.

The events in Atharratze emphasized the ancestral quality of the language and the power of oral transmission. The wise man, as a man of letters, might have been dedicated to writing, but the word was the protagonist of the action. Herein lies the key to the preservation of the language—the spoken word, inasmuch as it has no similar literary development. The beginning of written Euskara literature dates from the sixteenth century (1545), when the first literary text, the work of Mosen Bernart Dechepare, parish priest of Saint-Michel-le-Vieux in Nafarroa Beherea, was published in Euskara. In the seventeenth century an important, predominantly religious, movement arose in Lapurdi among the ecclesiasts, with Axular as its supreme example. But in spite of these literary efforts, Euskara did not become an integral part of political and administrative life, and it remained absent from nonliterary texts and documents. This lack of official recognition certainly had a negative effect on its natural development.

During the eighteenth century, literature remained in the hands of the clerics, and along with works of literary value there was an abundance of works intended to instruct the people in religious matters. These were written principally in the Lapurdin, Zuberoan, and Gipuzkoan dialects, which became the main vehicles for literary expression (Sarasola 1976:125–29).

Within Euskalerria, societies were dedicated to the development of the language and culture, and foreign scholars became interested in the scientific study of Euskara, an interest that continues to the present day. Among these scholars were Guillermo de Humboldt and Luis Luciano Bonaparte, who contributed important knowledge about the dialects and documented the quickly receding boundaries of Euskara in the Nafarroan valleys of Aezcoa, Salazar, and Roncal (ibid.:85–90).

Clerics and their religious themes continued to play a leading role throughout the nineteenth century. Just as the other dialects had done, the Bizkaian dialect served as a literary language. At the end of the century (1879) a Basque literary renaissance took place with the magazine *Euskal-Erria* as its principal voice. This movement included prose, poetry, theater, journalism, and the first attempts at novels, and it exhibited greater amplitude and diversity with regard to literary themes and genres (ibid.:135–41). According to Ibon Sarasola, Basque literature took off at that time. The renaissance had its ups and downs throughout the following century.

This century has seen the genesis of a movement broader than those that came before it, a movement that includes concern for the study of Euskara and the need for its literary development and faces the problems of receding boundaries, political oppression, and the need for systematization and unification of Euskara's various dialects. In the first quarter of the century specialized magazines were created, as well as cultural societies, among which Eusko Ikaskuntza-Sociedad de Estudios Vascos (the Society of Basque Studies) and especially Euskaltzaindia (the Academy of the Basque Language)[3] are noteworthy. The latter's first president, Resurrección Ma. de Azkue, published the *Diccionario Vasco-Español-Francés* in 1905 and *Morfología Vasca* in 1925; both of them can be considered supporting works of the era. The need for Batua, a unified Euskara (Villán and Población 1980:38–39), became apparent after 1964, and its official creation took place in 1968 in the Assembly of Aranzazu.[4] Batua was created in the midst of a powerful debate between those in favor of it and those opposed, a debate that still continues, although with less intensity.[5]

Just as the past and the present were joined in Atharratze, more recent conflicts have also disappeared, such as the incidence of internal and external migrations as a result of economic development and its effect on Euskara. The Spanish Civil War, for example, marked a period of strong political repression and a reduction in public support of Euskara. The task of ensuring the language's survival was relegated to the family, the church, informal nuclei, and individual efforts by scholars both inside and outside Euskalerria. This was a period of apparent immobility, but it allowed continuity and gave rise to a period in which greater development was experienced (ibid.:64,

72, 85–92). During this time (1940–75) economic development and migratory movements both inside and outside Euskalerria had a direct bearing on the restructuring of the social and geographic space of Euskara.

The most significant migratory movements of the twentieth century in southern Euskadi took place between 1941 and 1975, and especially between 1961 and 1965. The industrial development of the postwar period converted Euskadi into the focus of emigration within the Spanish state. Bizkaia registered the greatest influx during the years 1941–70, followed by Gipuzkoa, where the greatest growth was experienced from 1941 to 1965. Araba showed a rise in immigration after 1951 until 1976–80, followed by Nafarroa, where a slow recovery from the earlier exodus began during the 1970s. The period of development between 1951 and 1970 engendered the highest emigration balance everywhere but Nafarroa. The critical moment in the emigration decline began in 1971 and became more acute from 1975 on (Urrutia 1984:36–40). Later we will see how the opposite situation in Iparralde also had an influence on Euskara.

Such movements have resulted in an increase in Spanish speakers in the areas of industrial concentration, which has in turn had a direct impact on the decreasing use of Euskara by the established population. On the other hand, interior emigration has taken a significant number of people from the rural milieu to the urban, primarily Spanish-speaking, zones, increasing the presence of Euskara in these areas (Ruiz Olabuenaga 1984:51, 65); but in many cases this has also meant the loss of the language in the next generation.

Some of the principal developments in Euskara over the last few years include a rise in the number of ikastolas during the 1960s, adult literacy movements, the creation of Batua, the inauguration of the Euskal Udako Unibertsitatea (Basque University Summer School), the introduction of Euskara in university curricula, the development of a new literature featuring figures such as Gabriel Aresti and Joseba Sarraonaindia, the systematic development of linguistic studies by autochthonous and foreign researchers, the resurgence of bertsolarism and schools to teach it, television and press in Euskara, and new Basque songs and "euskal rock." Some of these developments arose during the years of Franco's political oppression, and all of them arose within the context of a minority language. They express in turn some of the paradoxes that Euskara has experienced through history: expansion-recession, continuity-discontinuity, and oppression-survival.

Extremes of the Life Cycle: Infancy and Old Age
as Indicators of Continuity

The importance of the socializing role of the family in the transmission of language, values, and ethnic identification is accentuated in the Basque case (Pérez-Agote 1984:88–92; Gurruchaga 1985:311–35). Moreover, the family's role is considered fundamental on the basis that "more than on a personal option, a linguistic phenomenon is based on the dynamic of an irreplaceable process of natural communication between parents and children" (Euskaltzaindia 1979:85). The preservation of Euskara is perceived as intimately tied to the family ambience and to the attitude demonstrated by parents, grandparents, and other relatives. The positive attitude of the family is indispensable for the preservation and development of the language (ibid.:85–101). However, because of the minority status of Euskara and the decrease in the number of people who speak it, generational continuity is being interrupted, and with it this natural form of transmission (Sánchez Carrión 1981:53–55).

In Korrika, this situation is transcended by updating the existence of natural transmission, in both the real and the symbolic planes. The continuity of the language is present in time, through the child-adult relationship and the generational tie that is indispensable for survival as a people. Likewise, the responsibility of the family in collaborating with other institutions such as schools, ikastolas, and *gau eskolas* (night schools) in the development of literacy in Euskara is acknowledged. Moreover, the family must support the passage of the language from the private to the public sector through an active presence outside the home.

THE LEADING ROLE OF CHILDREN

The experience of children in Korrika has a double dimension. On the one hand, they are incorporated into the action at the same time as the adults, and they share identical territory with them by assuming the role that corresponds to those who carry the testigo. Even in the first Korrika a child from the Oñati ikastola carried the baton in the second kilometer, received from the hands of José María Satrustegui (*La Gaceta del Norte*, February 25, 1980, p. 9), a member of Euskaltzaindia who declared that the race did not entail great effort

> since in the second kilometer I will be relieved by a child. This will be the deed that will occupy my thoughts during the thousand meters, since it is obvious that the schooling of the children in Euskara is the maximum guarantee for the survival of Euskara. (Ibid.:30)

The role of children is emphasized frequently throughout Korrika, especially on weekdays when they participate with their classmates. It is evident that they enjoy the race both when they carry the testigo and when they are a part of the crowd. They often leap into the air, impatiently awaiting the arrival of the group, and when they carry the testigo they run with pride, grasping it fiercely, looking ahead, smiling most of the time, and apparently conscious of the importance of the moment. There are exceptions, of course. A three-year-old girl burst into tears when her father picked her up in his arms and insisted that she carry the testigo on kilometer 1,074 in Biana. Sometimes they look about and seek the approval or support of the adults: parents, relatives, teachers who run beside them or follow close behind them, or grandparents who watch them with pride and approval from the doorway of the house or *baserri* (farmhouse) in the rural areas or from the street or the plaza in the towns and cities. It is obvious that they feel enveloped by the interest and caring of the adults.

The possibilities that Korrika offers for participation and coupling with autochthonous elements can act in a positive way as a vehicle of integration, at least in a certain sector of Basque society. I still remember the scene when Korrika, on its return through Bizkaia, left Bilbo behind and passed through Romo on the way to Getxo. A nine-year-old boy and his seven-year-old sister were running hand-in-hand in the first row next to the person carrying the testigo. When I asked them where they were coming from and where they were going, they said they did not know and kept running, oblivious to everything else. It appeared as if someone had put them in motion and they did not have the power to stop. They ran and ran amidst the confusion, the music, and the slogans, and as they began to tire they clasped hands even more fiercely. Then there emerged from the crowd a young man who had apparently come with them and had been following them closely throughout the race. Later I learned that they were children of workers who had emigrated from Extremadura to Euskadi a few years before.

Running in the first row holds a special attraction for the children. They compete with their companions to maintain the pace, getting ahead of the testigo, especially if it is being carried by someone older than they, and in many cases ignoring the directions of the organizers of the race. When the third Korrika passed through Zarautz at about one-thirty in the morning I was following the movements of two small boys who ran holding on to the back of the organizers' truck. Every so often they looked behind them and said excitedly, "Asko gendea" (a lot of people) and kept running. When that same race arrived at Gasteiz it was impossible to keep the groups of children in the crowd. They seemed caught up in the emotion emanating from rows and rows of people who cheered the passing of Korrika in the streets and plazas in spite of the intense cold. This, combined with music from the popular bands, the loudspeakers, the applause, and the voices, seemed to increase their interest in staying at the front of the crowd.

Linguistic standardization tied to the teaching of Euskara and teaching in Euskara begins with the ikastolas and other centers both public and private (Euskaltzaindia 1979:203–4; Gobierno Vasco 1983:197–201). Its importance is reinforced in Korrika through the children who represent the centers where they study. Groups of children are more likely to be seen on weekdays, when participation in the Korrika is included within school activities or is organized from there. The rapid entry of a group of children with their teachers injects enthusiasm and uproar into the race, and their young voices create a different tone for the slogans of "Herri bat gara, hizkuntza bat dugu" (We are one people, we have one language).

At some locations children representing local ikastolas or other centers wait for the Korrika to pass, as in Garralda (Nafarroa), where in the fourth Korrika they joined in with a placard they had made themselves featuring symbols like the *ikurriña* (Basque flag) and the *lauburu* (Basque emblem), and the slogan "Gora *korrika*, A E K, Gora Euskadi" (Long live *korrika*, A E K, Long live Euskadi). At other times they express slogans that call for the improvement of educational conditions. When the Korrika passed through Orduña the placards they carried read "Every day we go to Amurrio to study Euskara, why can't we study in Orduña?"

At times the children are highly visible, as in the passage through Nafarroa near the end of the race described in the field journal:

> In kilometer 2,024 a boy carries the testigo as representative of the ikastola along with a row of boys and girls each carrying a placard alluding to Korrika and Euskara that they had designed. The adult who carries the testigo during this kilometer carries a two-year-old boy on his shoulders. In the following kilometer two children join in, carrying a placard between them that says "Up with Korrika." The children in the group keep passing the testigo and, judging by their smiles, enjoying themselves.

The incorporation of different groups, the display of placards, and the chorus of slogans by young voices can be seen all along Korrika's route. The little ones are always carefully dressed in brightly colored jogging suits and running shoes that demonstrate painstaking preparation on the part of their mothers. In Basque culture much importance is given to dress, and the fact that the children are clean and well dressed reflects positively on their mothers' social prestige. We will encounter the issue of dress again later, when we examine the appearance of the women in Korrika. Fancy dress is a way of enhancing the festive character of Korrika, since in ordinary life there is a difference in the clothing worn on workdays and on holidays.

Whether it is a workday or a holiday has a bearing on the presence of mothers during the week and fathers on days off. The entire family may be present, especially during the evening. In the fourth Korrika the participation of whole families was especially noteworthy in Iparralde.

The reaffirmation of the family unit expresses itself all along the route of the race. Often women run as mothers, holding one or more children by the hand, smiling, with an air of satisfaction. There are times, generally outside working hours or on days off, when the men also join in the family group. Thus we observed small groups of several families and friends waiting for the arrival of Korrika in order to join in together. Once in the crowd, if the man is the one who takes the testigo, the rest of the family will remain at his side, holding hands. If a little boy or girl is carrying it, the parents will be involved in how he or she does it, encouraging the child and being attentive to any symptoms of exhaustion. If the child is small and grows tired, the father, or much more rarely the mother, will carry the youngster on his shoulders, and after a preliminary moment of uncertainty, of changing the perspective on what he or she sees, the child will smile joyfully and triumphantly. At all times the group is performing a joint action that helps in turn to visualize the family-language relationship. It is likewise an activity contextualized in public life, especially on holidays when it is normal to see family groups doing things together such as going for a walk or taking a stroll.

A second way of incorporating children into the race is through the *korrika txiki*, or "little Korrika," that is celebrated in many locations on the day before or on the same day that Korrika is going to pass through. The official race is reproduced, but on a scale appropriate to children and their comprehension. In the experience I described above, children joined in the Korrika of the adults; in the korrika txiki they reproduce the whole of the experience in miniature. I will single out the korrika txiki held in Iruñea on the day before the arrival of the fourth Korrika during a series of preparatory celebrations.

At ten-thirty in the morning on June 8 a good number of children were ready to begin their Korrika. The starting line was the Plaza de San Francisco, and the Plaza del Castillo was the finish line, just as it was to be in the official Korrika. All along the route through the streets of the Old Quarter the children chanted different slogans, such as "Korrika, korrika" and "Euskal Herria Euskaldunak."[6] The young runners stopped for a few moments before the town hall as a gesture of social protest against the decline of Euskara. When they arrived at the Plaza del Castillo they hung a banner with the slogan "Txikien korrika ez da txikia" (The little ones' Korrika is no little thing; *Navarra Hoy,* June 8, 1985). In korrika txiki, the children have the adults' experience on a reduced scale. They run through a territory, they chant slogans, they carry their banners and experience the start and the finish. They create their own universe modeled on that of the adults.

One comparison that leaps to mind is the *encierro txiki* (little running of the bulls) held during the Sanfermín festivities. Every morning during the seven days of the festival, before the "adult" running of the bulls, the stages of that activity are reproduced in a limited area in Estafeta Street. The children, dressed in white with the red *gerriko* (sash) around their waists, salute Sanfermín and chant "Viva" while nervously gripping a newspaper just as the adults do. Next, with mixed fear and expectation, they wait for the calves, which erupt in fright from a truck parked at the entrance to the street. Sometimes the calves seem to doubt whether they should leave the truck at all, and the moments of waiting contribute to the children's nervousness. The race is observed from the balconies and doorways of the houses, unlike the adults' event, when the street is left deserted for the runners. Alongside the children, observing them closely, are expert runners, members of the Peñas who follow the route and initiate the young boys in the way to run the bulls. The transmission of tradition takes place in the field, and within the same activity the youngsters learn to "feel" the bull, to "catch it." Along with the rules, the lesser show of skill and even the mixed emotions of fear and daring are recognized and reinforced. From both sides of the street, on the ground or from the balconies, the event is watched with interest and the children are bolstered by the spectators, many of whom are friends and family members. A masculine presence dominates both among the runners and among those who initiate them. The end of the running, with the recognition of a father who is a veteran runner and a final embrace from a mother or grandmother, completes the initiations. Later, when they reach the age of sixteen, they can take part in the adult running of the bulls.[7]

One difference between the encierro txiki and the korrika txiki is that the latter does not exclude participation in the official Korrika. Moreover, children can participate in both Korrikas and experience the differences of scale. In the case of the running of the bulls, however, children can participate only in the encierro txiki. The official entry into the adults' running implies a rite of passage into the world of adults where the boys, through their skill, quickness, and courage, demonstrate values associated with the masculine world. The encierro txiki prepares them for it. Some girls participate in the encierro txiki, but they almost never take part in the official running of the bulls.

THE INFORMAL PROCESS OF SOCIALIZATION
IN RELATION TO CULTURAL AND ETHNIC CONTEXTS

Korrika constitutes a form of informal socialization not only in the world of adults but also in the transmission of values and contexts identified as ethnic.

By taking place in public space and within a framework in which children have their own role, the event provides a series of powerful and varied experiences. It gives rise to an association between the identification of a situation and the commitment to do something associated with Euskara. The belief that the language is everyone's heritage does not prevent the adults, in practice, from making all the decisions, but, for a short time, at least, children are included in the experience of popular participation. In a society with a continual tradition of political and cultural movements and an experience close to linguistic and cultural oppression, nonconformity has become a part of Basque daily life. Thus Korrika and the way children are included in it can be seen as a socializing act where nonconformity and social involvement are experienced as positive adhesive elements. This occurs through the group experience, in mass participation, in slogans that speak of the unity of people and language, on the banners, and on the placards. This does not mean that these values correspond with reality, as we will see later, but they are transmitted as real throughout the race, and the children experience them in full measure (photo 2).

The individual role of the carrier of the testigo is balanced by the weight of the group. Whoever carries the testigo carries the symbol of Euskara, which is considered to be a collective patrimony. Often this meaning is expressed when passing the testigo from one runner to another. Furthermore, the one who carries it does so not based on individual talents or characteristics but rather as the representative of an ikastola or an association, or in the name of a father or a brother who is in jail for political reasons, or as the brother or son of a dead militant. However, knowledge of the language and a person's interests and acquaintances *can* be criteria considered at the time of selecting the person to carry the symbol. At least, that is how a ten-year-old boy in the Zurbaran neighborhood of Bilbo expressed it:

> Since my studies of Euskara in the Zurbaran school, they have told us that they were going to raffle off the testigo to the ones who knew a little because they were going to be pounding [Euskara] all the time . . . then they said they would choose one from among them. Then the teacher said he was going to raffle [it] among five or six, and I and two of my friends were chosen. More or less, [we were] those who knew more Euskara and were more comfortable [with the language].[8]

2. *Passing through Tutera in the fourth Korrika, the little ones express their cause on the banner. "Lokala-ikastolarentzat" asks for an ikastola to be located there.*

THE IMPORTANCE OF OLDER PEOPLE IN KORRIKA

Older participants are granted an importance similar to that attributed to the children who participate in Korrika, emphasizing in this way the two extremes of the generational demonstration. Although in numbers their participation is not as representative as that of the children or the young people, it is just as important. For that reason the echo of older runners' presence among the public is carefully evaluated. The presence of Pierre Lafitte in Iparralde or José Miguel de Barandiaran or the *berstolari*[9] Balentin Enbeita in Hegoalde (the southern part of Euskalerria) is just as valuable as the presence of other personalities with stronger local identification (photo 3). Thus each one's age, relevance, and the reasons why his or her presence is so meaningful are frequently mentioned. The photograph of Barandiaran in the newspapers on the day after he ran kilometer 92 in the first Korrika, and the fact that he endured the cold and rain of a harsh December morning at the age of ninety-one, was more powerful than any article on the commitment to take Euskara into the public sphere (photo 4). Furthermore, different generations can identify with different moments in Barandiaran's life. Some remember his younger years when they began working with him on the

3. The bertsolari Balentin Enbeita running his kilometer through Kortezubi
(Bizkaia) in Korrika 3 (Egin, December 11, 1983, p. 3).

archaeological sites in the caves of Santimamiñe and in the study of the dolmens in the sierras of Aralar and Urbasa. Others remember times of exile
when Barandiaran resided in the little town of Sara in Iparralde while he
continued his study of Basque culture. Among the young people there are
those who formed part of the Etniker research groups he founded upon his
return from exile. And many people followed his daily life in his native village of Ataun, where he lived and where he could be seen celebrating mass
early in the morning or taking his customary stroll in the nearby hills.

When Lafitte took up the testigo during kilometer 61 in the third Korrika,
he was acting out the metaphor that would be referred to a year later on
the occasion of his death: "He is unanimously recognized as the patriarch
of Basque letters in the French Basque country, he who took the torch from
the hands of the previous generation and passed it on to the next" (*Iker*
2:111). The photo that captured that moment was used in Korrika 4 to signify
Lafitte's eighty-four years of dedication to Basque language and culture and
was accompanied by the following sentence:

4. Neither his age nor the harsh weather kept José Miguel de Barandiaran from participating in the first Korrika.

Although yesterday's photo [taken] in Lapurdi is one of the best testaments in favor of Euskara, the Bascologist Pierre Lafitte, old and young at the same time, lent powerful support to the testigo carried by the young people in favor of Euskara. (*Egin*, December 4, 1983, p. 1)

Carrying the testigo in kilometer 1,729 in Bizkaia, the bertsolari Balentin Enbeita was compared to the language itself: "Balentin Enbeita and the testigo, two symbols united in yesterday's event" (*Egin*, December 11, 1983, p. 3).

These examples provide a picture of the continuity of Euskara; through them we experience the past inserted into the present. With the importance and leading role of children from the past-present, a projection toward the future is established, supported by the constant movement of Korrika and the ideology alluded to continually in the saying "Korrika does not stop." Associated with the symbolism of the testigo representing Euskara, this reinforces the impulse to move forward.

Faced with the reality of the progressive reduction in the number of people who speak Euskara and the fact that there are families where the language has been lost in the youngest generation, Korrika provides a powerful visualization of continuity through the presence of very young children and old people, as in the running between Lekeitio and Ondarru where children from three years old to people of more than seventy years were running, as recorded in the journal of the fourth Korrika:

> In kilometer 1,572 a little girl three years old runs holding her mother's hand, accompanied by children and adolescents in a rather numerous group. The most important block is that of the twenty- to thirty-year-olds and in lesser numbers that of the thirty- to forty-year-olds. Older people join in, and one seventy-year-old man who looks like an old *gudari* [Basque soldier] carries the testigo in the name of H[erri] B[atasuna]. A blind man who looks even a little older participates on the arm of a woman who runs with fist raised, and both took the testigo from the hands of the previous man. In the following kilometers, all the way to Ermua, boys and girls between ten and twelve years old carry the testigo, representing their respective centers. At times they pass the testigo happily among themselves.

The Role of Women

Women's most important contribution to the development of Euskara has been the transmission of the language, an activity associated with woman through her dominant role within the domestic group and her responsibility in the socialization of children (Barandiaran 1972, 5:135–37; del Valle et al. 1985:254). Her role, because it is associated with the family unit, does not achieve the recognition and social weight that it objectively deserves. Moreover, emphasizing and prioritizing that role reduces the possibilities of broader contributions from women, while it exempts men from responsibilities that should be shared and grants them a greater role in the public dimension of the language. Thus, the interest and work many women assume in the fulfillment of schooling in Euskara that, valued objectively, constitutes a significant contribution to the development of the language, is not as highly esteemed as men's work. Even the creation of the ikastolas is seen as linked to women's responsibility for caring for children.

Recognition of the continuity established by women, on the one hand, and at the same time their exclusion from the spheres where broad decisions are made about the language and where it has greater social prestige, contains a contradiction that can be resolved only be elevating women's role to a special category in which language would be considered as something inherent in the task of the woman as procreator. Seen in this way, woman as transmitter maintains the language's most intimate association with the house, the domestic universe, and the traditional world. The concept of procreation, of giving life, is likewise tied to the vitality of the language. Unfortunately, however, the public, the social universe, the linguistic and pedagogical techniques of the teaching of the language, and the institutionalization of Euskara generate more interest and social prestige. Thus the tasks carried out by Euskaltzaindia and the Unibertsitate Zerbitzuetarako Euskal Institutoa (UZEI), and the efforts of magazines like *Jakin* are considered more valuable than the tasks carried out by many women—tasks that down through the years have given life to the language in the family—and, on a public level, the tasks of those women who created and developed the ikastolas. Although the ikastolas are separate from the domestic realm, from their beginning a relationship was established between women's responsibility for the transmission of the language within the family and the creation of the ikastolas.

> The transmission of the language has been considered also as a direct consequence of the mother's role. The phrase that the *ikastolak* were born in the kitchen is a reality. Perhaps the first embryos of the future *ikastolak* were the Basque classes that the women of EAB [Emakume Abertzale Batza] organized for children in the location of "Emakume." Later, during the Franco era, the first clandestine *ikastolak* were organized in the kitchens of some houses. The responsibility for these first *ikastolak* was

in the hands of the women. As the development of Euskara began to be institutionalized and take on importance in the political arena, men assumed its direction. (del Valle et al. 1985:250)

Recognition labeled by gender has been attributed to specific persons who worked to advance the language. The recognition only recently given to Elvira Ziprita, in spite of her long years of dedication to the teaching of Euskara in the ikastolas and her central role in its development, cannot be compared with the recognition given to Manuel Lekuona, Pierre Lafitte, or Ricardo Arregui. However, if her work is evaluated not only from the point of view of the people to whom Ziprita transmitted the language but with regard to her contribution to the consolidation of the ikastolas, she deserves outstanding acclaim in the history of the birth and initial development of those institutions, especially in Gipuzkoa. It is not only the valuation of what a person does that is kept in mind, but rather a consideration of the social prestige that that work carries with it. And until the present, the activities and institutions related to Euskara that have had the most social prestige have been those led by men; none of them is associated with the home, with children, or with primary education. Rather, what is emphasized is the public dimension of the language, its presence in the communication media, in literary creation, in literacy, and in the performances and competitions of the bertsolari, fields where women have either been absent or where their presence is still in its infancy. When women do assume a major public presence in social activities, they do so principally in those areas related to Euskara and the betterment of the ikastolas. This demonstrates the importance women attribute to the language and the association they tend to establish with their family roles, even in these public demonstrations.

In this general setting, in which tradition carries great weight, new situations have begun to arise that represent qualitative changes in the social perception of women and their ability to generate important changes. The participation of women in fields heretofore considered masculine space and their access in recent years to teaching and research posts within the university can have a positive bearing on producing changes in the future. However, this cannot be achieved without effort, principally on the part of the women themselves. On the contrary, what women achieve can remain buried and subordinate to what men achieve. A good example of women's enlarged role is the participation by María José Azurmendi in the First Congress of Bascologists (Primer Congreso de Euskerólogos) held in Gernika in 1980 (*Punto y Hora*, no. 189–90:59), as well as the work she has been carrying out in sociolinguistics. In the field of linguistics, Karmele Rotaetxe stands out, and we can hope that the contributions of Feli Etxeberria, who unites her scientific preparation in the pedagogy of language with years of experience in the ikastolas, or those of Lourdes Oñaederra in the field of linguistics, will be well known in the near future. The number of women in areas of decisive responsibility over the language is still very limited. Carmen Garmendia, who serves as chief of linguistic policy in the Basque government, is an exception. Euskaltzaindia, considered to be the most prestigious association related to Euskara, is with one exception completely male. Miren Azkarate was selected to occupy the seat left vacant at Barandiaran's death.

The literary offerings of female writers from both sides of the border, including Arantza Urretavizcaya, Laura Mintegi, Teresita Irastorza, Itxaro Borda, and Mariasun Landa among others, is a demonstration of women's contribution to the literary genre beyond their traditional recognition as storytellers in the family ambience. *Emakumea idasle*, (Borda 1984), an anthology of works by fifteen writers who communicate their creativity in Euskara, is at the same time an affirmation of women's place in the creative process and a protest of the leadership that is granted to male writers when modern Basque literature is mentioned. In spite of the fact that women's contribution to Basque literature is still small, when evaluating it we must remember the social difficulties and the lack of a context that awakens the necessary interest and support, as well as the historical conditioning of Basque literature.

Even keeping in mind the general limitations of Basque literary development, it is curious that through four centuries, until 1976, the names of only four women appear: Vicenta Moguel (nineteenth century), identified as "the niece of Juan Antonio de Moguel," who apparently contributed only a translation of Aesop's fables to a book of Moguel's verses; Catalina de Elicegui, who wrote historical dramas in the years before the Spanish Civil War; and in recent times Arantza Urretavizcaya and Lourdes Iriondo, in poetry and theater for young people, respectively (Sarasola 1976:132, 146, 169, 170). On the one hand, women's exclusion from literary circles is an absence that needs to be investigated in the context of the cultural situation of women.[10] We would have to contemplate at the same time the fact that a good part of Basque literary production, at least until recent years, has been in the hands of the male clergy. The role that women have played or could have played in the transmission and conservation of the language beyond the domestic realm is yet to be written.

With this lack of a female literary tradition, real or assumed, it is understood that a woman writer is considered an exception, and she sees herself pressured by a series of expectations linked to the uniqueness of her situation. However, professional interest for the language appears in many of the women (49 percent in 1977) who participate in the Udako Euskal Unibertsitatea (Basque University Summer School; Villán and Población 1980:66), and women are beginning to appear in the publishing world and in newspaper and magazine editing.

Focusing on Korrika, within general participation, let us analyze how women's presence and behavior demonstrate some of the contradictions expressed previously, as well as aspects of the different ways women are evaluated. Likewise, I will point out aspects that, even within traditional positions, show a dynamic of change and those that could remain hidden when the participation of one sex or another is evaluated in its totality.

The presence of women in the race and the roles they assume vary in the different territories and locations, and in many cases their participation is defined by their family roles. At the beginning of Korrika 4 in the plaza of Atharratze, the women appeared to dominate. They were at the organizational tables signing up runners for the different kilometers, passing out the numbers worn by the runners, and being interviewed for local radio. At the same time they were taking care of the children who swarmed through the plaza, enchanted by the excitement that had invaded the center of their little town. Their sense of humor led them to ridicule, through masks and mime, situations in which women were forced to emigrate to Paris in search of work. Their versatility brought forth different posters which, along with the theme of Euskara, projected social change in the workplace and denounced unemployment (see photos 5 and 6): "There is unemployment in Zuberoa too," "Unemployment is everyone's problem," "It's time for the unemployed to wake up."

One group was dressed in blue work shirts. Five of them carried a big banner of purple cloth that headed the race with the slogan "Euskaraz eta kitto, AEK Herri Zerbitzu" (Basque and nothing else, AEK in service to the people). These slogans were in turn expressed in the message read by the representative of the unemployment commission and first carrier of the testigo. Amaia Fontán, AEK's representative in Iparralde, contributed to the projection of the feminine role in the genesis of Korrika when she read the proclamation that would correspond ten days later to the message read by Sagrario Alemán in the Plaza del Castillo of Iruñea. However, the most visible participation by women throughout the race through Iparralde, and more so as it approached the border—Baiona, Donibane, Hendaia—was associated with children and the importance of their schooling in Euskara.

There were also moments of leadership. When the race reached the border, the atmosphere was charged with tension when Asun García, a student of Euskara from Irun, waiting "in the so-called no-man's-land" to take up the testigo, was taken away by the police to verify her papers (*Egin*, June 2, 1985, p. 29) before they let her cross the border. Within seconds the forceful

5. *In the plaza of Atharratze moments before the beginning of Korrika 4 with the banner that would lead the runners: "AEK at the people's service," and a smaller one stating "In Zuberoa there is also unemployment."*

protests of those present filled the air. At last Asun took the testigo, and while another woman gave voice to an *irrintzi* and seven fireworks rockets were launched into the air, Korrika crossed the border to a background of rallying cries and music.[11]

The presence of groups of women and the frequency with which they carry the testigo vary not only with locality but also with the time of day and whether it is a workday or a holiday. Women's activities outside the home are limited by their responsibilities within the domestic realm (del Valle et al. 1985:166–69). Thus, for the working mother of a family, if her work is not related to teaching Euskara, it is difficult to find the time to participate except with her children and on her days off. The women who do participate are either young and have more free time or they take part while their children are in school. This is facilitated in small populations where everything is close at hand and communication, organization of activities, and moving from place to place are less complicated. In large populations and in the cities, the groups of women who participate in Korrika come from associations made up principally of young people.

During the running of the fourth Korrika from the border to Donostia, the number of women carrying the testigo increased. Thus, in Trintxerpe

6. *Slogans in support of social demands were present from the beginning of Korrika in Atharratze: "Unemployed people, it's time, wake up" and "Soule [Zuberoa] also has unemployment."*

and Alza the men dominated, while in the neighborhoods near the capital the presence of women grew. In the neighborhood of Egia, the father of Gladys del Estal carried the testigo in the name of the antinuclear committee to which his daughter belonged when she was killed by the civil guard in May 1979 in Tutera. The banner of one group of women linked their militancy with the memory of the same event: "Destroy Lemoiz," "Gladys, we remember you," "No nuclear power plant."

Later on, in the neighborhood of Gros, a woman took the testigo as a member of Euskal Herrian Euskaraz (Euskara in Euskalerria), and even when Txus Congil, the lieutenant mayor of Donostia, took the testigo in kilometer 251 for the Herri Batasuna coalition, two women occupied a central place in the first row. The feminine presence continued, associated with the Pro-Amnesty Movement or representing the ATS (Technical Sanitation Assistants), until a boy and girl shared the carrying of the testigo when the race arrived in Hernani.

In the run toward Donostia, the number of women carrying the testigo increased as the Korrika neared the city. Later, one of the few personalized recognitions was given to a woman when María Luisa Irizar, a Basque champion athlete, took up the testigo. With that action, the physical capability of resistance and coordination, traditionally valued in men, was exalted. In other places, however, women demonstrated the courage of carrying the testigo as a minority, as happened on a stretch in Nafarroa where out of fifty-two people passing the testigo, only four were women, all between the ages of twenty and thirty years.

Some runnings stand out because of the acts of women, independent of the fact that men outnumber them. One woman of sixty years took part by carrying the testigo in kilometer 453, accompanied by a good-sized group of people of both sexes who chanted the phrase "Total amnesty." When she could not keep up the pace, she gave way to someone who could try to accommodate the others.

The difficulty of the run, especially around the ports, did not seem to influence women's participation. The team noted a certain desire in runners to complete the race regardless of the difficulty. This appears to be a reflection of the feeling of responsibility to which I have alluded in other works, and it seems to affect women more than men (del Valle 1983:254–56; del Valle et al. 1985:152, 188–89, 292; photo 7). In the exchange of the testigo, as recorded in the team's field journal, we see reflected the generational passing on of the symbol of the language:

> In kilometer 453 between Leitza and Ezkurra a sixty-year-old woman hugs a twenty-year-old when she takes the testigo. Young men and women enter the race with letters that form the words "Total Amnesty." The woman carries the testigo with her right arm raised. They shout "Free the prisoners—total amnesty," and she conducts the chant with the testigo. At last she cannot keep up the pace and she gives way. She wears a shirt with orange and green squares and at her side a young woman accompanies her carrying an amnesty poster and a Basque flag on her shoulder. The hill is steep, the sun beats down. The woman holds up well, and when she arrives at the top more than fifty people join her while a group of people receive them with applause.

Continuing through Nafarroa, a woman of sixty-five took the testigo on kilometer 604 in the Nafarroan town of Abaurre Gaiña. Again, the moment was recorded in our field journal.

> She is somberly dressed, wearing short boots, and it's difficult for her to run. She looks serious and carries the testigo as if it were a candle. Several youngsters from the school accompany her, along with a young girl who is apparently her daughter and who relieves her in the last stretch. . . . In kilometer 511 a girl of eighteen carries the testigo accompanied by the person who just finished carrying it and a young girl

7. *Passing through Araba almost alone and running uphill. In the background the caravan of cars with an organization car in front carrying the ikurriña.*

who has been running for twenty-three kilometers. It is noon and we continue climbing toward Belate. She is left alone for a moment, but two women and a man immediately emerge from a car and join the race.

Later on, in the valley of Ulzama at two-thirty in the morning, a mixed group of young people ran at an incredible pace. This was in contrast to the relay of kilometer 547, where only a girl carrying the testigo and her female companion were running. Nevertheless, they were smiling, in spite of the fact that it was three-fifteen in the morning.

Woman's never-ending task of passing on the language is expressed well in an interview with one of the women responsible for the organization of Korrika in Rentería:

I think that Euskara is something that today you give a grain of sand, tomorrow another, on the next day they take two grains away from you, and you keep adding sand. It's a little . . . the struggle . . . it's a social struggle, no? Well, I notice in this struggle that today I give and tomorrow they take away from me, but I keep giving; that is, I don't stop. All this is a social statement that it is necessary to introduce Euskara into the lives of everyone; I think it's the process of recovering a language.[12]

One memorable character we encountered was a thirty-eight-year-old woman running kilometer 606 with the testigo. She began her run with pride and dash. When she began to tire and someone suggested relieving her, she said that she had to finish what she had started. A few meters later, as she passed a Guardia Civil post, she lifted the testigo in a gesture of defiance and shouted, "Gora euskara" (Long live Euskara). Eventually she was picked up by the organization truck, and when we entered Abaurre Gaiña she got out to run again, head high, self-satisfied, and proud. This was repeated at the entrance to the town of Ezkaroz, where she lived. Taking the megaphone she began to shout slogans while telling us, "You have to get the people from here moving." She later commented that in this once Euskara-speaking region there remain only a few old people who speak the old language. A native of Gipuzkoa, she had lived in Eskaroz since marrying a man from that area. In spite of being in the minority, she still had a feeling for Euskara, and she had to do something about it.

There is a proud spirit in the women's participation, transmitted in the way they run, the way they carry the testigo high in the air, and in their animated expressions. This is maintained even by older women who cannot keep up the pace but refuse to give up their role, even though they slow the rhythm of the run. They are committed to finishing, and when they must delegate the testigo to someone else, it seems that this is not as hard if it is the daughter running alongside who finishes the task. It is another form of continuity.

Both the children and the women take pride in their appearance (del Valle et al., 1985:219–20). It shows in women of all ages, independent of their economic level. In Iparralde women and children adopted a rather informal air, while in Hegoalde both young and old appeared in attractive sport clothes; in some cases women color-coordinated their outfits with their children's. Some said that they were wearing a jogging suit for the first time. The generation difference appeared in the kinds of apparel they chose and in the freedom with which they expressed their personal likes over social convention. Thus, only women over forty wore street dress of skirts or shirtdresses, although some women of that age and older had adopted sport clothes, a sign of change, or of adhering to current fashion.

In Korrika women sometimes participate more directly in elements of change. In Hernani, where unemployment is a particular problem, an assembly convened on the morning of the race designated a woman to carry the testigo. The assembly decided "that a woman should carry it, since it seemed that the problem of unemployment was only a man's problem and they wanted to shatter that image, and since there was no other woman available, I was the one" (field journal). Interviews with the local people responsible for Korrika 4 point up the initiative and seriousness with which women assume their responsibilities as well as their capacity for introducing change:

> This year we made the schools participants, it's another thing if you come out better or worse, those are problems to analyze from a different angle. On the village level what I intend to do is involve all of them, everyone. For me it's the criterion, what happens is that the Korrika as such has a political *kutxu* [taint], understand . . . that I . . . plan to break with that because there are certain kinds of acts that are very slanted toward one side or the other, and to me, as far as my responsibility goes, I make the effort; the group of people here agrees with that.[13]

Korrika appears as an activity loaded with physical and symbolic energy, playing principally with elements that are associated with the masculine universe. One of the images that appears most frequently in Korrika publicity is the enormous groups that participate and advance through different localities. A poster for Korrika 3 perhaps best expresses this affirmation. Its visual impression is that Korrika advances and overtakes one. It was taken from a photo that captured the avalanche of people as the race passed through Bilbo in Korrika 3, and those in the front row, all men, can hardly be contained (photo 8). It is a vision of united strength, of masculine power, or *indarra*, transmitted through the compactness of the group of men and their interlaced arms. One could guess that it was taken at the moment of arrival at an important town and that the pace of the run had let up to accommodate the multitude that had joined in. The poster drew criticism at the time from women who protested the masculine vision it gave of Korrika as well as its lack of correspondence with reality. Publicity for the next Korrika gave a greater role to women.

A poster from Korrika 3 represents the face of a young woman with her hair blown by the wind as if she were running (photo 9). Her face is shortened. It is an isolated face that we assume is emerging from among a group of people. The drawing of the hair relates it to a magic, surrealist world close to science fiction, where velocity can reach unimaginable limits. However, it is a face that in turn connects with specific realities through dress appropriate to young people who appreciate the comfort of sports attire and can be found dressed just that way in the race. The detail of the safety pin that fastens her number to her clothing emphasizes the presence of the ordinary in Korrika. The number is placed there only for the race, to "do" the Korrika, and it indicates the temporariness of the action. She runs on impulse, and

8. Photo used for the official poster for Korrika 3. It captures the passage of Korrika 2 through the neighborhood of Deusto.

we suppose with effort, but in this representation all that suggests effort disappears and a festive, amusing quality dominates; the smile motivates and encourages participation.

I said earlier that in Korrika contradictions appear with respect to the appreciation of women in the development and transmission of the language. On one level there is a continuity in the association of women with children, socialization, family, and the domestic universe, even when they are defending interests that have to do with schooling. It is a separate universe that exists on a level of lesser recognition. The personalization of the principal characteristics of Korrika, such as strength, cohesion, and action, are projected as masculine and principally through male characters, although the women who participate in Korrika contribute with their own strength, pride, and capacity for initiative and change. However, women symbolize Korrika only in an evocative, unreal, humorous sense. The faces of the women who are singled out appear in order to make us feel the presence of those who are absent: political prisoners and others who have contributed to the Basque political or cultural cause. Only Gladys del Estal appeared as a feminine protagonist actually commemorated, and in her case it was her father who represented her.

9. When women are included in Korrika publicity, they are generally represented humorously.

The participation of women in the organization of Korrika principally embraces the prerace groundwork, as revealed in Bizkaia where nine women and nine men worked on Korrika 4 as coordinators of a certain stage.[14] In Erribera the coordination of the relays was shared by a Gipuzkoan woman and a young man from Tutera. In contrast, at the higher levels of the organization women are scarce. The fact that the idea for Korrika emerged among a group of men has perhaps resulted in the greater masculine role in directing the race. In Korrika 4 there were only two women on the organizing team that participated directly in the race.

The presence of women's groups and organizations in Korrika varies from one place to the next. In Iparralde the presence of unemployment is clear, and women represented the cause along with men. This in turn indicates a change that associates women with the labor question, something already noted in the case of Hernani. Groups of women representing the feminist movement were absent in Iparralde, although they did appear in the other territories. Among the alternative groups present in Korrika the presence of women with specific social causes, such as the right to free abortions, was more notable in Bizkaia than in the other territories. In Barakaldo six women carried a placard reading "No to NATO and the police, yes to Euskara."[15] At kilometer 1,264 near Bilbo, a young woman of eighteen took up the testigo, accompanied by five women belonging to a cultural group who shouted, "Women, too, in favor of Euskara." In Bilbo the Assembly of Women from Bizkaia ran the relay on the high part of Miraflores upon leaving the city. At kilometer 1,449 a young woman of twenty-five took the testigo, accompanied by six others who carried signs with the feminist symbol and two slogans: "Korrika Abortatzeko eskubidea" (which can be interpreted as "Korrika the right to abortion" or "The right to abortion running") and "Emakumearen agresionaren aurka" (Against violence against women). In Ermua one placard with white letters on a purple background and the feminist symbol protested "Against the closing of the planning," which, according to one of the six young women carrying it, pointed out the fact that "they are making a health plan and tedious problems like that." The Group of Women from Arrate ran kilometer 1,748. The only feminist group that appeared in Araba was in the neighborhood of Zaramaga, in Gasteiz, where the testigo was taken by a woman accompanied by a group with a placard bearing the feminist symbol and the words "Euskararen alde [sic] Zaramagako emakumeen taldea" (The group of women from Zaramaga in favor of Euskara). In Nafarroa the presence of women's associations was limited to Tutera, where a group of women carried the testigo in kilometer 927, and to Iruñea. At kilometer 2,049 the testigo was taken by the group AIZAN,[16] with their sign "Jo Ta Ke, euskararen alde" (Passionately in favor of Euskara). They passed the testigo amongst themselves, shouting, "Passionately until we win," "Up with the feminist struggle," and slogans about political prisoners. However, it was principally in towns in Bizkaia and Nafarroa (El Baztan and Erribera) where a more egalitarian participation among the young people of both sexes who organized themselves to run as groups of friends was apparent.

One last aspect of the presence of women concerns the evocative power of the Korrika, a theme I will analyze in chapter 5.

The Resolution of Discontinuities and Contradictions

Let us return to the beginning of the fourth Korrika in the plaza of Atharratze. Taking that space, open and closed at the same time, as a symbol of Euskalerria, we see that many of the discontinuities and contradictions that exist in Basque society are indicated or represented in the plaza in embryonic form. I have already pointed out some of these discontinuities and contradictions in my discussion of the history of the situation of Euskara, and others will appear during the running of Korrika. Principally they have to do with the language, the territory, and the responsibility for the transmission of the language. The Korrika is an attempt to transcend these disruptive factors, and this has already begun in Atharratze with the continuity-discontinuity of the language in time and space.

In the plaza events that I have described, we experience the continuity of existence of the language from prehistory up to the current moment in the encounter that takes place between the cave man and the scientist, during which the latter is able to identify the cave man's language and at the same time communicate with the crowd in that same language. The past is brought into the plaza through the reference to habitat—the way the prehistoric man obtains his food, and his clothing. The present is there, too, visible in the atmosphere, the plaza, the placards with slogans, and all the economic problems of Iparralde, reinforced by the carrier of the testigo, who represents the unemployment commission. Nevertheless, in this representation of continuity between the distant past and the present, history is reduced to a nonhistorical time where centuries, events, and the vicissitudes that Euskara has experienced disappear in an attempt to unite the two extremes of the spectrum that they connect. The past is inserted into a popular event in such a way that it can occur simultaneously with the present in an effective manner. The present and the past are transcended, leaving continuity as the dominant element.

We are powerfully reminded of the mystery of the origin of Euskara, something that has held a unique attraction for linguists and historians interested in deciphering its roots. In the plaza we meet a character who could solve some of the unknowns. But the character seems interested only in the continuation of the language and in passing on the amulet of the prehistoric—as the first person who spoke Euskara—to the representative of the unemployment commission who is to carry the *testigo*, the symbol of the language, and transmit it kilometer by kilometer through Euskalerria.

In this scene we take a step toward recognizing the universal value of science, transcending local circumstances, at the moment the scientist recognizes the contribution that the knowledge of the origins of Euskara would bring to linguistics. Then, although this remains explicit in a way, it is set aside because symbolic transmission is not accomplished through the scientist or his actions or words, but directly from the prehistoric carrier of the *testigo* to the modern Basque person. An interpretation could be made here about the relationship between science and the people. It is not that science is rejected; rather, through this act, it is recognized, although as subordinate to the people. The scientific value of Euskara is based on its antiquity, on the mystery of its origins; but at the same time the events in the plaza attempt to transcend science and its institutions. They are an affirmation that without the people who give life to Euskara, the language could not survive. A language lives because the people re-create it as they transmit it. With the cave man's knowledge we could open up the secrets of Euskara's origins, but that possibility is set aside because it is not of great importance for the survival and existence of the language. On the other hand, setting aside that issue means that even if the origins of the language were known, and advances in linguistics may make this possible, it would not affect the importance that Euskara has for the people. The transmission of the language is what makes it live and re-create itself. Prehistory and the carrier of the *testigo* represent the people in the past and in the present, and a symbolic transmission occurs between them, beyond all the historical vicissitudes: recession-expansion, discontinuity-continuity. Likewise transmission occurs in a space, the plaza, that represents a united Euskalerria through the presence of people from both sides of the *muga* and establishes a limited, liminal area in which all this is possible. Moreover, transmission can be considered a partial actualization of what Korrika expresses without stopping, kilometer after kilometer for nine days, until it returns to put it into effect in the plaza at the finish line: Iruñea.

The scientist's leading role suggests an acknowledgment that institutions, be they scientific or political, are the owners of the language, while Korrika tries to demonstrate that the people possess the language, and in the past they have been the true protagonists in its preservation. The movement, the advancement of Korrika that we are seeing, is interpreted as the active participation of the "people," a concept that has its own meaning. In the past the language survived in spite of the absence of institutionalization and in spite of its late literary development. Thus the oral tradition and family responsibility played an important role. Nevertheless, the lack of official support has been detrimental to the development and expansion of the language. In this first part of Korrika, the importance of survival and the role of the people is what has priority, and in order to make it so, the importance of the institutions becomes relative. Later we will see how the need for their support is emphasized, but only after it is clear that the people are the protagonists of the language and that they have given it continuity.

The allusion to the importance of survival is implicit in the additional knowledge the prehistoric figure transmits by handing over the amulet of the animal killed in the hunt. The association of physical survival provided by the hunt, based in turn on the familiarization with habitat and mastery of specific techniques, is related to the wisdom that suggests preserving the language and is not tied to either science or the institutions that propagate it. This knowledge is passed on not to the scientist but to the people. With all that, it transcends the paradox of discontinuity in time that appears in historical analysis and in modern statistics, and, on the other hand, transcends the difficulties that survival carries with it when there is a lack of institutionalization and when political oppression is present. I should point out that the elements of change that appear in Korrika are principally associated with the marginal and the subversive: the women who protest against unemployment and who reclaim their right to work make it everyone's problem; the feminist groups who reclaim the right to decide about their own bodies are indications that women are tending, on the one hand, toward greater individualization, and, on the other, toward projecting themselves in society beyond the responsibilities and spaces of the domestic universe. There is an attempt to break the association of language with woman's function as procreator and socializer because support for Euskara in a public act like Korrika, even when the principal role offered to women emphasizes their domestic functions, has a broader interpretation. On the part of the women change can be read in the slogans that demand their right to participate directly and to obtain the recognition that they deserve within the public function of the language from which they have historically felt excluded and in which they are fighting to excel and to contribute. The participation of women in Korrika is complex and includes not only contradictions but possibilities for resolution and self-improvement. Korrika is a way of transcending the framework of nature that presupposes "domesticity" and the family universe with which women have been associated. Although Euskara clearly belongs to the entire culture, women have begun working at the variety of tasks involved in the total development of the language. Korrika shows indications that, although diffuse, are an expression of change and, like the contradictions, respond in turn to those perceived within the broader linguistic framework.

Conclusions

In this introduction to the dynamics of Korrika we have seen the importance bestowed upon the continuity of Euskara: in history, down through the generations, and in the family. To this end there are recurrent demonstrations that evoke a positive response in the people by their content and the way in which they are presented.

The different groups that I have described capture the significance of a comical representation such as that in the plaza of Atharratze in transcending the conflicting discontinuous historical experience and the modern reality. The myth that emphasizes the language and its origins serves to unite the varied crowd from both sides of the border and inserts itself in turn into the problems of the tangible present. The ritual of linguistic transmission through the symbol of the dead animal takes place in a temporally limited space—a space that is geographically identifiable, a space both involved in and separate from the activities of everyday life, a space that permits the resolution of the historical and generational discontinuity. In order for this space to transcend time, time must stop in the plaza. The plaza's spatial limitations can be interpreted as the creation of a liminal space where time disappears and we experience the nonhistorical moment where the two extremes—prehistory and the current moment—are united. Everything that has occurred in between has no relevance; the important thing is affirming that the language spoken by the prehistoric figure, and thereby the ancient inhabitants of Euskalerria, is still spoken, as the scientist demonstrated when he understood and transmitted the message to the crowd, and as it was carried out in symbolic transmission to the carrier of the testigo. The myth of Euskara's origins is jointly validated by the people and by science, but the role of the former and their sovereignty over the latter are strongly emphasized.

From the experience of the nonhistorical moment, we moved on to contemplate what occurs diachronically when the generations are taken as an important element in the transmission of the language. On the one hand, we are considering two extremes, children and old people, and uniting them through the participation of both in the Korrika. But we also see the intermediate steps—how people of other ages participate, the passing on of the testigo, and thus the chronological concatenation. With this, the generation break is eliminated, and the importance of transmission in all its dynamic aspects is presented. No rupture exists, only continuity, and this in turn evokes what has been happening from the prehistoric past to the present of the carrier of the testigo. The presence of different generations is another way of evoking the centuries through the personalization of time, without having to bring in historical dates. The effect is powerful. It deals with continuity on a reduced scale. In historical time the mythical recurs, overcoming discontinuities, while on a generational scale it is expressed, acted out, and visualized.

Finally, we have seen that woman is capable of transcending her marginalization from the more public tasks of the language by reclaiming the marginal and subversive in the public space of language and carrying it beyond the traditional associations with home, children, and family. It is clear that she plays a more important role than that communicated by the graphic visions on posters and the symbols with which she is identified, and that she is capable of expressing herself directly in a social way in the public arena.

The symbolic power given to continuity on different levels, and the occurrence of Korrika in a time separated from the ordinary, help to overcome historical discontinuities by acting as a revitalizing element and agent.

Chapter Two

The Creation of Korrika

The organization of Korrika is intimately linked to the history, objectives, and organizational structure of A E K, a body that was born and developed within Euskaltzaindia (the Academy of the Basque Language). A E K came into being in 1966 in the midst of the Franco dictatorship when certain members of Euskaltzaindia, conscious of the repression and retrogression that Euskara was experiencing, saw the necessity of promoting a literacy movement among the population. Thus a commission was created within the academy with dual objectives: teach the language to those who do not know it, and provide the means for those who speak the language to learn to read and write it. At the forefront of this movement was Ricardo Arregui, the "leader of the literacy movement, fundamentally, but also of the Euskara teaching movement, in Euskadi" (*Punto y Hora* 1982, no. 266:10). In 1966 Arregui wrote a letter to José María Satrustegui, a member of Euskaltzaindia, expressing the need to give official form to the teaching of Euskara to nonspeakers, a process that is known today by the term *euskaldunización*. The letter constitutes, in turn, recognition of the role granted to Euskaltzaindia in this task. A translation of that letter, which was placed inside the testigo during the first and second Korrikas, follows:

From Andoain, January 17, 1966
Dear Father:
   Having taken into consideration what you said to me in Baiona, some young collaborators and I wish to complete our task from within Euskaltzaindia. In order to do that, along with our companions, we thought about an act that consists of teaching Basque speakers who do not know how to read and write. I am sending two duplicated pages for your verification that were sent to the rest of the members to demonstrate our intention. Moreover, since you are Navarrese, I want to ask you something: could you carry out a similar scheme with other Navarrese Basques? We are a group of young men ready for anything. Those [sic] and we ourselves, along with responsible parties in Nafarroa, could see if it is suitable to establish contact. You, better than any other person,

might know, and that is why I am asking you. We think you might accept our plans to some degree, and if you agree with us, you might vote in favor of our proposal. Moreover, if you could come for this and if your opinion of our proposal is affirmative, we ask with the greatest respect that you write to Euskaltzaindia as soon as possible, giving them your opinion.

In the belief that we have not wasted your time and extending our thanks beforehand, I am your faithful servant . . . [1]

The objective of the euskaldunización proposed here was amplified into an initial plan, and the activities of the corresponding commission were oriented toward adults, since it was understood that the ikastolas were already dealing with the needs of schooling the children. This was a response to the cultural movement of the 1970s, mainly after the death of Franco, when a great interest in learning Euskara was registered, an interest that translated into a demand for centers where courses oriented toward people with different levels of knowledge of the language would be offered. The interest in Euskara affected young people and adults, and it brought people of different occupations and social sectors into the classrooms. By 1975 Alfabetatze Euskalduntze Koordinakundea was beginning to be recognized as a group that arose from the need to coordinate the teaching efforts in all the territories.

Interest was clearly there, and in the school year 1976–77 forty thousand registrations were recorded. The dates of matriculation for the pilot centers of the University of Deusto and Bilbo's neighborhood of Santutxu had to be moved up because the classes were full. Broad sectors of the population began learning Euskara: workers, students, businessmen; people of both sexes and a wide variety of ages. Their interests varied from those who saw Euskara as a form of identification and support for the Basque cultural movement to those who were learning it to use on the job or in their search for work. Learning the language constituted in turn a way for those born outside Euskadi to penetrate the society.

As demand grew, a need was seen for an organization that could respond both to the many people who were drawn to the classes and to the demands of developing appropriate methods for teaching the language, keeping in mind the specific situation in which Euskara found itself. Thus were created the first academies with a fixed program and schedule that would try to adapt to the variety represented by the student body; and a team dedicated to the development of didactic aspects of teaching was created. The importance bestowed on intensive study led to summer courses with a boarding-school regimen, which people could attend during their summer vacation. Later, intensive courses of several months' duration were organized in places where Euskara was the predominant language. Some of those courses were aimed at teaching the language and others at the preparation of language teachers. All the courses were in great demand, and by their collective dynamic they aided in the formation of groups that held together beyond the course itself and continued to reunite after the participants had returned to their residences and their normal activities.

When the Basque Nationalist party (PNV) came into power in 1979 through the first elections in which they emerged as the majority Basque party, AEK hoped to be considered on its own merits as an official public service and as such to be included in the government's budget. The autonomy that AEK wanted to maintain did not appear compatible with official recognition, however, and in the opinion of the Basque government, budgetary support would have to carry with it greater governmental control of the organization. Although the number of students in AEK-sponsored courses varied depending on the current strength of the cultural movement, AEK responded to a considerable demand. Progressively, and through its multiple activities oriented toward teaching and the development of the language, it managed to establish itself in the four territories of southern Euskadi and in the three northern territories as well.

Something Had to Be Done

At the end of the 1970s, and in spite of the fact that the cultural unease initiated in the previous epochs was continuing, it was believed that Euskara was in grave danger, and drastic solutions were needed. While the work of the ikastolas was socially valued and recognized, that of the literacy movement was not. From that situation arose the need for a public demonstration that would attract attention, make known the work that had been done, and point out the deficiencies that still plagued euskaldunización. The demonstration would also give a powerful boost to AEK at a time when it was not clear how much recognition the organization was going to get from the Basque government.

Likewise, we must keep in mind the positive climate that was being created by a series of milestone events organized between 1977 and 1980, including the inauguration of the Bai Euskarari campaign in 1978 and all the events that followed until 1980 and the "march of liberty" in 1979.[2] Although each event had different objectives, together they provoked massive popular demonstrations that owed their success to the coordinated work of many

people who participated within the broad spectrum of the different nationalist currents. Likewise, a national concept was developed that encompassed
all seven Basque territories. In the popular fiesta Bai Euskarari (Yes to Euskara), the people experienced the cohesive quality of Euskara through the
crowds that flocked to the soccer stadium at San Mamés in Bilbo in 1978.
The image-making campaign carried out by specialists was evaluated positively, as were the utilization of aesthetic symbols such as the dove designed
by Nestor Basterrechea and the hymn composed by Telesforo Monzón. The
march of liberty constituted an important indicator of the power of action for
expressing the idea of a people in movement. Enough money was collected
from the different events to defray Euskaltzaindia's expenses and support
future work. All this served as a reference point and as an organizational
experience on a very broad level when the time came to plan the public
projection of the language.

In spite of the fact that interviews with people from the organization and
with those involved in the gestation of the event made action and improvisation appear to be important characteristics, which were in turn key elements
of Basque culture, Korrika also was based on previous experiences, actions,
and mobilizations on behalf of Euskara, especially those led by the ikastolas
in the different territories in the north and south of Euskadi.

> It is 1980. Here and there campaigns, demonstrations in favor of Eus-
> kara, have been organized: KILOMETROAK, the IBILALDIA
> march . . . and the daily work is often hard and heavy. Tiring as well.
> But it is something that always has to be done. While we were involved
> in that, after a dinner, it occurred to AEK to organize KORRIKA,
> KORRIKA 1. (*Aizu,* November 8, 1983)[3]

The circumstance most closely related to the birth of Korrika took place
during an after-dinner conversation among friends in the house of Julen
Kalzada in Busturia in December 1979, in which Kalzada expounded upon
AEK's precarious economic situation.

"We need five million pesetas," he said. Also present were Alberto Gabika,
Bittor Artola, and Jesús Naberan, all of whom were related to the popular euskaldunización movement, and some members of Bai Euskarari. My
informants spoke of that moment as the "dinner/meeting that catalyzed"
everything that developed afterward.

From that moment on, these people began to work with the idea of organizing an event to earn money. The impression I have received from the
informants is that a period of time passed in which a jumble of different
ideas were rejected in search of something original that would capture the
attention of the public. I cannot identify the specific idea of the relay race

with a single person or a specific moment. I was told that "the idea emerged; there was a meeting; something occurred to somebody; then it was evaluated a little; they began to say maybe yes, maybe no; they began making the first tests and look, well, let's go forward; and that's how it emerged."[4] Some people told me that "it emerged from a dinner among friends, from a 'mala manga' like so many things in this country." Others said that "different ideas were shuffled about until they centered on the idea of action and on the presence of the symbol of Euskara." The experience of the march for liberty led to an idea. The organizers thought they would follow the march's model of distributing four testigos, one from each territory, in order to bring them together in the same place. However, that seemed to be dividing the language when what they wanted to do was emphasize unity, Batua, and so the search centered on something that would combine action with the unity of the language beyond geographical divisions. That was how the idea arose of a race in which the language is transmitted in a symbolic way. They thought of a giant *kilometro*. One of them pointed out that "the march for liberty and the *kilometroak* were milestones that made us think in terms of a giant *kilometroak* that would take off locally and embrace all of Euskalerria." What does seem clear is that it was a cumulative process: "The idea did not occur to anyone in particular and nobody wanted to repeat systems that were already known, they wanted something new." The same process of shuffling interests and objectives would have a lot to do with the concepts and symbolism we are going to encounter as we analyze Korrika throughout this book.[5]

Nor is the way in which Korrika arose unusual. The informal character of something planned at a dinner has deep roots in Basque culture. On the one hand, it is based on the importance given to the informal associations called *cuadrilla* and their socializing and communicative function. Both Alfonso Pérez-Agote (1984:105–10) and Ander Gurrutxaga (1985:365–74) emphasize the importance of the cuadrilla—even more so during Franco's regime—in the development of nationalist conscience and activity. Later we will see its importance in the organization of and participation in Korrika.

In the context of a cuadrilla, a conversation initiated during dinner easily goes on for one or more hours. Topics move quickly from banal commentary and jokes to profound philosophical conversation. Thus it is not difficult to imagine how a serious project could arise in this friendly, relaxed context where exposition, confrontation, and group participation convert an individual idea into a group product. Moreover, there are times when who suggested the idea is not remembered, but the discussion is, especially if it was heated, and the final decision is remembered. That generates the necessary energy for carrying out the action and transcends the specific moment in which the idea is born.

Improvisation and action form part of the ordinary experience in Basque culture. Joseba Zulaika establishes a parallel between the bertsolari's capacity for improvisation and ETA's (Euskadi ta Askatasuna, or Basque Homeland and Freedom) activism (1988:230–35). Likewise he speaks of a mentality for action in which efficiency is based on repetitive physical action. The image of work in rural culture is linked to the image of the hands and the body in motion (ibid.:371). By means of this image we can affirm that a Basque person is defined by and communicates by doing, a fact that is reflected in sayings taken from popular oral tradition. In Ataun, they say in the Gipuzcoan dialect, "Zenbat lan? Eginala lan!" (How much work is there? As much as you can do!) or "Lan lasterra lan alferra" (Quick work is lazy work) or "Lanik ez duenari, lan emok" (Give work to the person who has none). The latter is said ironically of people who have obligations but waste their time in futile labors (Thalamas 1931). I want to emphasize that I offer this "doing" as a form of discourse in which there is a thought, a reflection, or an experience of content, and often it may even contain abstraction and speculation or be the path to speculation. I underscore this because at times this "doing" contrasts with thinking, affirming that the first excludes the second. In the Basque case, I would say "doing" in the sense of "being." It is a "doing" that can arise from improvisation, as is the case with the beginning of Korrika.

> The first Korrika was organized as best it could be, nobody knew very well what it was, nobody knew very well how to put it on, nobody knew very well what was going to happen. But what we did know was that something had to be done, and it had to be done well, and that we engaged to do thoroughly.[6]

In spite of the fact that Korrika requires careful preparation carried out over several months, improvisation is always present in the race, and the ability to improvise constitutes one of the personal qualities valued when the time comes to select or choose the organizers of each stage. Korrika in turn can be considered as *ekintza* (action) in the sense that all of it is a demonstration of the value of movement as an expression of the importance of the language and the word. It implies a physical effort because it generates, manifests, and consumes indarra (biological energy). Also it confirms how, faced with a deficiency or difficulty, an almost primary need appears for "doing" that carries physical movement implicitly within it. Action can represent a cultural way of resolving a concern through the visible experiential act of movement. It provides a sensation of already being part of the solution to the problem. When this action occurs in a group, it has a power that can prolong the enthusiasm of the moment and carry over to specific actions within ordinary life.

The connection between the initial plan, a product of improvisation, and the cumulative group experience was carried out through the organizational structure of AEK and with the support of members of Bai Euskarari. In the words of my informants: "AEK gathers together the power of Bai Euskarari."

AEK Defined

AEK defines itself as a popular autonomous group whose activities are directed toward the euskaldunización of adults through the direct, popular, and participatory teaching of Euskara. Its field of action includes the seven historical territories, and democratic management is emphasized in its organization. This is reflected in the participation of the different groups that function at the levels of village, district, and territory, and in their representation on AEK's national board through elected members. Participation of both teachers and students is promoted.

At the lowest level, AEK is teaching centers (night school, boarding school), in every one of which a representative is elected; these in turn elect representatives who carry out coordination at the district level. These latter representatives coordinate the processes of the *eskualde* (district): the price of matriculation, teachers, teaching materials, and other matters. In turn they form the coordinating body of the *herrialde* (territory) and are responsible for teaching services and the preparation of teachers. The representatives of each territory form a *batzorde* (assembly) at which information is disseminated and general plans of AEK action are prepared for all Euskalerria. In the case of Korrika, it is at the batzorde that general decisions are made, to be implemented later at the different levels, as I have indicated in figure 1.

Within each euskaltegi and boarding school students participate through regular meetings that permit them to take part in decisions that affect the development of the course. Participation of members of a group doing an intensive four-month course is proportionally greater than that of those who attend a daily two-hour class. At the same time, participation of teachers through their contractual tie with AEK is greater than that of the students, although student participation is considered important.[7] The teaching approach is based on the communicative method of language teaching and on the insertion of the student into the social milieu. It is based on the affirmation that a language is not lost because those who do not know it do not learn it, but because those who *do* know it do not use it. "It is the example

FIGURE 1

The organizational levels of Korrika (adapted from AEK, "Korrika-4—
Aurreproiektoa" (AEK document, 1985).

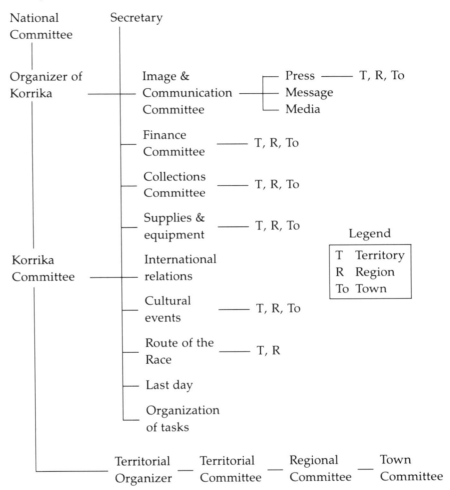

of . . . those who speak Basque, that must motivate those who do not know
it to learn it" (*Egin*, November 5, 1983, p. 31). This thought materializes more
clearly in the intensive courses, in which the group is inserted into the social
milieu of the locality where the course is taught. My experience in the course
in Lekeitio speaks in favor of this type of integration. Outside of the six
hours of class, it was up to each person to involve himself or herself in the
Basque community. Initially this was done through people in the town who
offered to act as a liaison between the student and the milieu, so that what

was being learned in class could be put into practice outside the classroom, and vice versa.

Moreover, specific activities took place within the class context, including interviews and visits to different organizations and businesses with the object of practicing Euskara. The visits to small plants, factories, baserris, cooperatives, and schools, to cite a few, provided situations where vocabulary and linguistic structures could be assimilated in their proper context. Likewise, although the course centered on the teaching of Batua, these contacts with local people made possible a familiarity with dialectal forms.

The organization of AEK is based, on the one hand, on the distribution of responsibilities to groups, and, on the other, on the participation of each group and upper-level coordination for their normal functioning. AEK's power resides in the organization of the total experience at each level (town, district, and historical territory), and within each tier it resides in the leading role and degree of decision-making power allotted to each group, always within the general plan of the organization.

AEK's didactic orientation exhibits concern about inserting the learning of the language into the context of a population that continues to use Euskara as an ordinary means of communication. The result not only benefits those who are learning Euskara; it also has reinforcing effects on those who communicate in it. In both cases, the experience gives validity to the continuity of the language over time and demonstrates its intrinsic capacity to respond to the communication needs of the present moment.

Objectives of Korrika

Certain pedagogical, cultural, and political nuances can be appreciated within the fundamental objectives of the organization of Korrika. The first objective consists of publicizing the work that AEK carries out in its task of developing and empowering Euskara in Euskalerria, maintaining as its ultimate goal the implantation of Euskara as the principal language. The second objective is directed at encouraging the learning or perfecting of Euskara, principally among adults, with the end of creating a Basque atmosphere in both the public and the private realms. And the third is to acquire through economic contributions the necessary support for continuing their work.

Those objectives have remained constant during the short history of Korrika, while others have been added that respond to new situations. Thus, in the second running, the organizers considered one objective to be acquiring the Basque government's recognition of AEK as a public entity on the basis of its sixteen years of dedication and its 206 centers devoted to the service of the literacy movement and the euskaldunización of Euskalerria. The principal goal here was to acquire public financing. Along with that funding AEK would have to allow the government to direct spending, but members insisted that they be allowed to maintain their autonomy in teaching.

Apart from official objectives, as we will see later, Korrika's capacity for adaptation provides for the incorporation of a varied set of problems. "Korrika is good for something more than extending the language. It is a social statement for any type of people's problems."[8] It is for that reason that I distinguish between official objectives and those of different groups with varied problems. I will examine this further in chapter 5 when I speak of Korrika's integrating capacity.

It is interesting to substantiate Korrika's objectives through the slogans and messages that go into the testigo in each Korrika. In the first, the slogan was "Korrika Euskal Herria!" and in the second, "Herriaren Erantzuna Euskararen Alde" (The people's response in favor of Euskara). In both, the message consisted of the letter from Arregui to Satrustegui quoted earlier. The slogans allude to the relationship of the language with the territory and an active people that supports it. The concept of movement is present in the letter, in which the need to give a quick, committed response to advance the practice of Euskara is recognized.

"Euskara eta kitto," which can be translated as "Basque is enough," was the slogan of the third Korrika, suggesting a radical position of support for the supremacy of Euskara. With this slogan the organizers intended to channel the broader effort when it came time to pull together all the people involved in promoting Euskara in order to convert the language into the basis of communication for all the people.[9] The testigo carried in the third Korrika contained a poem by Gabriel Aresti:

HIBAI UGARIA

Herri isilaren aho biribila.
Hibai ugaria,
zeineko ura
zoineko hura
da,
gure gogoak
janzten zuen
hickunza eskuarra,
egiak esateko
euskara
klaroa,

asmaketetatik eta eldarnioetatik
minzaera
garbitua,
pucu ilun batetik
datorrena,
orain ixas zabal batera
lasterrean
doana.

(Poemak II:44-45)

The silent people's round mouth. Abundant river, whose water is that tonic, our own language in which our spirit is dressed, sparkling Euskara for telling truths, language free of inventions and heaviness, that comes from a dark pit, that now runs toward the wide sea.

"One people, one language" was the slogan of the fourth Korrika, and inside the testigo was an excerpt from the speech given by Pierre Lafitte on the occasion of the homage paid to Euskaltzaindia in Ustaritz on May 23, 1983, a speech charged with patriotic and religious feelings:

Something that has moved me in these latter times is a group of young men and women who have come to Euskara with new spirit, with new vision, and with new ways of researching the language, not superficially but deeply and extensively. I have become aware of this marvelous springtime, not only after reading this book, but [also after] some other thesis and grammar reports written by men and women.

My God, my time is almost up. You can take me to your side. There I see those who come after me, following the Basque path I began. It seems to me that they will achieve the salvation of the Basque culture. Long live the youth. So be it. (*Egin*, June 10, 1985, p. 7)

In the fifth Korrika, the slogan "Euskera, zeurea" (Your Euskara) personalized the language in such a way that reading the slogan and hearing it evoked a response of positive responsibility. On that occasion within the testigo there were poems by Lauaxeta and by the bertsolari Balentin Enbeita, both of which point out the power of the language for Basque identity:

Euskera euskaldunok dogu
lenengo premia
horretaz dudarik duena
ez dadila deitua duena.

(Lauaxeta)

We Basques have Euskara, our basic necessity, whoever doubts it shall not be called Basque.

Euskadi ez da Euskalerria
bere hizkuntzarik gabe
eta etsaiek argi ta garbi
hori gaur ikusten dabe
Euskeran alde jaiki gaitezan
lan egin dagigun trebe
Euskerarekin egingo gara
geure Herriaren jabe.

Euskera dogu Euskalerriko
izaki guztien ama
Euskeragaitik daukan fama
Euskera dogu gure babesa
Herri bizi ta anima
euskaldunaren espiritua
Euskerak berak darama.
(Balentin Enbeita)

Euskadi is not Euskalerria without its language, and our enemies see that very clearly today. Let us rise up on behalf of Euskara, let us work hard, with Euskara we will make ourselves masters of our people.

Everyone in Euskalerria has Euskara for a mother, Euskara is our protection, the life and soul of our people, the spirit of what is Basque is contained in Euskara.

The interrelationship of the three general objectives makes Korrika a complex act that can be examined from several angles and can evoke varied reactions in different sectors of the Basque population. The leadership AEK proclaims in language pedagogy is presented in opposition to that claimed by HABE, an institution promoted by the PNV that receives strong official backing. AEK's unconditional support of Batua excludes the support of those sectors that, although in the minority, oppose the unified language. For that reason what appeared in the first Korrika to be an action called to unify people of different political strengths in favor of Euskara to accept the cultural project as their own is being more and more identified as a political project of the abertzale Left, more specifically, with Herri Batasuna. Moreover, as we will see later, even within this group, discrepancies arise over the form in which the linguistic realities of the present moment and their development in the future are interpreted in Korrika.

The Bases of Popular Participation in
the Organization of Korrika

A key element for the success of mass participation in Korrika is its organizational base, which brings together people from all parts of Euskadi who, while aware of the global nature of their task, are associated with local contexts (see fig. 1). Decisions about the celebration of Korrika are initially made in the General Assembly of AEK. From that moment on, responsibilities are divided through various committees whose tasks are implemented at different levels: town, district, and territory. Each committee assumes a series of responsibilities that take shape in specific locations, within general guidelines and criteria established for all of Korrika. The importance attributed to the lowest levels contributes to Korrika's success. It is at the lower levels that the union with the local people takes place; the activities that are planned, whether politically relevant or festive, have their link with concrete reality; and symbols have a greater capacity for popular interpretation.

The openness of Korrika is one of the characteristics mentioned most frequently in the interviews my team and I conducted, although contrary opinions were also voiced:

> The work of the Korrika campaign is open to everyone. A series of commissions are formed, such as publicity, the race route, funding, placards, posters, etc. Participation in the organization is free; everyone can participate in it.[10]

One teacher from AEK evaluated her participation in the preparation of the second Korrika as follows:

> We had to divide the work. Some set up sales booths, others ran, it fell to me and two other people to go by car through the towns to give runners' numbers to the race participants who were waiting for us at the points of departure. We had to leave at four in the morning, but you are always ready to do these things because, what's more, you have a good time. I would do it again without hesitation.[11]

Even in areas with large populations such as Bilbo, which is divided into different sectors for organizational purposes, participation is the key:

> Neither the organization nor the development are closed things, it's done for the people and with the people. All the political parties and associations take part, everyone who wants to collaborate, for that reason it is a Korrika for everyone.[12]

When Korrika in general is evaluated, its success is attributed mainly to local organization.

I think that this year participation has been greater than in other Korrikas. We managed to set up organizing committees in all the towns in Euskadi, including zones historically more reluctant because of their special "erdeldun" situation such as the Navarrese Ribera, the Araban Rioja, or the Encartaciones. This year it turned out very well since there were Korrika committees in all the towns, and you can see that participation is increasing.[13]

However, some of those we interviewed emphasized that the same people always participate in the organization or that major responsibilities fall on a small group. That was the opinion expressed by Juana Mari and Marta when they were interviewed on the eve of Korrika's passage through Isaba:

When the time comes to run, because it has to do with a festive event, people will participate more than when it's time to organize it. There were four or five of us who organized and, in contrast, there will be at least thirty of us running.[14]

Anabel, the director of the Korrika organization in Tutera, reflected a similar opinion:

All the people who have participated by running should have had to contribute to the organization more than they did. Before beginning to prepare Korrika a meeting was held with all the people who potentially would have been disposed to help us and who later ran, and the majority said yes. But when the moment of truth came, four people got stuck doing everything. There were very few of us, and even though it all turned out fine in the end, the people should have had to contribute more.[15]

In Iruñea the representative of the Peña Anaitasuna expressed the opinion that while anyone could participate in the organizing activities, some people were discriminated against for not knowing Euskara; for example, the musical group Barricada, which had offered to perform. "In the end, there was no musical group from Pamplona, because none of them from here know Basque, and leaving them out is not a good thing."[16]

In order to achieve a broader participation it is necessary to work with the local environment in mind. Thus the utilization of public space for announcing Korrika has its importance, as could be seen in the small Araban town of Kanpezu, whose most important point of social reference is the plaza.

In the plaza there is a showcase, the bakery's showcase, that fulfills the function of official public bulletin board, and there you could find everything that referred to Korrika mixed in with bus schedules, announcements of excursions, publicity for the Red Cross, some municipal notice, and all kinds of offers to sell stuff.[17]

In Zalduondo (136 inhabitants) publicity for Korrika 4 was placed on the fronton where the festival is celebrated, in the bar, and on three stands where drinks are served.

In each town there is one person responsible for organization and another for the sale of kilometers. Euskaltegis and night schools have an important function, and their members form part of the local organizing committee. Other urban entities that want to collaborate are also included on the local organizing committee. Neighborhood associations, political parties, women's groups, ecology committees, antinuclear committees, alternative radio operators, and business groups are all welcome, with the object of involving the greatest possible number of people through them. These local commissions are coordinated with those from the district and the territory, and together with the central commission they carry the weight of the campaign. The local commissions do everything necessary for the execution of the campaign in each town: organizing their stretch of the race, selling campaign products, spreading publicity, organizing buses for the last day, and organizing events in support of Korrika in each location—Korrika txiki, parties on the eve of the race, meals, and cultural events.

Focusing on contact with groups rather than with individuals ensures that many people are involved. This sort of organization through groups is important in Basque culture, given the capacity for organization and mobilization that those associations have. In the case of the fourth Korrika, the involvement of schools was perceived as an advancement toward the broader participation that is one of Korrika's objectives.

The definition of Korrika as open and participatory is important when it comes time to involve different groups; however, the same objectives of action, orientation, and an ideological basis to identify with may bias the selection of participants toward nationalists and even people from the abertzale Left on the basis of the connotations their support or participation might have. The bilingual situation of the language at times leads to the exclusion of people who want to participate, given that, on the one hand, mass participation is desired but, on the other, Korrika's goal is to supply a vision of the strength of the language, and that verbal expression will be in Euskara. In the local contexts, however, both native speakers and those who were learning Euskara carried the testigo.

The Economic Dimension

In spite of the fact that cultural objectives appear to be Korrika's priorities, the petition for funding is also important in planning the campaign. In fact, it is continuously present. The kilometers of the race have an economic translation. "The objective of Korrika is not to acquire money, but Korrika's funding team has a great goal, and it is to obtain the greatest sum possible." [18]

Each race campaign is carried out with anticipation and is directed at different sectors of the public. Within each location, the most selective campaign consists of personal visits from the person coordinating the funding to public and private agencies such as territorial and municipal governments, banks and savings institutions, businesses, and professional societies, as well as specific persons. In 1985 the Municipal Government of Donostia approved the underwriting of Korrika 4 with 800,000 pesetas (*Egin,* May 25, 1985). In the cases of public entities, where support is submitted for approval to the representatives of the different political parties, approval or the lack of it reflects in turn the positions of those bodies in relation to Korrika. Thus there are cases in which underwriting was granted but the opposition the move evoked was well known, and other cases in which changes in support took place from one Korrika to the next.

The popular focus embraces different activities: the sale of kilometers, selling publicity material such as bumper stickers and metal plates, the sale of "o kilometers" in each location, requests for funding in cities and towns, and the support of local patrons. Every kilometer is purchased in its entirety, and its price depends on its location and the importance attributed to it. Prices vary, as table 3 shows for the third and fourth Korrikas.

Most of the time, kilometers are bought by entities, associations, and institutions that pay the corresponding fee. Sometimes members of a group or cuadrilla chip in until they arrive at the total price of the kilometer. In every case the group decides on the person who will carry the testigo and wear the official racing number that corresponds to the number of the kilometer. From that moment on, the kilometer is assigned to that group; thus one hears of the "ikastola's kilometer" or the "kilometer of the Women's Assembly of Donostia" or that of the "Hernani Municipal Government." There are times when an individual, or, more frequently, an entity, sponsors the participation of a person who possesses outstanding cultural significance. Thus in the third Korrika, the Provincial Savings Bank of Gipuzkoa paid for the kilometer in which the singer Mikel Laboa carried the testigo. The cost of each kilometer corresponds to the importance of that stretch. Thus, the Boulevard kilometer in Donostia is more expensive than the Amara, since the centrality of the first ensures a large concentration of people and there-

TABLE 3

Comparative Cost of Kilometers in Korrikas 3 and 4 (in pesetas)

Location	Korrika 3	Korrika 4
Capital cities	150,000–250,000	150,000–300,000
Big cities	75,000–150,000	75,000–150,000
Towns	20,000–75,000	30,000–75,000
Unpopulated areas	10,000	20,000

Sources: AEK, *Korrika 3. Finantziaketarako aurreproiektoa* (no date); AEK, *Korrika 4. Finantziaketa Aurreproiektoa* (1984).

fore a stronger public projection. Also, in each Korrika there are kilometers "reserved" beforehand by the organization; for example, the last kilometer always belongs to members of AEK.

Within a specific city or town, a person can contribute to Korrika through voluntary donations, or "kilometer o." The kilometer o category allows purchasers to be "officially" involved in the race; that is, they wear a small runner's tag with the number o; this category is especially popular within the stretches in the cities and towns, and anybody can participate. In order to enter the kilometer o the person contributes money, with no set minimum required.

Implicit in the buying and selling of kilometers is much activity involving contacts and personal visits that demonstrate the degree of cooperation and the variations it represents.

Specifically, the officials of the Diputación and the Municipal Government of Iruñea, students, members of the Caja Laboral Popular, Tavernkeepers of Iruñea, Peñas, Ortzadar and business committees like Eaton, Union Carbide, Seat, Super Ser, Copeleche, Imenasa, and so on, have already bought their corresponding kilometer. (*Egin,* May 24, 1985, p. 21)

The most important collection takes place one week to a few days before the beginning of Korrika, with separate dates for the cities and the towns, and still different days for the capitals. In the third Korrika in Donostia the collection took place on November 27, and in Gasteiz, Iruñea, and Bilbo on November 29. In contrast, in the fourth Korrika the collection was carried out on the same day in all the capitals (on the weekend), and in the towns on weekdays. Collection tables are placed at strategic locations, and volunteers are charged with asking for donations on the streets and in central locations. Contributions are voluntary, and the effort is directed at those who have not purchased kilometers. The bumper stickers that are distributed in exchange for a donation are a way of announcing the Korrika; at the same time, with different symbols or colors, they constitute an up-to-date point of reference and mark continuity with previous runnings.

Organizers recommend a festive ambience for the collection sites, created through activities such as korrika txiki; participation of *txarangak* (popular bands), *txistulariak,* and people in costume; and car caravans with loud-speakers that contribute "noisily" to announcing the event, since "a festive atmosphere makes the collection easier."[19] Imagination and ingenuity are necessary correlates here.

At each level local sponsors play a relevant role in building a foundation of support and effective networking that multiplies their effectiveness. This relates to what I said earlier about the importance of contacts through groups and institutions. Contributions are solicited from businesses, bars, and small factories, which in turn receive a poster that recognizes their contribution; this is generally placed in the display window or some other visible location. Thus, when I took a stroll through the Old Quarter of Bilbo before the last Korrika, I was able to determine at a glance those who had contributed to Korrika. It is a direct way to transmit a message of patriotism and also to evoke commentary in those opposed to the event. These places also provide additional information about Korrika, such as the location of the starting line and the schedule of the buses that are organized to take people to the place where the end of the Korrika is being celebrated.

At any moment, in any given kilometer, people can take part whether or not they have made a monetary contribution. When the different forms of participation are mentioned it is said, "If the money were missing from it all, simply running. Because, although we need the economic support, moral support also is appreciated."[20] Participation is promoted, recorded, and highly valued throughout the race. Moreover, in the general evaluation of Korrika, one of the things that is mentioned most frequently is the num-ber of participants and the presence of "active" and "mass" kilometers. The relationship between economic participation and the group is expressed in a full-page announcement that appeared in *Egin* on the occasion of the third Korrika (November 26, 1983, p. 9). In the foreground is a compact group of runners linked arm in arm, and in the background, a giant piggy bank with the emblems of AEK and Korrika 3 and the slogan "Euskara is in the bank."

Another form of subsidy is in the help provided by festive and cultural ac-tivities. These are sponsored by local entities, or the participants (musicians, artists, and dancers) donate their services as a way of supporting Euskara. If the activity accrues a deficit, the local coordinator can ask for payment from the general fund.

Once the expenses of the race are covered, the contributions to Korrika are earmarked for the support of AEK's existing activities and for creating new ones. For example, in the third Korrika, 41 million pesetas was received in gross revenues. Of that amount, 15 million was committed to the "Consciousness in Favor of Euskara" and the "Attraction of New Students" campaigns and to the costs of organizing and putting on the race. The 26 million remaining pesetas went for the following:

—Teaching services for education in the areas of traditionally smaller attendance such as Nafarroa (Erribera, Lizarra), Araba (Errioxa), and Bizkaia (Mehatzeta)

—New learning centers (euskaleskolas) in Nafarroa (Erribera, Erronkari), Araba (Errioxa), Bizkaia (Barrios of Bilbo, Mehatzeta, Lea-Artibai), and Iparralde (Zuberoa, Lapurdi)

—New centers for accelerated courses in basic Euskara, on a four-month boarding basis, in Lekeitio, Otxandio, Lakuntza, Errigoiti, Etxarri-Aranaz, and Leitza

—Organization, at different points in Euskalerria, of cultural weeks, bertsolari festivals, *kantaldis* (singing contests), and parades as a means of enabling and spreading Euskara[21]

The emphasis on economic objectives evoked opinions that, although there is a need for financial support, "it is really sad to have to resort to Korrika to obtain money." But the reality is that AEK needs to face up to its annual deficit, and the very act of trying to cover it emphasizes the discriminatory situation to which AEK is subjected for lack of greater institutional support.

Preparing the Action

Since the first Korrika, and within the preparatory campaign, activities related to promoting the Basque language and culture have been carried out in a progressively intensified manner, generated by the organizing committee of Korrika. The prerace activities are aimed at creating an atmosphere of receptivity and support among the general public, attracting the interest of the press, and projecting an image of group support, on the part of both organizing groups and the people who join them. These activities are held during the days or weeks before the Korrika begins.

Presentation to the press is considered very important, as the third and fourth Korrikas demonstrate. In the third, a celebration was held in the Korrilla cider shop in Zarautz in the form of a dinner organized by Carlos Argiñano, one of the most highly regarded chefs in the New Basque cuisine.[22] The dinner was attended by representatives from AEK and the communications media and Basque cultural personalities. In an atmosphere of comraderie, and after "enjoying a simple menu but one that is very us" (*La Voz*, December 2, 1985), Urtsa Errasti, general coordinator of Korrika, spoke about general objectives and about what the third Korrika was going to mean. Xabier Amuritza[23] intervened and contributed a note of artistic improvisation through his *bertsoak* (verses) and his good humor and jokes.

In the fourth Korrika these official publicity events increased in number. The first took place on May 7 in the Gastronomic Society in the heart of the Old Quarter of Donostia, this time attracting a group more broadly representative of Basque culture. Representatives from northern Euskadi such as Jone Etxeberri (in the name of SEASKA)[24] and the writer Daniel Landart shared a typical meal with Natxo de Felipe of the musical group Oskorri[25] from Bilbo; musician Pablo Sorozabal, a resident of Madrid; and María Josefa Ganuza, the widow of Telesforo Monzón, who came from Bergara. There was also a representative from Nájera (La Rioja), who came to petition the organizers to allow the Korrika to pass through that locale (for further details see chapter 3).

Both presentations attempted to achieve the same objectives through representatives from the worlds of sports, business, culture, and Basque politics. At the dinner in the Café Iruña in Bilbo, attended by three members of my team, the organizers of Korrika asked us to explain our work, and this information appeared in detail in *Egin* on the following day (May 19, 1985, p. 28). Volunteering locations and organizing dinners are considered contributions to and public support of Korrika. I should emphasize the informal atmosphere surrounding a dinner after which references are made to Korrika. This relates to what I said earlier when I spoke of the creation of Korrika and the importance of formal and informal contacts. Likewise, it is an atmosphere in which men predominate. In the case of the Bilbo dinner, only two of the thirty persons invited were women, a reflection once more of the value of masculine social roles in Basque culture. A similar proportion of the sexes appeared at the other two publicity events I have mentioned.[26]

In all the Korrikas, preparatory events have been celebrated days before the beginning of the race, and their importance and geographic extension have been increasing. Cultural activities were organized throughout Euskalerria to publicize the fourth Korrika, and a good number of writers and poets participated in them in Euskara. These were opportunities to present works by writers from northern Euskadi—Pierre Xarriton, Itxaro Borda, and

José Luis Duvant—as well as from southern Euskadi—Luis Maria Mujika, Laura Mintegi, and Xabier Gereño, among others. Likewise, participants answered questions relative to the production of books in Euskara and the problems it involves; literary themes; different genres—essay, poetry, and novel—and the presentation of works such as "Ni ez naiz hemengoa," by Joseba Sarraionandia, written from prison; and the new magazines that have come into being in the last few years in Nafarroa. They also spoke of theatrical productions and the presence of Euskara in the streets. In the presence of the numerous crowds that gathered in the different capitals—Iruñea, Bilbo, Donostia, Gasteiz, and Baiona—they publicized the activity that has been generated around Euskara in the last few years. In general the perspectives presented during these activities gave rise to hope; when there is a creative process, the language is alive and constitutes a very important form of expression. Likewise, it reveals a specific situation and atmosphere.[27]

Cartoon videos on the occasion of the third Korrika were run on television channels[28] (Televisión española, Telenorte, Telenavarra, and Euskal Telebista, or Basque television) and in movie theaters to publicize the event, and several broadcasting stations contributed with radio programs in the days preceding the beginning of Korrika. As in all sports activities, the warmup is indispensable. The activities that precede the race are intended to create an atmosphere favorable to its support and to the comprehension of the message it attempts to transmit. To that end everything that can help generate interest and capture attention is put into play. The communications media (press, radio, and television) are combined with forms of casual association in an attempt to put a familiar, informal face on the precampaign, while keeping it oriented toward awakening a sense of responsibility toward Euskara.

Contradictions and Conflicts

In my introduction I referred to the importance of Korrika as an act that encompasses and expresses many of the contradictions that exist in an important area of Basque society.

The conflicts within Korrika arise at times from the internal dynamics of the Left, but they are also related to a broader sector of political life. However, the continuous internal conflict present from the second through the fourth Korrikas was a result of the confrontation of the two bodies that currently assume responsibility for the euskaldunización of Euskadi: AEK and HABE. Likewise, the conflicts can be said to have originated and developed as a result of the actions of the government in Madrid, and from that government's perception of the situation and the validity of Basque social claims, as we will see in this chapter with regard to Nafarroa and in the next as we follow the route of Korrika through Treviño.

I have already spoken of the creation and development of AEK. In September 1981 the Basque government created HABE through the Ministry of Culture, directed by Ramón Labaien, and appointed Joxe Joan G. de Txabarri as director. HABE depends on a large budget and the support of the territorial governments of Araba, Bizkaia, and Gipuzkoa. This new body was formed to promote the normalization of Euskara, in Basque institutions and through the protection of Article 6 of the Statute of Gernika. In theory the HABE guidelines speak of all Euskalerria, although its area of operations is limited to the Basque Autonomous Community. HABE's objectives are directed toward the education of the adult population, the preparation of teachers, the development of a technical Euskara that permits its incorporation into modern life, and the development of an up-to-date pedagogical method.

In the 1981–82 academic year, schools of Euskara were opened in Bilbo, Gasteiz, Donostia, and Hondarribia—a boarding school in the latter—and in the summer of 1982 they were opened in Arrasate, Ermua, and Urretxu. At its inception HABE was generally directed toward the same tasks that AEK was already performing, although with a different philosophy and orientation. While exposing the differences that exist between these two bodies, I will present the more polemical points, those with greater public projection, that reflect on the dynamics of Korrika. One could say that at the basis of every project lie different concepts of the roles institutions play. In HABE's view, the democratic process gives legitimacy to the leading role of the Basque government in the development of Euskara and authorizes it to take corresponding steps. In contrast, AEK claims a leading role in that field based on its previous work and asks for institutional support and sufficient economic backing. That is how the creation of HABE is interpreted in circles of the Basque cultural Left. Prior to creating HABE, the Basque government made several offers to AEK that AEK did not consider acceptable, and vice versa:

The first attempt dates from the academic year 79–80 when the CGV [Consejo General Vasco] through the Ministry of Culture proposed the first project to them for institutionalizing the popular movement of the Gau-Eskolas, and AEK responded to the above-mentioned project with another that had nothing to do with the one presented and at the base of which there lay an entire political philosophy: self-management, the role of administration from which it was banished, giving it [the government] only the role of economic patron, a popular movement.[29]

When the Basque government realized that it could not acquire AEK, it created an organism over which it could exercise control.

The competitive situation and the position of economic disadvantage in which AEK found itself after HABE began to receive direct funding from the government gave rise to an ideology of confrontation and the continual practice of comparisons and conflicts. Many educators left AEK to work for HABE because the latter offered better work conditions and salaries. In fact, the number of teachers on HABE's payroll jumped from 92 in 1981–82 to 152 in 1982–83 (*HABE Plan de actuación*, academic year 1982–83). The politics of student selection in HABE, where potential students have to pass a preliminary exam, has tainted it with charges of discrimination, especially in the face of AEK's open policy of accepting any person who wants to learn Euskara.

AEK's constant goal throughout the years has been to obtain official recognition from the Basque government in the form of funding proportional to that received by HABE, thus bringing to an end the imbalance that exists (see table 4). AEK wants it understood that official funding does not imply control; that must continue in the hands of AEK itself. In contrast, from the beginning, the opinion of the Basque government has been that private entities should be funded with public monies only under the condition of economic, pedagogical, and professional control delimited by the government's own centers.[30]

The initial AEK-HABE conflict arose in the middle of the first Korrika when the handwritten letter from Arregui to Satrustegui disappeared from inside the testigo, apparently without anyone realizing it. At the end of that Korrika, Julen Kalzada, the representative of AEK in Bizkaia, read a message with a different text than the one that had been introduced in Oñati. This new text stressed that the objectives associated with Korrika were intended to make the people aware that Euskadi does not exist without Euskara and that AEK, as an organization, is capable of carrying out the process of euskaldunización. In addition, the new text asked Basque institutions to recognize AEK as a public entity within the seven historical territories and to create a single self-governing organism on behalf of Euskara. According to opinions I gathered from informants, that message caused uneasiness in the Ministry of Education and Culture because it alluded specifically to the ministry's lack of recognition of AEK as a public entity. Dionisio Amundarain's letter

TABLE 4
Activities and Government Support in Euskara-teaching Institutions,
1983–84 Academic Year

Institution	Number of students	Hours taught	Financing (pesetas)
HABE	4,612 (8.6%)	1,742,209 (17.54%)	648,453,405 (63.75%)
AEK	31,995 (56.62%)	5,274,183 (53.65%)	201,541,844 (19.82%)
Others*	19,905 (35.22%)	2,814,115 (28.63%)	167,003,751 (16.47%)
Totals	56,512 (100%)	9,831,207 (100%)	1,016,999,000 (100%)

Source: Euzkadi 184 (April 4, 1985): 24.
*Includes various private, local small-scale teaching enterprises.

published in *Egin* (February 1, 1981, p. 15),[31] indicates that the reading of the text had not pleased certain members of Euskaltzaindia either. The letter alludes to the note published by the academy at the meeting held in Azpeitia on January 23–24, 1981, which said that Euskaltzaindia did not agree with the content of the communication read at the final event of Korrika in Bilbo. In Amundarain's analysis, an initial discrepancy between the direction taken by AEK, made clear in Korrika, and that proposed by the academy comes to light, and he refers to it in order to explain Euskaltzaindia's negative reaction. After the end of the first Korrika, it was clear that although AEK was born out of Euskaltzaindia, it was following an independent course that was going to take shape in the next runnings of the race. Thus, although AEK was a part of Euskaltzaindia for fifteen years, "in 1980 it became an Autonomous Organism with deep roots throughout Euskal Herria."[32]

In 1982, when AEK decided to organize the second Korrika from May 22 to May 30, the principal reasons put forward—beyond those given for the first running—were economic, tied in turn to AEK's need for recognition as a public entity by the Basque government. On May 14 the Euskadi Buru Batzar[33] (EBB) issued a statement asking its members not to support the programs of the second Korrika. This represented a change; in the first Korrika representatives of that party took part by carrying the testigo, running, contributing monetarily, and supporting the organizers of the race. The statement was interpreted as an obvious rejection of Korrika, and therefore of the organizing body. The EBB's withdrawal echoed loudly in the press, where the PNV gave the following reasons for not participating:

1. In the first Korrika a final statement very different from the one initially known and adopted was substituted.
2. PNV's affiliation has been repeatedly utilized for other ends besides the diffusion of Euskera.
3. AEK's true goals go beyond euskaldunización, and Korrika 2 goes beyond the mere collection of funds, by presenting itself as an alternative to the Basque government's plans for teaching, including suggesting confrontation.
4. AEK demands recognition of their public service without admitting minimal guarantees such as public hiring of professors and parliamentary control.
5. The funding from the Basque government that AEK claims is meager climbed to 68 million pesetas for the academic year 1981–82, being dependent on the results of the exams established by HABE, which they do not recognize.
6. AEK officials in Bilbo rejected funding to the tune of 4.75 million pesetas for the publication of didactic material because they could not accept the condition that the name of the funding agency, the Basque government, be cited in the publication of that material.

The interesting part of this whole debate is that the opposition awakened by Korrika has served to make it stronger. Its opponents give Korrika, and therefore its organizers, a power—a strength—whose very intangibility makes it more powerful. Korrika has been accused of manipulation, deception, utilizing a social cause as a means of pressure, and "proposing goals" that are not expressed but are there nonetheless (Legarreta 1982). Korrika has also been accused of plotting to swindle thousands of people:

> If in the first running it began like an angelic campaign to gather volunteers on behalf of Euskara and ended with a public statement remembering the dead, those rotting in the jails, those tortured in police stations, and even those who live in anguish because some day they will be tortured (a clear reference to the Bienaventuranzas), in this second running that begins as a social cause, the ending can be magnificent. (Taldea 1982)

AEK's response was prompt, and its statement presents a different version of the goals attributed to it by the PNV. First of all, the statement expresses the surprise felt by the National Board of AEK upon reading that letter, since they considered that "AEK had made very clear what their philosophy and situation was, as well as their reasons for promoting Korrika" through the press. They had in turn handed over an explanatory document to the Basque government. The fact that AEK is a popular supporter of Euskara did not mean, as was stated in point 3 of the message, that it had shown itself to be an alternative to the government's plans, although the board recognized that it was "logical that AEK's alternatives and those of the government's Department of Culture not be identical." AEK officials recognized the longevity of AEK in spite of the fact that public bodies had not given it the recognition it deserved. They made a statement categorically denying point 5: "AEK has never received 68 million pesetas from the Basque government, and even if that had been the figure, it would have been a meager amount for teaching Basque to 25,000 students. In contrast HABE has disposed of 120 million pesetas for only 800 students." They felt the gravity suggested by the boycott of "the greatest popular demonstration ever seen in this country on behalf of our language." Another article in which the EBB's statement is criticized in detail responds to point 1, a point that is not addressed in AEK's communiqué:

> The so-called substitution of the final statement of the 1980 Korrika was not that at all. As the press was opportunely informed, the message contained in the "testigo" of Korrika 1 went astray of its trajectory, very much in spite of AEK's will. For that reason AEK officials went on to read the note of thanks that was written by AEK's National Committee for the final event, a note that they were planning to read anyway along with the message contained in the Korrika testigo. (Haitzerre 1982)

When I asked about the matter, I received several answers. People from the AEK organization affirmed that

> evidently it [the original message] was lost and Euskaltzaindia manipulated the situation. Two things could have happened: one, when the testigo was dropped (I saw it dropped myself), the one who picked it up did not realize it and closed it without noticing that the message was not inside, and the other, if some voluntary pawn made it disappear, so-and-so from Euskaltzaindia, they could have had something to do with it.

Other comments always made reference to the "mysterious" character of the disappearance and to a certain "magic" that is evident during Korrika; at certain moments, the responsibility for apparently inexplicable actions was attributed to that magic.

The results of the journalistic exposition and the comments of my informants are contradictory and confusing to the point that it may not be possible to decipher the "truth" of the matter. In the end, "history will say who is right" (*Deia,* May 30, 1982). Already people speak of the "testigo of

discord" when referring to the symbol that carried the two different mes-
sages (Garcia 1982:32), and one newspaper with socialist leanings said that
"Basque is confronting the PNV with the abertzale Left" (*Cabrero Tribuna
Vasca*, May 14, 1982).

The PNV's position and accusations had repercussions in various institutions, especially in city halls, and whether or not to support Korrika was
transformed into an object of debate, with the different political parties
taking the following positions. Where PNV had a majority, party members
demonstrated against participation, as in Gernika (*El Correo Español*, May 29,
1982) and Portugalete (*Tribuna Vasca*, May 19, 1982), where it was felt that
"the teaching of Euskara belongs in the institutions and the organization of
Korrika is outside them" (*Egin*, May 20, 1982, p. 17). In contrast, in other
locations Korrika achieved not only moral but economic support as well.
Thus in Barakaldo it was funded with 250,000 pesetas, the fruit of favorable
votes by PSE-PSOE (Partido Socialista Español–Partido Socialista Obrero
Español) and HB, six votes in all, while PNV voted three against, and UCD
(Unión de Centro Democrática) abstained (*Tribuna Vasca*, May 2, 1982). In
Iruñea the city hall awarded a budget of 110,000 pesetas, 10 percent more
than in the previous Korrika, a result of six votes from HB and PSOE, with
UCD and UPN (Unión del Pueblo Navarro) voting against (*Deia*, May 27,
1982). In Eibar a majority voted to support the Korrika and gave 10,000 pesetas (*Egin*, May 20, 1982). Larrabetzu not only supported it but went on to
say that "this City Hall recognizes AEK officially as the only institution that
can carry out the euskaldunización of adults" (*Egin*, May 15, 1982). There
were also groups within PNV who demonstrated in favor of Korrika, such
as the euskaltegi in Gasteiz, in spite of the EBB's nay-saying (*Tribuna Vasca*,
May 20, 1982).

The causes that AEK has supported over the years, and the conflicts these
have generated, were incorporated into the third and fourth Korrikas. At the
end of the third, AEK raised a protest because of the "shameful discriminatory treatment" that *Deia* had given the final events of that Korrika. Other
newspapers such as *El Correo*, *La Hoja del Lunes* in Bilbo, *La Voz*, and *Navarra
Hoy* had dedicated not only more space than *Deia* but had treated the race
as worthy of notice. Broadcast programs like "Euskadi Irratia," "Populares,"
and "Gure Irratia" (the latter from Iparralde) followed the end of the race,
and even ETB and TVE[34] had reported "more than *Deia*" ("AEK considera
vergonzoso," *Egin*, 1983).

However, one of the most noteworthy conflicts took place when the fourth
Korrika passed through Gasteiz, and it reflects the different positions within
AEK over the hunger strike led by seven AEK teachers from Gasteiz.

With the goal of calling the public's attention to the Basque government's position on Euskara, a group of seven teachers spent more than fifteen days on a hunger strike in the office of the Neighbors' Association of the Old Quarter of Gasteiz. They asked that the AEK faculty receive official recognition equal to that of HABE faculty and denounced discrimination against AEK in matters of government funding. When the Korrika passed through the center of the city and arrived at the Plaza de la Virgen Blanca, the carrier of the testigo entered the building where the hunger strikers had shut themselves in, and from the balcony he presented the testigo to the applause of the crowd that filled the square. One of the hunger strikers read a statement in Euskara expressing the strikers' desire to continue with the campaign for the euskaldunización of adults in spite of the scant support received from official institutions. As a background to all this, various banners, some held aloft by balloons, bobbed in the air to catch the audience's attention. Thus one could read "Kilometer 1927. With no money. We want to learn Euskara. Up with AEK." Another banner read "No discrimination."

The climax came when one of the hunger strikers tied the testigo to a banner that said "Public money for AEK too. Solidarity." With that act the strikers symbolized both their inability to carry the testigo and the circumstances that obliged them to remain locked in, precisely because they wanted to realize one of Korrika's objectives: institutional recognition. The banner that symbolized the cause of their protest carried the testigo (the language) through the city. With this action the protest itself was ritualized, personalized, and converted into a protagonist. An act of deep meaning took place in the plaza, a public place par excellence, and it was interpreted positively by the crowd, who applauded the gesture.

Opinions about the hunger strike varied from an HABE comment that it was a good strategy to begin the Korrika with propaganda directed at the people of HB rather than at the people of PNV (who did not support the Korrika), to those who said that it corresponded to differences within AEK:

What real meaning do the serious incidents that happened during the development of Korrika in Gasteiz have? How can we interpret the scant support that the hunger strikers from the euskaltegi in the Araban capital have received from AEK in their recent protest action against the Autonomous Government? (*Zer Egin* 1985, no. 194, p. 12)

The conflicts that exist among the different positions of the abertzale Left also appear in evaluations of the race. On the one hand, emphasis is placed on the Left's "not inconsiderable capacity for social incidence, on their considerable resources for popular mobilization," manifested in Korrika, while, on the other hand, the ideology represented by the central slogans of the last Korrika—"Herri bat, hizkuntza bat" (One people, one language) and "Herri bat gara, hizkuntza bat dugu" (We are one people, we have one language)— has been strongly criticized. It was imputed that these slogans proclaim a definition of Basque identity, an identity centered on Euskara as the essential element, reduced in turn to the abstract.

> It has to do with something much more general and abstract: it has to do with recovering a faultily drawn national identity, a deterio-rated national identity, a national identity and differentiations centered, clearly, on Euskara. (*Zer Egin,* ibid.)

Critics noted the existence of an essentialist ideology closer to the racist statements of the first nationalism than to the complex social and political reality of modern Euskadi.

> The Basque people are made up of archetypes as different as the fisher-man of Ondarroa, the peasant of Cascante, the emigrant worker of Bara-caldo, the office worker of downtown Donostia or the "Cuchi" punk of Gasteiz. . . . Those and many others. This entire complex and varied community makes up the Basque people. Along with it, with the ma-jority, we aspire to create a revolution of communist orientation. Ac-cording to one leading point of view, no one is more Basque than anyone else. (Ibid.:13)

Another source of the conflicts exhibited in Korrika is the government in Madrid or its representatives. In the case of the second Korrika, the initial prohibition against the passage of Korrika through Nafarroa handed down by the civil governor drove several bodies, including the PNV, to demon-strate their disagreement. Thus protests came from institutions as varied as the Carlist party, the Central Nacional de Trabajadores of Iruñea (CNT), the PNV's Junta Municipal of Baztan, the Asamblea de Trabajadores from Eaton, Euskal Herrian Euskaraz, the Langile Abertzale Iraultzaileen Aldun-dia (LAIA), and PSOE.[35] I should point out that the support that Korrika received in the second running, reflected in these protests, demonstrated a range of political options that progressively disappeared in the following years as the race's objectives and their attainment were better defined politi-cally. The protests mentioned above clearly contained political overtones: "The CNT of Iruñea thinks that the 'prohibition of the Korrika is the ulti-mate in total absence of freedom and it is part of the plan to separate Navarra from the rest of Euskadi, through total political repression.' "[36] For the Junta of Baztan it suggested "a negation of free movement of citizens recognized in the Universal Declaration of the Rights of Man, a charter that evidently the civil governor of Navarra is not familiar with." [37] Even *Deia* dedicated part of an editorial to the subject:

> If the prohibition is maintained, it is another political error. Without going into a debate of the statement of the cultural demonstration, in which there are people and groups for and against (for example, the majority Basque party does not support it), democracy has to give all possibilities to the different expressions of civic, political, and social life, as long as they fall within legal norms. To not respect this democratic climate is to fall into arbitrariness. There is still time for the civil government of Navarra to facilitate the celebration of "Korrika-2" in the old Kingdom. ("Una decisión equivocada," 1982)

Egin provided definitive interpretations of this prohibitive act when it published a statement by HB's National Board that affirmed that both the PNV's public boycott as well as the governor of Nafarroa's prohibition constituted "a terrorist imposition against Basque culture, against Euskara and against the broad democratic feel of the Basque Country" (May 20, 1982, p. 3).

Korrika left Iruñea once AEK's representatives had negotiated the demands of the civil government, including altering the urban route. Instead of leaving from the Plaza del Castillo the race departed from the Plaza de los Fueros and avoided passing by official buildings (*Egin*, May 22, 1981, p. 31). With the civil government's prohibition of the race in Nafarroa, one of Korrika's aspects of conflict once more became evident: the territorial concept of Euskalerria.

Conclusions

At the political moment at which Korrika emerged, six years after the death of Franco, the cohesion among the different political forces in Euskadi brought about by opposition to the dictator had ceased to exist, and the focus was on the division of power among the nationalist parties. Korrika was organized three years after the PNV became the majority party and two years after the creation of HB as a coalition of the so-called abertzale Left. Moreover, Korrika began the month following the inauguration of the Basque Parliament at which HB members refused to occupy their seats, just as they had done previously in the Spanish Parliament. Their politics call for HB members to be absent from institutions born of the Spanish Constitution or from the Statute of Gernika, laws that the majority of them disagree with.

For that reason the political climate in Euskadi was full of conflict and confrontation within the nationalist arena. Departing from that reality, only something related with Euskara would have enough charisma and power to evoke a united stand; and, indeed, Korrika at first inspired support from the most diverse political factions. However, Korrika also contains elements that make it contradictory—subversive for some, absurd for others, and manipulative for more than a few. The danger and the fear are perceived through the strength of Korrika's representativeness and its symbolic content. These same elements led its initial support to diminish, and the issue of associating or not associating with Korrika came to be interpreted in a broader context of Basque political life. There is no longer united support from the nationalist forces or from the abertzale Left. The PNV officially withdrew its support, while the PSOE demonstrated in favor of Korrika in the municipalities. Moreover, the conflicts that emerged in the fourth Korrika make evident important discrepancies within the abertzale Left. Statements that appear alien to Korrika influence it because, as we have begun to see, Korrika represents something more than an event of several days' duration.

If we analyze the event from its organizational structure, it becomes evident that Korrika contains powerful elements. Its organization reproduces many of AEK's dynamics, and it possesses elements that can evoke the necessary volunteerism for carrying out tasks that require much time, dedication, and energy. Organizing a Korrika requires action directed outward; it is necessary to combine efforts toward objectives whose results will be seen over a long period with the need for many months' work requiring immediate compensation. Thus, in the organization of the long-term work, emphasis is placed on the group dimension, informal contacts, and personalization of negotiations through people already known in the town, neighborhood, or city. At the same time, each person's or group's contribution to the broader organization is always known and appreciated, and all of it carries Korrika to completion. The attainment of small objectives that provide immediate gratification has the power to maintain enthusiasm for a project that requires a long time to realize. The division of tasks with objectives and concrete actions—fund-raising, publicity, organizing the route, cultural events, and the sale of kilometers—within contexts close to the people who are carrying them out is key to the participation and support that Korrika receives. Finally, the ritualization of the opposition transcends concrete moments, such as Korrika's encounter with the hunger strikers in Gasteiz. It is a valuation of the posture of opposition when this is defined in relation to a cause that is considered significant—in this case, the institutional support that Euskara needs.

The conflict between AEK and HABE is expressed in two different discourses that are directed not at listening and compromise but rather at convincing and pulling the followers of one ideology to espouse the other. The central problem in each discourse is that of independent management, which responds in turn to the dominant statements presented in the nationalist ideologies that sustain them. The contradictions must be seen as expressions or explanations of each contradictory situation rather than as the presence or absence of "truth," and their logic can be found in local contexts.

Chapter Three

The Significance of Territorial Boundaries

Crossing the *muga* was mentioned from the very beginning of the fourth Korrika in the plaza of Atharratze, and it was stressed more and more often as Korrika advanced through Maule, Garazi, Uztaritz, and Baiona, as it ran through the cities and towns of the three territories of Iparralde. A mixture of anxiety, worry, and expectation permeated the crowds. The border is considered one of the "hot spots" of the race, and it is always possible that problems can arise there; at the same time, the conflictive character of the crossing augured meaningful and outstanding participation.

The atmosphere began to intensify during kilometer 205, after the race passed through Urrugne, ten kilometers from the border. The crowd was growing as Korrika traversed a bucolic landscape of fields and *baserriak* (farms) where animals were intent on their grazing and oblivious to the passage of the race. The transfer of the testigo from Julen Madariaga, one of the founders of ETA[1] and a resident of Iparralde, to the bertsolari Xanpun was recognized by applause from the crowd. As the race passed through Hendaia the sound of horns, cries of "Euskalerrian Euskaraz," continual references to the muga, and the atmosphere of expectation grew moment by moment. The people followed the passage of Korrika from the doors of shops, and the DYA[2] ambulance sirens contributed to the overall jitteriness. The dominant tone was set by fathers and mothers accompanied by their children, many of them riding on their parents' shoulders. Groups of children carried placards alluding to schooling: "Ikastola Herri eskola" (Ikastola, the school of the people) and "Euskaraz bizi nahi dut" (I want to live in Euskara). As the runners ascended the hill close to the muga, the rhythm slowed and the shouts and cries increased. When the group waiting on the other side of the border came into view, the volume of voices rose, as did the emotional charge being transmitted. The festive sounds of the *trikititxa* were mixed with cries about the current deterioration of Euskara in Hegoalde.[3]

The atmosphere was charged with tension when Asun García, a student of Euskara at an AEK institute in Irun who was waiting "in the so-called no-man's-land" to receive the testigo, was taken away by the police to verify her documentation (*Egin*, June 2, 1985, p. 29) before they let her cross the

10. People from Iparralde watch Korrika disappear across the border. The barricades and building mark the border.

border. A few seconds passed, and the protests of those present were heard in force. Finally, Asun collected the testigo, and, while one woman gave voice to an irrintzi and seven fireworks rockets were launched into the air, Korrika crossed the muga to a background of shouts and music and was received by banners and a group of people who joined the race to continue on to Irun. On the other side, the participants left behind lingered and watched for a while, some with a nostalgic air, political exiles among them, until the silhouettes of the korrikalariak disappeared in the countryside (photo 10). It was five o'clock in the afternoon on Saturday, June 2, and it was obvious that an opposition between muga and border had been established in Korrika. Through the ritualization of the crossing of the muga, a symbolic attempt was made to abolish the border. For one moment the metaphor of Basque unity was actualized.

I have been pointing out the importance in Korrika of certain concepts and practices with strong roots in Basque cultural tradition. One concept concerns ways of establishing territorial or spatial limits, and this is a key to understanding how, in Korrika, through action, the delineation of a territory that has a political identity is emphasized in a ritualized way. Thus, a discussion of muga and border is necessary to understanding Korrika's full impact.

The Muga in Tradition

The word *muga* refers to the dividing lines established in the land to delimit the boundaries of private or individual property (Barandiaran 1972, 1:173). The most important lines are those that delineate the communal lands of a group, those that run between two or more communities, and those that signal the division of land whose ownership or use has given rise to conflicts and disputes.

Long, partially buried stones called *mugarriak* (boundary markers or terminal stones; ibid.) are used to mark these borders, although natural landmarks can serve in some cases. Thus the sign of the cross on a rock can transform it into a boundary marker (Zubiaur Carreño 1978:256). When placing the boundary marker it is customary to deposit pieces of roof tile and charcoal underneath it, in the presence of the interested parties and two men acting as witnesses, as Barandiaran relates is done in Ataun (ibid.). This helps to distinguish whether a stone is a simple stone or a boundary marker. The stones used for this purpose are generally between 0.2 and 1.5 meters high, the larger ones corresponding to the borders between villages. There are some even larger stones, as in Otxandio (Bizkaia), where the boundary marker at the edge of Azpikoarri is 2.7 meters tall, 0.9 meters wide, and 0.4 meters thick; the stone at Mugarrioaundi is 2 meters in height (Aguirre Franco 1971:198).

In boundary marking, specific properties are used as geographical points of reference. Gardens, orchards, walnut groves, and vineyards may be used, always with reference to their owner and/or to place-names that are deeply rooted in the community. The boundary marker is engraved with the name of the village—as in the zone of La Barranca, bordered on the north by the bulk of Aralar (ibid.)—or with a cross. In order to help it stand out from its surroundings, smaller stones are placed beside it like witnesses. Part of this is illustrated in a document from the year 1568 about the placement of forty-six boundary markers on "Carnicería" lands destined for communal pasture to fatten cattle in the community of San Martín de Unx in Nafarroa (Zubiaur Carreño 1977:255–56, 261, 271):

> The first was placed at the Ermita del Salvador, to the left of the Olite road in the straight stretch called Vida-Paso. The second below the Ermita in the middle of the Abadia plot—over that royal road that

goes to Olite—. The third of that region at a distance of three shots of the crossbow to the right on the upper road of Varatajado. The fourth [boundary marker or mugarri] on top of the Hill of Cabezo of the Levada in Remico, in sight of Fuenfria and Varatajado—on a rock on which a cross was made to serve as the sign of the boundary marker—. The fifth at the foot of said hill on the sunny side. The sixth next to the plot of Sebastian de Castellano, in sight of Fuenfria. . . . The tenth, a stone with its cross was placed and two witnesses, in front of that stone. The eleventh was placed by turning to the left toward the villa, on top of María Castellano's plot, one crossbow's shot away from the preceding boundary marker and a stone with its cross and witnesses was placed— next to the straight stretch called "gravel of wounds." (Ibid.:278)

In many cases, as in Gipuzkoa and Nafarroa, the boundary markers were placed among dolmens and cromlechs (Barandiaran 1972, 1:173–74), and there are indications of the use of discoidal steles for this purpose as well (Zubiaur Carreño 1978:258).

Marking with signals takes on particular importance when it deals with establishing the boundaries between two communities, and even more so when it is necessary to mediate an agreement about the "combined usage of pasture by two or more towns or valleys for each of the contracting parties' flocks of sheep." These contracts were known by the term *facería* (Fairén Guillén 1955:507). In the case of the Pyrenees, and keeping in mind the importance of livestock to the local economy, the objective was to find a peaceful solution to conflicts that arose over the use of pasture on both sides of the mountains. Finding such solutions became even thornier when the towns or communities involved belonged to or were subject to different political jurisdictions and the solutions became international treaties (ibid.). However, the tradition of the agreements, as we will see later when we examine ritual, has been lost down through time although it existed long before the formation of the Spanish and French states.

The term *muga*, therefore, possesses great strength; its use evokes a shared history in which divisions or limits between territories and towns were negotiated with participation by the people directly involved, especially in the small communities. It is likewise a history of conflicts that in many cases led to the ritualization of the agreements as a way of reinforcing compliance and sanctioning violations. The communal character of both the properties and the agreements is reflected in ritualized trips to the boundary markers that demonstrate the power of disposition over one's own surroundings, ratifying the boundaries established by the community.

In Otxandio (Bizkaia) a ritual related to the Araban valley of Aramaiona is celebrated annually on the third Sunday in September. Its object is the reaffirmation of the property in a zone called "El limitado: the product of an ancient argument between the two communities." On that date members of the city government, accompanied by a good many neighbors, walk along the muga and draw up a certificate concerning the boundary markers' situation. The ritual occurs within a festive context, and the committee stops along the way at different points to be fêted with food and drink (Homobono 1982:98).

At other times the division of a territory that once constituted a single ethnicity is ritualized, as in the case of the separation agreed upon in the sixteenth century among villages of Burunda. The division gave rise to conflicts that ended with the symbolic division of the local shrine. Thus two separate celebrations are held, one in Alsasua on Saint Peter's Day, and the other in Urdiain on the following Sunday. However, the positive feeling of sharing a territory is expressed in the celebration held by two other villages in Burunda—Iturmendi and Bakaikoa—every year at the shrine of Santa Marina, in which the villagers remember and mark their past common usage of an area in the Sierra of Urbasa around the shrine. Perhaps the most relevant boundary ritual is the one known as the "Tribute of the three cows," of which I will have more to say later. Other rituals of boundary take place in other areas of Bizkaia and in communities outside Euskadi that abut the province of Burgos (ibid.:98–100).

The importance attributed to the establishment of the muga also appears in legends. Sometimes the legends explain how the agreement was arrived at; for example, the border between Goizueta and Leitza. There it was decided that a young village woman would leave from the center of each town at the same time and run in the direction of the other town. At the place where they met, a boundary marker was placed. Their meeting took place closer to Goizueta than to Leitza because, while the woman from Leitza ran without stopping, the one from Goizueta took time to fix her hair. In the demarcation of the borders between Ataun and Amezketa in Gipuzkoa, the race was run by two young men. In this case, the man who marked the place for the boundary stone was the one from Ataun, who grew tired and lay down to sleep before reaching the halfway point.

Moving a boundary marker is a great offense subject to severe punishment. There are various stories of individuals who changed the stones and then wandered about unable to find peace or rest, even after death. Only by returning the marker to its place can the damage be repaired.

A shepherd from Aranaz heard these words on the mountain every night. "Where will I put this boundary marker?" The shepherd answered: "Put it where you found it." From that time on he never heard the mysterious voice again. (Barandiaran 1972, 1:174)

The importance of the marking of territory likewise appears in literature and in numerous words associated with *muga*. A wealth of words has arisen to express degrees of closeness, such as *mugakin* (nearby) and *mugatsuan* (almost on the border), while the infinite (*muga gabe*) is less frequently represented. Compound words such as *muga herri* (nearby town), *muga etxe* (customs office), and *muga txartel* (passport) indicate in turn a certain progression in time, the last two representing contradictory meanings between *muga* and *border* on a symbolic plane. The terms *mugarri* (boundary marker), *mugaketa* (the placing of boundary markers), *muga kendu* (removal of boundary markers), and *mugarritzaile* (the person who carries out those actions) have a relationship that expresses the spatial association of the human being with a material *harri* (stone) and a specific territory. Crossing the muga *mugatsi* (for purposes of smuggling contraband) indicates a specific activity and a way of life that is found anywhere there is a border.

Borders and Their Relation to the Spoken Word: Mugarri-Hitz

The principal element of the action of setting limits is the *mugarri*. The stone is not something that is brought from far away or from outside but rather an element that is taken from nearby surroundings. In some cases it is chiseled into shape; in others a natural rock or stone is used; and sometimes prehistoric monuments serve as markers, the work of time and human beings. As I pointed out earlier, points in the surrounding area are taken as references for the markers. Thus it is said that one boundary marker is placed alongside the property of the widow of Celigüeta, the neighbor of San Martín, and the next one "on the plot of Sancho Maiz of the same neighborhood" (Zubiaur Carreño 1981:270–71), a phrasing that suggests the affirmation of the permanence of private property. When trees, streams, and hills are used for orientation, nature is incorporated as a witness to the contract that is established in the demarcation, and more so when a stone or rock from the surrounding area is used as a mugarri. The inclusion of vineyards, sown fields, and fruit trees can be interpreted as a recognition of the nobility of the human labor of modifying the surroundings as the means necessary for survival. Barandiaran mentions that a priest participates in the annual visit made by the city government of Ataun, blessing the people from each boundary marker and conjuring storms, and this practice has been preserved

in other locations (1972). However, the strongest association is established
through the meaning of the stone in relation to the word.

The *mugarri-hitz* association is clearly demonstrated in the ritual of the
"Tribute of the three cows" celebrated each July 13 by representatives of the
Roncal and Baretous valleys; it is a ritual outstanding for its antiquity and
the continuity that it represents. Likewise, the historical and political evolution of the communities sponsoring the ritual is of interest for the analysis of
superpositions that can arise in the symbolic contents of the terms *muga* and
border. The ritual's legendary origins date from the seventh century. Detailed
documentation exists in the Sentencia de Ansó of 1375 and in the Treaty of
Bayonne (Baiona) of 1856 and its third annex of 1858. The Sentencia says:

> Attention to the years of antiquity with which the Valley of Bretons
> [Baretous] has paid the tribute of the three cows to the Valley of Roncal,
> it is determined that they will continue to comply from now into per-
> petuity, without looking for any excuse or pretext, on July 13 of each
> year. And so they declared about that part of the port where the foun-
> tain was located [that it was] the Roncal Valley's fountain and not the
> Bretons Valley's, likewise making known that they [from Baretous Val-
> ley] could never arrive directly to that fountain. And with regard to the
> deaths that occurred during the war . . . the sentence be allowed with-
> out recourse, under the payment of 3,000 silver marks, expressed in the
> arbitration oath. Item, the arbitration judges declared that three cows
> would be handed over every year at the Port of Hernaz and the muga
> of San Martín, and that on that day the Alcalde of Isaba and the Adju-
> dicators of the Valley of the Bretons would hold an audience to discover
> the cases that had occurred during the year with other providences that
> were included in those pacts of compromise, one of them being that the
> arbitration judges had to go in person to the port of Hernaz and the
> muga of San Martín, where they ordered that the boundary markers be
> fixed where they would have to celebrate the handing over of the three
> cows. (Quoted in Fairén Guillén 1946:275–76)

The importance of the stone appears in the 1375 document where it says
that "they ordered that the boundary markers be fixed where they would
have to celebrate the handing over of the three cows" (ibid.:275–76). Years
later, the historian V. Alenson wrote that the meeting of the adjudicators of
the villas of the valleys of Roncal and Baretous took place on the summit of
the Pyrenees in a place called Arnace (ibid.:276) "where there is a stone a
rod and a half high that serves as a muga and limit" (quoted in ibid.:277).

Likewise the importance of the word is evident at the beginning of the ritual when the people from Roncal

ask the Bearnese if they want to swear in the usual manner to the conditions of Peace. And when they consented the Roncalese replied and said to the Bearnese that they should extend their lance on the ground along the limits to make the Cross over which they must swear. Once the Bearnese had executed this maneuver, the Roncalese crossed the metal toward Bearne to form the head of the Cross. Standing in this position, the Scribe of Bareton received the solemn oath from each side over the cross of lances and over the gospel to keep and observe all the pacts and customary conditions according to the titles and ordinances expedited on this point. To this they responded by saying five times out loud "Paz avant" which means that Peace will continue from that time on. (Quoted in ibid.:277)

In a legendary narrative, an informant from Mendibe (Benafarroa) alludes in general to the changing of location of the *mugarriak* and the corresponding punishment and adds: "Once your word is given, you must comply; otherwise, after you die, your soul will wander" (Barandiaran 1972, 1:175).

The act of placing a boundary marker is equivalent to the deed of giving one's word, something that is highly valued in Basque society. Joseba Zulaika emphasizes the importance of the oath, and even among second-generation Basques in the United States this value is mentioned as one of the characteristics that distinguishes them as a group (Douglass 1980:128). Thus, the mugarri could be defined as an agreement about spatial limitation that implies the recognition of the existence of a property, be it private or communal. Giving one's word is in turn a way of establishing limits with respect to one's relationship with another person. It can be interpreted as a cultural way of breaking with ambiguity and indefinition; one knows what to depend on. The mugarri thus symbolizes the given word. It is a permanent and visible document both in space and in relationships and time. A parallel exists between the mugarri, which marks limits on a physical level, and the word, which does so on a symbolic level.

Delving more deeply into this association, going back on one's word is considered a very serious offense, and that is just how serious changing the location of the mugarri is considered to be. Whether it has to do with private or communal property, the legends say that this act provokes a loss of inner peace that cannot be recovered until the person reverses the action. On the one hand, it deals with an external deed (the changing of the mugarri's location), and, on the other, it affects a person's subjective, intangible inner world. The boundary marker symbolizes the word, and the individual who does not keep his word, or, in this case the person who does not comply with an agreement over ownership of the land, is sanctioned. However, the meaning is broader and transcends the concrete into the negativity of the transgression of going back on one's word in general. When one does not keep one's word, one must deal with the consequent punishment—that is, with the unkept word that is converted into a liability. Another story tells us that the transgressor "after he dies wanders about burdened with roof tiles through the night and crying: 'What a burden!'" He will be free of his burden only when he returns the stone to its rightful place (Barandiaran 1972, 1:174). A word that is kept does not weigh anything because "it is in its place," while the one that is not kept weighs heavily because it has been taken from its place and must be carried symbolically. From the point of view of Basque culture, I believe that it is better to break one's word than never to have given it; in this last case one never knows where the other's limits are.

Thus the weight of the word does not reside in the sanctioning of the existence of a property but rather in the action itself, in placing the mugarri (giving one's word). This is what permits the event to transcend the here and now and constitute the expression of broader meanings. The connection between *mugarri* and *hitz* is what makes an individual act, such as breaking one's word about rights to use a property, transcend pure individuality, because that action has been sanctioned by the community, by the people. In turn, that word, when given in concrete language, has—apart from its meaning—the value attributed to it as an element of communication, of identity; it is a symbol of permanence.

In Korrika, this association between the delimitation of a territory and its relationship with the language, Euskara, is expressed through the physical act of running, which symbolically marks the territory, and through the new signs (mugarri) that are left and the ritual recognition of those that are already present. This relationship and delimitation is reaffirmed in time and especially in space.

The Establishment and Development of the Border

The general characteristics with regard to the nature of borders and territorial limits described by William A. Douglass (1978:[39]) can be applied here.

> First, taking into account the viewpoint of the states, the border serves to limit the movements of people, business dealings and in many cases ideas. Second, the border rarely has the same meaning for those who

live in the interior of the state as for the border population. Third, the bases for defining international borders vary considerably and are reflections of different historical and geopolitical realities. Fourth, the modern delimitation of a border can coincide with natural barriers and/or with ethnic differences, or they can be entirely arbitrary. And last, due to an interrelationship of all the factors mentioned above, each international border is in some aspects unique.

In the case of the French-Spanish border in the western Pyrenees, there are two distinguishing characteristics. On the one hand, since the Napoleonic invasion there has been no international military confrontation even though the last two centuries have witnessed frequent remodeling of the international borders of Western Europe. On the other hand, although the Pyrenees constitute a natural barrier, the placement of the borderline on the crests of the range violates the ethnic and linguistic unity of the border peoples, especially in the Basque lands (ibid.:39–40), which constitute a geographic unity. Moreover, along the greater part of the route, the border is superimposed on mugak that have been there for centuries but signified a different kind of boundary and were placed there through radically different agreements. That is why I maintain that the muga-border opposition proclaimed by Korrika has its explanation in the historical analysis of the development of both muga and border. In some cases, however, there is no opposition, but rather a difference with distinct levels of meaning.

The 435-kilometer-long range of mountains running from the Mediterranean Sea to the Atlantic Ocean reaches a width of 140 kilometers at its center, separating the Ebro Valley on the south from the lands of the Aquitania plain. This natural delimitation of the border continues along almost two-thirds of the fluvial trench. Other mountainous masses in the region present great variety: abrupt summits, broad sloping pastures, valleys, hidden villages, and an economy based on herding, agriculture, forest development, and tourism. The mountains form a culturally different region that is notable for its diversity and is divided politically between the two neighboring states, Spain and France (Gómez-Ibañez 1975:1, 9).

The economic and social organization of the borderlands is based in several valleys. The valley is the context within which social life, economic transactions, and interchanges throughout history have been realized. Perhaps ten or twelve villages might have existed within a single valley, but the existence of the inhabitants was outlined or delimited by the valley's borders, and this was the people's principal form of identification when they tried to inform a stranger about their origins.

The cohesion of the valley's inhabitants was a response to the topographi-

cal variety within it and to the three categories into which the valley's lands
were traditionally divided. The first included the more fertile lands along the
rivers and streams, where settlements were located and intensive cultivation
was carried out. The second was a zone of intermediate altitude with spring
and fall pastures and forests. The third, and the farthest from the villages,
contained summer pastures and included the highest altitudes and moun-
taintops. Each area was used during its corresponding time, and the seasons
marked the movement of the inhabitants of the valley. The most important
movements were related to the livestock that united the region of summer
pastures in the high altitudes with the pastures and fields at the bottom of
the valley. Thus the movement of the livestock marked the activity of the
population. The herders remained in the mountains until the cold weather
came; in many places their descent was fixed by tradition on September 29,
the Feast of Saint Michael, or, if the climate was more temperate, on November 1, All Saints' Day. The return to the villages occurred after the harvest,
and thus the livestock could make use of the stubble and fertilize the earth
at the same time.

In spite of this ecological and economic variety, the valleys were not self-
sufficient. For that reason the pride of belonging to a certain valley and the
jealousy with which the inhabitants guarded their autonomy had to be balanced with the interdependence on other valleys necessary to repair any
deficiencies in their resources. Relationships and treaties were thus an important part of the history of this area, especially as far as they pertained to
livestock and, within that realm, to transhumance. Livestock moved about
within a single valley or in conjunction with other valleys or areas that involved long routes. For example, the livestock from the Salazar and Roncal
valleys were herded eighty kilometers toward the south to the Bardenas
Reales; and the herders of Ste. Engrace took their flocks as far as Burdeos
(Gómez-Ibañez 1975:24–27).

The needs of transhumance delimited property and especially land use
in the mountains, and many of the pasturage agreements known as *facerías* in Spanish and *traités de liés et passeries* in French date from the twelfth
and thirteenth centuries (ibid.:44–45). The agreement of Pesaldea, near Iri-
burieta, was signed by the valleys of Cize and Aezkoa in 1556 (Fairén Guillén
1955:518). The facerías were intended to resolve disputes over the use of the
pastures located on both sides of the crests of contiguous valleys through
an agreement to share the valuable lands on the sides. There were numerous such treaties among the Pyrenees people, not only between valleys that
were later separated by the international border but also between adjacent
valleys in the same declivity. In the western Pyrenees every valley carried
out agreements with its neighbors (Gómez-Ibañez 1975:44–45), and Victor

Fairén Guillén says that the Pyreneen border from the Cantábrico to Andorra "approximately, appears riddled" with treaties dealing with cattle (1955:507–508). The agreements varied from place to place, but the majority established common zones all along the borders where the livestock of either side could pasture together. They specified the type of livestock that could share the pasture, the time, and the area. In general the livestock could pasture freely throughout the facería. Sometimes the privileges were not reciprocal, and those who enjoyed them had to pay a small fee. This sometimes happened even in cases of a reciprocal agreement. The agreement named guards who were to ensure that all the clauses of the treaty were complied with, and measures were also established to deal with infractions, measures that at times consisted of seizing the trespassing livestock (Gómez-Ibañez 1975:45).

The facerías have passed through three stages. The oldest stage was purely economic. Then they took on a political tint after the sixteenth century with the goal of achieving peace between the valleys and emphasizing their neutrality in the conflicts among the sovereigns of Nafarroa, France, and Spain. Later, after the formation of France and Spain and the end of the French-Spanish wars, the agreements, and compliance with them, returned to their initial objective: the economic one (Descheemaeker n.d.:295).

In this analysis the most important meaning of the "Tribute of the three cows" would be the economic contract signed by the communities of Bearn and Roncal for the use of the pasture and water of Leja and Ernas, to which the people of Bearn still accede for twenty-eight days each year, a practice that dates, as we have seen, at least from the fourteenth century (Fairén Guillén 1946:292). Passage into territory is regulated more by references to the agricultural cycle and the position of the sun in the heavens than by the physical acts of opening or closing it. Thus in the facería cited above, the livestock of Baretous and Roncal are authorized to pasture in parts of Ernaz and Leja from sun to sun, but they cannot spend the night there. The people of Bearn may use the pasture during twenty-eight days from July 10 onward, and the Nafarroans then use it until December 25, the day when the territory is forbidden to all. The obligation to return and spend the night on one's own land is considered fulfilled if the livestock manage to cross the muga before nightfall (ibid.:287). The livestock treaties also served as commercial and political instruments because, with the goal of promoting commerce within the mountain region, they protected the passage of persons and goods.

The valley constituted a political entity that even in the feudal epoch was seen to be exempt from obligations; many valleys functioned like autonomous republics. Of course, there were attempts by feudal lords in the lowlands to exercise dominion over the valleys of the western Pyrenees, but they were never effective due to the valleys' isolation and the fact that they did not offer great economic rewards. In time, the feudal lords negotiated the granting of *fueros* (codes of laws) to specific valleys. Thus, in a process that lasted two hundred years and was completed around 1300, the valley community arose as the most important political unit in the mountains (ibid.:24, 32). Even today, in spite of the development of the modern states of France and Spain, the valley people have been able to maintain independence with regard to their property and the administration of the communal lands. The identity of the valley continues, and we will see this later when we follow the Korrika through some of these areas.

The inhabitants of a valley could ask for help from their neighbors. In some cases valleys made peace treaties independently from the state powers of France and Spain. After the fifteenth century, and in spite of the continuing wars between France and Spain, there were treaties between valleys that promised to maintain the peace independently of the battles that their respective sovereigns initiated. In some cases inhabitants of the valleys refused to take up arms in the service of either France or Spain, citing their obligations to the medieval facerías as their reason. Later, once the border was established and ratified, there were cases, such as during the Napoleonic campaign on the peninsula in 1812, when inhabitants of the valleys from both sides of the border refused to participate and collaborated in maintaining peace in the mountain zone. During the three centuries of wars between France and Spain, the Pyrenees were rarely affected (Gómez-Ibañez 1975:44–45).

Linguistic continuity is another significant aspect of the relationships between valleys. It is based on the extension and reach of the various dialects and subdialects, which have little to do with the concordance of current political divisions (ibid.:20). Thus, inhabitants of the Baigorri Valley and the Aezkoa Valley speak the same dialect of Western Behe-nafarrera but different subdialects. Eastern Behe-nafarrera is spoken as much in the valley of Cize as it is in the Salazar Valley (Yrizar 1981, 1:[206a]), and Zuberoan with various subdialects has been spoken in the valleys of Baretous and Roncal (ibid.). Apart from the valleys this linguistic continuity could be extended across the border to other areas, as with the Lapurdin dialect, which predominates in Iparralde and has also been spoken in Zugarramurdi and in Urdax in Nafarroa (ibid.:[198a]). Poets sing of this unity to affirm the existing contradiction between continuity and the border divisions.

The borderline established by Spain and France dates from 1659, when representatives of both powers—Luis de Haro for Felipe IV and Cardinal Mazarin for the French prime minister—signed the Treaty of the Pyrenees on the Isle of Faisanes in the middle of the Bidasoa River. Although the treaty contained clauses about the border limitations between the two states, it was directed principally at ending the conflicts between France and Spain. The exact placement of the border was not described, and it was not determined precisely until the Treaty of Baiona (1856–66; see Gómez-Ibañez 1975:43–45, 47). The fundamental character of the treaty consisted of establishing juridical rules applicable to each of the involved parties and creating the permanent international organ known as the Commission of the Pyrenees (Descheemaeker 1941–45:242–43). In the great majority of cases, the division followed the ancient divisions established between the valleys and sanctioned in the facerías, to such an extent that many of the border markers had already been recognized as mugarri for more than five centuries (Gómez-Ibañez 1975:47). After 1856 the facerías remained grouped in four categories presenting varieties of continuity: (1) those that had been established between valleys situated on the same side of the slope and whose clauses were respected as such; (2) those established with valleys situated on the other side of the slope that were subject to negotiation every five years; (3) those that were maintained in perpetuity, such as the ones established between the valleys of Cize and Aezkoa as documented in 1556 and that between the valleys of Baretous and Roncal with the ritual known as the "Tribute of the three cows"; and (4) those of the "Fifth Country," which are considered a special case and affect the valleys of Baigorri and Erro (Descheemaeker 1941–45:260–61, 267).

However, the officially established border had a different, unnatural feel; it suggested a superposition. It implied the recognition of divisions established long ago, but now those same divisions fell within a new category, that of border. They were legitimized through the legal recognition of France and Spain, powers whom the inhabitants of the valleys had ignored throughout history when they were making their own economic pacts and peace treaties. The latter, as I have mentioned, were intended precisely to demonstrate the independence of the inhabitants of the valleys from the objectives and acts of war proclaimed and executed by the sovereigns of their respective states.

The ratification of limits does not implicitly carry with it impenetrability. Moreover, Douglass emphasizes the importance of the "porousness" of the frontier on the basis of the relevance of the relationships of lineage and affinity, contraband, and economic factors such as contracts established either in verbal form or document form for the utilization of lands, hunting rights, or fishing; and men and women who cross the frontier to work temporarily in Iparralde and in France (Douglass 1978:40–52).

With the facerías in mind, let us now turn to smuggling. This activity, called *gaulana*, or "night work," consists of the interchange of products from one of the two states to the other according to demand, influenced in turn by international political events. This interchange became smuggling when

Spain and France established the border; before that, for a very long time, free commerce had existed between the different valleys. This commerce was so well established when the border was created that it was clear to both Spain and France that it would be difficult to control. It was impossible to guard all the places where one could cross the border, more so when it came to "prohibiting the people—especially a people as furiously independent as these—from following their ancient customs" (Gómez-Ibañez 1975:47). Commerce dealing with livestock, grain, textiles, oil, and other necessities continued uninterrupted until the nineteenth century (ibid.:48).

Smuggling in the western Pyrenees is a well-organized business that is supported by a few rich people, who never touch the merchandise, and is carried out by many people who in turn never see those who promote the activity. It began to take on importance during the nineteenth century and gained in significance during the two world wars. Thus during the Second World War (1936–48), while France was occupied by German troops, many of the basic necessities, and almost all luxury items, were scarce. Medicine and other items crossed the border, from Euskadi, especially penicillin, alcohol, buttons, lace, thread, sugar, olive oil, lemons, oranges, and even tomatoes. In the other direction went spices, jewels, and gold. Although the border remained officially closed when the war ended, smuggling from the north to the south continued in the form of parts for cars and machines, copper, precision instruments, and other manufactured articles; while from the south came alcohol, mules, sheep, cattle, and horses (ibid.:125–26). Euskadi's isolation, a product of Franco's neutral position during the Second World War, allowed smuggling to acquire great importance between 1940 and 1960, although it diminished progressively after that (Douglass 1978:45). Generally speaking, smuggling made a positive contribution to the economy of the border populations, as documented by Douglass with regard to Etxalar (1977, 2:24–27). In addition to being profitable, smuggling is quite a respectable way of life for those who engage in it (Gómez-Ibañez 1975:54). Smugglers have to depend on contacts with people from the other side of the border, and in these cases, blood relationships, affinity, and friendship are indispensable. Along with this, familiarity with one's surroundings is key to choosing the most appropriate point of passage for the cargo being transported.

In spite of the fact that all international treaties refer to the border, and circumstances continually emphasize its presence—customs, border guards, passports, and checkpoints, better known as "filter operations"—the concept of muga, and within that, of "porousness," continues to be in vogue even today.

The Border in Recent Times: Muga, Yes, Border, No

Recognition of the muga as the only meaningful division, because it is based on unity of language, is expressed by the poet Orixe (Nicolas Ormaetxea) in his most significant work, "Euskaldunak," written between 1931 and 1934 when he noted the existence of, and consequent rejection of, the borderline:

> Zazpi aizparen gai dan oiala
> ebakirikan erditik
> alde batera iru soineko,
> utzirikan lau besterik.
> Guraiziakin bereizi arren,
> bakoitza bere aldetik,
> ezagutzen da jantzi diral-
> zazpiak oial batekin.
>
> Oialtzat artu zagun Euskera,
> guraizitat Bidasoa,
> -ibai koxkor bat besterik ez da;
> utsa . . . balitz itsasoa-.
> Elkarren urbil dauda zazpiak;
> muga deitzen da Pausoa.
> Zergaitik izan ez bear degu
> family bakar osoa?
>
> Arbola baten zainetatikan
> sortzen diran landareak
> bezela gera, Bidasoa'ren
> bi aldetako jendeak.
> Berdinak dira gure jatorri,
> oitura eta legeak.
> Ama Euskerak magal berean
> Azitako senideak.
> (Ormaetxea 1972:195–96)

Having cut in half the cloth that dresses the seven sisters: three dressed in one part and four in the other, even though the scissors have separated them on their respective sides, it is well known that the seven sisters have adorned themselves with the same cloth.

Let's call the cloth Euskara and the scissors the Bidasoa River. That river is no more than a stream. So what if it were a sea. The seven are side by side; they call the Pass a border. Why must we not become a single family?

We peoples who live on both sides of the Bidasoa are like plants that sprout from the same tree. Our origins, customs and laws are the same. We are brothers raised in the lap of Mother Euskera.

The language-territory relationship is apparent in the poet's metaphors, and in light of this poem the representation in the plaza of Atharratze with which I began this book takes on deeper meaning. Language is like clothing that is in direct contact with the body, while the border is described as something superimposed—a kerchief "that barely touches the skin" and therefore does not affect one's essence. The muga is close to nature and to the human condition; one could almost say, interpreting the poet, close to the essence of being Basque. The border cuts apart a family of seven sisters, the seven territories. The river symbolizes the division, because the natural delimitation of the border follows almost two-thirds the length of the Bidasoa River, and in Irun the so-called international bridge, or bridge of Santiago, over the Bidasoa displays the flags of Spain and France. This natural boundary, this muga, was converted into a symbol of division when it was used to sanction a borderline. The muga does not imply a cutting but rather a form of differentiating one territory from another (one sister from another). However, when "they call the Pass a border," division takes place.

The other image in the poem is that of Mother Euskera representing Euskara, for the relationship between the sisters springs from the language. Although the presence of "ama lur," or Mother Earth, is not explicit, it is implied (these two associations are mentioned in Zulaika 1988; del Valle et al. 1985, and Aretxaga 1988).

In Iparralde the bertsolari Fernando Aire, known as Xalbador, notes the division of his land of origin in one of his best poems, dedicated to Nafarroa, which was divided by the political interests of Spain and France in 1512. He speaks of how this arbitrary separation has divided the Nafarroans, and he refers to the treaties as empty words and to the limits of the frontier as mere appearances (Aulestia 1982:459).

The tradition of the border towns on either side serving as refuges or places of political exile, illustrated so well in the case of Etxalar (see Douglass 1978:41), has continued. During the Spanish Civil War and in the years following the end of the Franco regime, the border populations on the north side, such as Hendaia, Baiona, and Donibane Lohitzun, played an important role in the history of the Basque resistance. The mugalari, an expert at crossing the border without being seen, was a key character in the border crossings of political refugees and members of clandestine organizations. At the same time the existence of the border and the crossing of it served to bring together a number of refugees in Iparralde, and that area served as a base for clandestine activities that were later carried out on the Hegoalde side. This refugee presence served in turn as a catalyst for the development and reinforcement of nationalist sentiment in Iparralde.

In more recent years, the assassinations of political refugees and ETA militants in Iparralde have contributed to strengthening the significance of the muga-border opposition by ritualizing its crossing, as pointed out by Begoña Aretxaga (1988:23). The symbolic importance of crossing the muga-border is emphasized when the body of a political exile is taken across it, and both the people who bid it farewell as well as those who wait to receive it

> shout the same slogans and sing the same songs. The symbolism of the territorial unity of Euskadi for which the dead person has offered up his life takes on strength at the moment of crossing the border that separates the French and Spanish states and divides the Basque Country into North and South. This symbolism is reinforced by the presence of the family members, especially the mother. The image of the divided family, of the forced separation of the child, unites with that of the divided *aberria*, or country. (Ibid.:30–31)

The same sentiment was expressed in 1981 when the body of Telesforo Monzón, former minister of the Basque government and voluntary exile, was moved from his place of residence in Donibane Lohitzun to his native village of Bergara (Gipuzkoa). On the border some four hundred people and numerous cars carried *ikurrinak* (Basque flags) covered with black crepe and paid tribute to him, a moment that was captured graphically in the newspaper *Deia* with the following photo caption: "The mortal remains of Telesforo Monzón cross over into southern Euskadi in a hearse" (March 12, 1981, p. 7; note that reference to the border is avoided).

There are situations where the greatest significance lies not in crossing the border but in closing it. This is always clearly identified with the border-line because although the muga is regulated with references to time, it does not close. Two significant border incidents took place in March and April 1985. The first concerned the PNV's tribute to José Antonio Agirre on the twenty-fifth anniversary of his death that was scheduled to be celebrated in Donibane Lohitzun on the morning of March 23. In the early hours, the French authorities closed the border, shutting out the highest officials of the Basque government, the *lehendakari*,[4] and José Antonio Ardanza, among others.

The delegate of the French government who accompanied the security forces charged with physically executing the closing said that the people could stand "only behind the flags where it is no longer French territory," while the people shouted slogans such as "Iparralde is Euzkadi" or "Gure herritik aldegin" (Get out of our village). Likewise, when the French delegate indicated that the lehendakari could cross, his answer was: "I know that I am authorized to cross, but you will understand that if the people do not cross, I cannot cross" (*Deia*, March 24, 1985, p. 10).

Fourteen days later the border was closed again to prevent the crossing of a group celebrating the memory of Xabier Galdeano, a correspondent for the newspaper *Egin*, and protesting his assassination in Iparralde. In protest, workers from *Egin* demonstrated on the south side of the border. The tribute was carried out anyway, however, and "thousands of refugees and friends of Xabier Galdeano *who were able to cross the muga clandestinely* gathered on Friday at the municipal fronton in Donibane Lohitzun to say their final goodbyes" (*Deia*, April 7, 1985, p. 2; italics mine).

Conclusions

Throughout this chapter we have seen the differences in meaning that exist between the terms *muga* and *border*. The first is lost in time, associated with the equal and proportional distribution of some of the sources of wealth essential to an agricultural and livestock-based economy: pastures, water, and wood. The divisions of territory very often turn out to be problematic; they are flexible or rigid according to the demands of economic interests. The mugak constitute part of local history, and they designate in a spatial context the value of the word symbolized in the stone that must remain in place until its position can be renegotiated. Rituals reinforce the pact and make it more enduring through means of the importance given to words. In order for it to be respected, a moral value is attributed to the word, and it constitutes a way of recognizing outside rights and maintaining a value that carries weight for the individual and for groups.

The border, in contrast, is the result of international treaties associated with the creation of states. Although in many areas the Spanish-French border is based on the muga, its meaning is different, and it does not have the same significance for border populations that it does for those who live farther away. Along with the border go the benefits border people obtain from its proximity, especially in commerce. However, commerce and exchange become smuggling when a border is imposed, and with borders comes the regulation of traffic of both people and products. In the case of political friction between the involved states, crossing the border becomes a criminal or subversive activity. The border is maintained and ratified from the centers of state power, Madrid and Paris in the Basque case, and is sanctioned by the ratification of the written laws in which its characteristics are specified. The external symbols of the border's existence are evident in the presence of police mechanisms: barricades, customs posts, the requirements of passports or identity documents, and the definitive ways in which states open or close the border. On many occasions the border between France and Spain has given rise to clandestine economic and political activities. On other occasions it has been seen as a barrier to communicating political causes that contravene the dominant states. The border is a place of differentiation where demonstrations and social protests acquire unique power.

Independently of the economic benefit that the border has provided to individuals and communities because of circumstances present in the Basque case, many see it as an external imposition, the product more of international agreements than of internal negotiations. Because of political circumstances during the Franco era and the events of recent years, the border is for many the symbol of oppression, an aspect that has also been recognized in oral and written literature.

In Korrika the aspect of division and the muga-border counterpoint dominate, and that is ritualized in each celebration of Korrika at the moment it crosses the muga. Divergence from reality is ritualized when the runners attempt to abolish the border symbolically or, to put it better, to transcend its existence. Whatever the different reactions it evokes, however, the border is there, both when its existence is recognized and when it is ignored. These contradictions are also present in the different actions that Korrika generates. As we will see in the next chapter, as the race passes through the different territories, Korrika will recognize the mugak between one territory and another, and between the different valleys. At the same time it will create its own system of signals through which the concept of one united Euskalerria will be delineated. The posters and other Korrika publicity frequently use the symbol of the mugarri, sometimes as proof of its passing, and at other times as a goal to be reached. Thus Korrika will ratify the relationship that is established between language and territory.

Chapter Four

The Ritualization of Territorial Integrity

Faced with the different political powers that claim and protect the border division in Euskalerria, Korrika projects a powerful image of territorial unity at the same time that it recognizes divisions between territories, municipalities, towns, and neighborhoods. The message is transmitted in various forms on posters, in slogans, and especially in the very act of running through the territory. Signs (mugarriak) are left about the countryside attesting to the passage of Korrika and expressing the different contexts of territoriality, including the expansion of the current borders on the basis of political, historical, and geographic concepts of the past. That same movement of expansion is a way of symbolically recovering the territory, rather like putting the mugarri back in its place. During the action of running, two constant movements take place, one advancing toward the final point and the other circling, surrounding, physically expressing the reclamation of a specific territory.

Ever since the first Korrika, the figure of the entire map of Euskalerria has appeared on its posters, but without references to territories, borders, and continents. The silhouette appears isolated, cut away, outside any European, peninsular, or geographic context; as far as the design is concerned, the territory depicted could be an island or a continent (figure 2). The only references are internal ones associated with the running of Korrika and emphasizing the names of places such as the capitals of the territories, the points of departure, and the finish line. Even more, in a design that appeared frequently on announcements for the first Korrika, we see only the line of the route enclosed by an outline that looks more like a world map than an abstraction of the place through which the race will pass.

With Korrika's progressive advancement from the first running to the fifth, the importance of graphics increased, as did the number of posters and the care taken with color and design. Also, the representation of Euskalerria was more carefully elaborated, adding elements that affected only the internal representation, while the isolated external vision remained constant. Thus, on a poster from Korrika 2, arrows indicate the route from the beginning in Iruñea to the end in Donostia. On one of the posters of the third Korrika

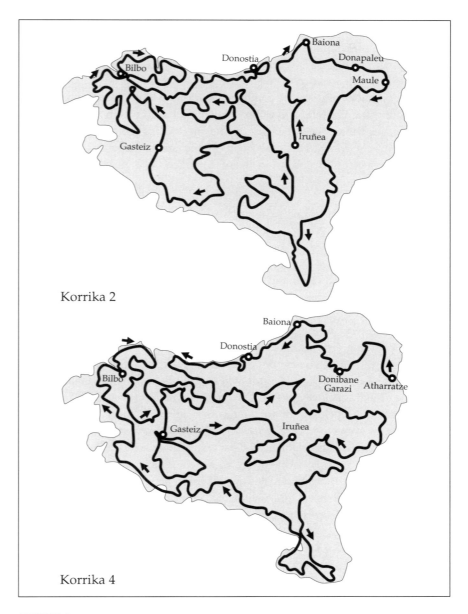

Korrika 2

Korrika 4

FIGURE 2
*Maps showing the routes of the second and fourth Korrikas in which the most
important towns have been indicated* (Korrika 4: Enbata, *April 25, 1985,
no. 867*).

the outline of Euskalerria in green on a blue background might make one think that the race was to take place on an important island in the midst of an unknown ocean. Within Korrika, this principal reference alludes only to dates and places meaningful to the race. Thus the route is marked by a huge fuse, and next to it, as if it were a road, appear the dates, days, and places where Korrika will arrive at the beginning of each day. There are also boundary markers that announce the principal locations: Maule, Donibane Garazi, Iruñea, Donostia, Gasteiz, and Bilbo. Likewise a modification is emphasized that expresses the territorial entity of Euskalerria, for the line of the route leaves the map to include the county of Trebiño, which makes up part of the Spanish province of Burgos, an inclusion to which I will refer later.

The Tradition of the Korrikalariak

Continuing with the importance of traditional cultural practices defined in chapter 3, I will go on to expound on the relationship that exists between the concept of *indarra* and races and marches.

In Basque culture great importance is placed on the display of indarra, the biological energy applicable to human beings, animals, or things that makes possible the execution of movements such as carrying, taking, lowering, pushing, pressing, and transporting. Indarra can apply to people, animals, things, thoughts, and voices (del Valle et al. 1985:175–76).[1] Its importance is emphasized in the many legends whose final denouement is carried out by means of extraordinary physical strength (Aguirre Franco 1971:199–200). Applied to human beings, indarra suggests a capability for realizing a series of continuous movements in which are projected a notable inversion of energy. Its greatest expression is in rural sports in a variety of forms such as stone lifting, tree cutting, stone dragging, bowling, grass cutting, races, and regattas that are still celebrated today. All these activities have in common the way in which physical energy is used with the goal of making the best possible effort, taking care not to put one's corporal integrity in danger, and, of course, wagering. Footraces known as korrikas are a traditional Basque way of expressing and testing indarra. The similarities between these ancient competitions and modern Korrika are striking.

The competitions take place when two wagering participants run for a distance of 10 to 20 kilometers, although on some extraordinary occasions the distance has been more than 100 kilometers. Traditionally, they were held out-of-doors on roads and highways. Today, they are also held in plazas, frontons, and especially in enclosed areas such as bullrings. More than a display of mere strength, such as that required in stone lifting, this footrace represents resistance to exhaustion and inclement weather—cold, heat, rain, or snow—adaptation to running night or day; the ability to expend, economize, and save energy; a sense of orientation for knowing where one is at every moment; and familiarity with the route so that one can choose the shortest trajectory. Traditionally, the route was not precisely fixed; rather, the point of departure and the finish line were established and the runner was free to find his or her own shortcuts. The runner could also run or walk quickly carrying a hazelwood staff in the right hand. Little by little more restrictions have been imposed on the routes, and the free runs that were once so important are rare now. When they became more spectacle than competition, the celebrations moved into enclosed areas. Just as in other sports, the energy required is principally manifested by men, since they are the protagonists in these competitions. Only on rare occasions have women participated, although it is recognized that women have indarra.

The tradition of running races that was made famous by those competitions still exists. For example, in Gipuzkoa there are the races of Zarautz–Aia: from Aia to Getaria and back; 17 kilometers between Billabona and Aia over flat land (from Billabona to Asteasu), uphill (from Asteasu to Andazarrate), and downhill (from Andazarrate to Aia); and one from Pasaia or Rentería to the top of Gaintzurizketa and back. In Bizkaia there is the Llaudio–Bilbo race, which leaves from the Plaza del Ayuntamiento of the first town and ends in the Plaza Circular of the city after an 18-kilometer cross-country route. And in the opposite direction there is the Durango–Bilbo race, which sometimes doubles back. In Nafarroa the 6,040-meter route called Lengua de Lekunberri is famous for the difficulty of the slope; during the last few years runners have been trying to break the standing record of twenty minutes.

There have also been solely cross-country races like the one from Baraibar to Igaratxa (Aralar) or the one between Alzoazpi and the Usalde herder's hut in the municipality of Azkarate (Nafarroa), in which the two competitors ran a route of approximately 13 kilometers, cross-country one way, and the other on the highway.

The Tolosa–Iruñea–Tolosa race became famous among these long-distance tests. Forty-seven-year-old Nicomedes Azpeitia ran the 126-kilometer race in seventeen hours and fifty-three minutes. Another noteworthy runner from north Euskadi was Marquestan, who, in October 1903 at the age of sixty-four, broke all the distance records by running the 600 kilometers between Burdeos and Paris on a bet.

It is important to point out that the majority of these competitions were carried out in a popular context. The competitors had supporters, and their triumphs or defeats were celebrated or commented on by a group or community. Many of these challenges took place between herders, especially the races requiring a detailed knowledge of the road through the woods, like those of Aralar. Occasionally the challenges transcended a community, and two towns would face off. Then, in order to avoid any influence luck might have on the outcome, an effort was made to establish fixed routes like those I mentioned above. The people of the respective towns gathered at the finish line, and the race and its end became a festival, as mentioned by Orixe in "Euskaldunak."

> Egun artxantxe Lekunberri'n zan
> anka jaso zezakena;
> denen aurretik erri ontako
> umeteri nabarmena.
> Goizetik Koxko ingu-minguru
> zer atera zebillena:
> durua nola, mutilla zertan,
> emanez guri kemena.
> (Quoted in Aguirre Franco 1971:331, 332)

On that day everyone came to Lecumberri who could get there by foot. Ahead of them all the daring children of our village. Koxko was occupied from early morning with how the money was handled, what the boy was doing, encouraging us all.

Miquelets (Gipuzkoan policemen) sometimes accompanied the athletes in relays in more populated places, keeping order among the followers who lined both sides of the highway. "With his boina and his cape fluttering in the wind, he trotted at the runner's side during the difficult moments of the race, especially at the beginning and near the end" (ibid.:304–5).

In these wagers it was expected that the people would support the hometown runner, and when that was not the case it was seen as a betrayal, as Orixe comments:

> Itsusigorik! Bai bide-duzu
> errikoaren buruzki
> diru-egina. Orrelakoak
> ez du besterik merezi.
> Egun artantxe atz egin zion
> bein ta berriz kazkarrari!
> Or dabil orain astelenako
> buru-begiak ernari.
> (Quoted in Aguirre Franco 1971:332)

What a dishonorable thing! There appears to have been someone in town who wagered money against his fellow citizen. Such a person is good for nothing. On that day he scratched his head a lot! There he goes now, head down and eyes like Monday morning.

All of this shows how well received these competitions were and how they captured the people's interest, inspired wagers, and celebrated skill and physical ability. They transcended individual interest by pulling together the followers and identifying runners with their town of origin or with the place where the competition originated.

How Physical Dominion of Territory Is Established

By observing how Korrika's route is laid out and achieved, we can appreciate this modern event's link with tradition, with the ritualization of the muga as noted in chapter 3, and with the tradition of the *korrikalariak* (runners). The dynamics of Korrika, as we will see, allows the reflection, integration, and transformation of traditional elements.

Korrika's relationship with rituals concerning limits can be analyzed using different routes as examples. One of the examples will be the Erribera route from where it leaves Kaparroso in kilometer 811 to beyond Ribaforada and a little before reaching Buñuel in kilometer 907. The other example will be the route through the urban area of Tutera in Nafarroa. Both routes use a variety of signs for marking the territory, especially for marking the end of each kilometer and the place where the relay runner must receive the testigo. The most frequent signs are the boundary markers along the highway, eighty-seven altogether. Placing the Korrika's numbers over the boundary markers can be interpreted as an act that converts the markers into mugarriak. Traditionally, it was the sign of the cross or the name of the town that converted a stone or rock from the surrounding area into a marker. But here, whether we are dealing with boundary markers on the highway or other signs—lightposts, barricades, balconies, bridges, churches, factories, or gas stations—they receive validation in Korrika through the kilometer number that corresponds to the Korrika route (for example, "K-872"). These signs frequently appear on the ground next to the monument or structure that is used as a reference; in Iparralde numbers are inscribed on pennants placed alongside the road. This numbering can be interpreted as equivalent to the transformational power of the cross or the name of the town.

Korrika's route sets its own boundary markers, creating a concept of muga that, by assuming local divisions and limits, moves on to establish the dividing line that transmits the concept of territorial unity that we have seen reflected in posters and chanted in slogans.

Other forms of sign marking physically express the passage of Korrika, such as markers recognizing specific persons who have some connection with the support of the Basque language and culture. This recognition is incorporated into what is now recognized as the "Korrika tradition." When Korrika 2 passed through Etxarri-Aranaz, a bouquet of flowers was deposited on the spot where young Xabier Exeberri was struck and killed by a car as he was returning home after participating in the first Korrika. A stone monument has been erected in his memory, and an offering of flowers is made in every Korrika. When the fourth Korrika arrived in Ustaritz while passing through Iparralde, tribute was paid to Pierre Lafitte, and a commemorative plaque was placed on the spot where he "did his kilometer" the year before (*Egin*, June 2, 1985, p. 29). Later, when Korrika arrived at Bilbo, tribute was paid to the poet Gabriel Aresti and to politician Santi Brouard;[2] in both cases the memorials became established locally. In the case of Aresti, it was done by planting an oak sprig, brought from Mount Gorbea, in front of the Museum of Fine Arts and placing a plaque there with one of his poems inscribed on it (*Egin*, June 7, 1985, p. 3).

> Irrintzi gorri batekin
> estaldun nituen
> egunaren eta gauaren
> ate meharrak.
> Sega zorrotz batekin
> ebaki nituen
> pagadiaren
> azken
> lukurreriak.
> Teneza gogor batekin
> atera nituen
> debekazaleen
> aginak.
> Gero hil nintzen.
> (Aresti 1976, 1:488–91)

With a red shout I blocked the narrow doors of day and night. With a sharpened scythe I cut the beech grove's final usuries. With a hard pair of pliers I pulled the teeth of the prohibitors. Then I died.

In Brouard's case the remembrance had a more ephemeral symbolism. People of all ages, especially women and children, filled the doorway of the house where he was assassinated on November 20, 1984, with red carnations. Shouts of "Santi gogoan zaitugu" (Santi we will remember you) reverberated in the background. At other moments in Korrika, I heard the route through the Alameda de Recalde identified as "Santi's kilometer." In this way, the passing of Korrika reproduces the presence of the abertzale leader who is remembered carrying the testigo through the streets of Bilbo in Korrika 3 (*Gaceta,* June 6, 1985) as a member of the National Board of Herri Batasuna, and his photo was included in a publicity pamphlet for Korrika. During the development of the "tradition of Korrika," this route through the Alameda de Recalde has been institutionalized as a tribute to and memory of Brouard, and in the fifth Korrika the participants returned to ritualize the spot in front of "Santi's house."

Just as the traditional marking of the mugak used workplaces as references, today other elements of modern society such as factories and public buildings are incorporated. Thus the relay of kilometer 859 was taken at boundary marker 114 beside the Biarometal factory; kilometer 829, in the leg from Castejón to Corella, went from the School to the Ebro bridge. The highway crossroads served as an orientation point; thus the relay for kilometer 857 went from the boundary marker to the intersection with the general highway. In Tutera a traffic light marked the relay point for the people running from the Plaza Nueva as far as the monument at the Fueros. The presence of the group that waited around the "mugarri" visually demonstrated the continuity of the reclamation of the urban territory taking place, step by step.

Many of the physical qualities attributed to the traditional runners are present in those who participate in Korrika. The route of the race represents the ecological diversity of Euskalerria, and for that reason a great variety of terrains is incorporated: flatlands, mountain passes, and highways along the sea, together with marked differences in climate even within the same season. Korrikas have been celebrated in both winter (Korrika 1 and Korrika 3) and spring (Korrika 2, Korrika 4, and Korrika 5), providing very different climatological conditions for the runners. The success of Korrika does not depend on the race passing through easy terrain or on good weather, although this can facilitate participation. Rather, difficult mountainous terrain, solitary locations, and low temperatures provide an incentive and a different value when it comes time to evaluate the success of the race. Thus the crossing of the muga at Luzaide in the first Korrika, after the port had been closed for three days and the townspeople had to help open the road so that Korrika could pass, is remembered as a special moment when the local people's help in surmounting physical difficulties was interpreted as special support of the event.[3] At other times one can hear on the uphill routes: "These kilometers are worth twice the flat ones!"; or the exclamation "Kilometro madarikatua. Goian dago!" (Blasted kilometer! It's a steep one!)

Sometimes low temperatures decrease participation, and at other times they are ignored. In 1985, when passing through Gasteiz with "a temperature of three above zero, Korrika was 'getting fatter' the closer it got to down-town" (*Egin*, December 9, 1983, p. 23). I remember my impressions from various scenes of the third Korrika. It was three in the morning along the route at the edge of the sea between Zarautz and Getaria and a fog covered everything. The runners came out to integrate themselves into the race, and it seemed that they were coming out of the stone walls along the road. Another time, only three runners maintained their pace in the middle of the cold December night on the solitary stretch of the Araban plain between Kanpezu and Viana. One of the organizers commented, "This impresses me more than anything, more than the huge crowds because there you have a certain leadership role, you are accompanied, while here there is noth-ing like that. This lifts my morale and breaks all my preconceived notions." Later, someone else commented "that the climb to Arrate had been exciting because of the difficulty of the slope and because it was raining hard."

In the fourth Korrika, the places that put endurance to the test were the stretches through the mountain villages and through Erribera. At those times interactions between the runners increased, as well as those between run-ners and organizers, and they joked and teased one another. In the first kilometers, "the sun beat down and the slopes were steep." In kilometer 511, the climb to the port of Belate at noon on a June day required tremen-dous effort for the main group of women, who managed to succeed in spite of their exhaustion. The descent in the following kilometers was greeted with enthusiasm and shouts of "Korrika, Korrika" and "Euskalerrian Eus-karaz," and it was difficult to get the runners to adjust to the pace of the race. In kilometer 538, the pace set through the Valle de Ulzama was incred-ible, in spite of the fact that some of those in the group had already been running for five kilometers. Fifteen kilometers later, only two people ran through the silent moonlit night. The rain, a rather habitual phenomenon, did not generally discourage the runners, who joked and interacted with the organizers traveling in the cars: "What a great way to go, that way you don't get wet," a commentary that received the immediate response: "It's so you can refresh yourselves and run better; so they won't say that the Nafa-rroan . . ." In Erribera the hardest parts were the long distances through the monotonous countryside. On the route between Corella and Tutera, fifteen kilometers without a single town, the sun was setting. The person who took the testigo in kilometer 941 started running at full speed; when he tired, he slowed down and asked for water, but he was told: "No, when you reach the boundary marker, because if you drink now you'll die."

The popular context, the local identification, and the competitive participation associated with traditional runners are also true of Korrika. When the race is being planned, the general organizers lay out the general route, and each town establishes its own internal route and takes charge of covering the kilometers that correspond to it and organizing festive and cultural activities to increase participation and emphasize the arrival of Korrika. Each place demonstrates its capacity for initiative and publicity, and nearby neighborhoods or towns compete, especially if a rivalry already exists.

Korrika's route is fixed beforehand, and the places and times the race will pass are specified and announced through the media. In addition, every day the schedule is published in the newspapers and announced on the radio. However, there are times when the route is changed on the move for reasons generally having to do with local circumstances. That happened in the fifth Korrika. The route through Erribera was different than the one programmed beforehand, as we were able to confirm on the move. The officials in charge of organizing the relays in that area had made the change, but the general organizers of the race had not been notified. The new route was designed to achieve the greatest collaboration from people in an area where Euskara is absolutely in the minority and where the participation of the students of the gau eskola of Cientruénigo was important. In the original plan, Korrika was supposed to pass by in the morning when the people were working in the fields harvesting the asparagus, one of the most important agricultural products in the area. Young boys could thus come directly from the fields to run their kilometer, and afterward go back to work. But the route was changed so that the race could pass through Cientruénigo at a time when the students could participate, supporting with their presence the first year of existence of the night school for Euskara.

In the Araban towns of Araia and Zalduondo, located four kilometers apart and sporting an ancient rivalry, it was said that the people from "Araia had stolen a kilometer upon the exit from Zalduondo for which the Korrika organizers were responsible and they even treated the people of Araia like imperialists." The next day the townspeople expressed satisfaction over the passing of Korrika and recognized that the fact that it had coincided with local festivals meant that people from outside were present. One person added:

The people from Korrika calculate things well, they pass through the capitals on the best days and at the best times, through the towns whenever they happen to, but we were lucky (even though they knew what they were doing when they did it) that it coincided with the festivals. There would have been darn few people from Araia because in addition to the lousy time, it was freezing cold.

Of the 700 inhabitants of Araia, 27 participated. In Zalduondo the villagers complained that the general organizers had made all the arrangements for the race; but "next time . . . we will be the ones who prepare the route in our municipality."[4] It is interesting to note that this demand for a greater role took place in a town of 136 inhabitants with an area of twenty-three square kilometers.[5]

The enthusiasm of the people from the different towns competing through participation in Korrika is often captured through comments overheard between the local organizers and the runners. In Korrika 4 an overheard conversation indicated that there had been problems with the people from Buñuel, who had committed themselves to four kilometers but in the end had only taken two. Later, someone commented that Buñuel "is the most conservative town in the Ribera." Many times runners identify one another by the names of their towns, an indicator of the weight given to local identity. Thus I heard those from Cascante say: "Ablitas [residents of a town in Erribera] don't run anymore." When the group from Murchante was running, someone shouted at them: "Cheer up, cheer up, you look like a losing team." Sometimes shouted phrases allude to towns along the route, such as when the person who took the testigo in kilometer 1,021 shouted: "We did half the Korrika between Lerin and Allo." He was pointing out that between those two towns they had taken charge of running twenty-three kilometers. On the route from Tafalla to Olite, someone commented on seeing the runners in the crowd dance and sing: "You should see the people of Tafalla"; to which they replied, "Drunk and proud" and continued their boisterous celebration.

Recovering Territory

There are times in Korrika when the route can be interpreted not only as a reclamation of the entire territory but also as an action intended for the symbolic recovery of a part of it, incorporating the most diverse social causes into the geographic limitations of Euskalerria by means of specific actions. One way of reclaiming the unity of the territory and reinforcing the concept lies in crossing the border, when the borderline is eliminated, at least for a few moments. Another way has to do with expanding possible limits by incorporating new territories on the basis of where they belonged in antiquity. If, as I said before, marking the territory with the passing of Korrika is one way of placing boundary markers that signal limits beyond the political concept of France and Spain and imposing a united Euskalerria in its place, at other times the same act incorporates territories on the basis of social movements of the distant past. In a figurative sense, it is as if the boundary markers had been wrongfully moved, and now an attempt is being made to recover them, returning them to their proper places. Thus the legends about uncertainty and anxiety in people who dared to change the location of the markers have echoes in the present day in the continuous protests against the closing of the frontier and the prohibition against crossing, in the demonstrations on both sides of the border barricades, and in the affirmations made with relation to the other territories the organizers want to incorporate.

In Korrika, crossing the muga may take place in either direction and at any time of the day, depending on the points established for the beginning and end of the race. In the first two Korrikas, the race crossed from Hegoalde. In Korrika 1 the crossing was made during the last hours of Sunday, November 30, 1980, when the mayor of Hondarribia crossed the muga into Nafarroa after all the relays had been run in Iparralde (*Punto y Hora* 1980, no. 205, p. 44). In the second Korrika, the race crossed the border on a Sunday morning in May 1982, returning to cross again through Nafarroa on Monday at three in the morning. The third Korrika, which began in Baiona, crossed through Izpegi around five in the morning on December 14, 1983; the fourth crossed on Saturday, June 2, 1985, at five in the afternoon. So far the muga has been ritually crossed in both directions, at different points and at different times of the day, night, season, and year. It is not an activity like *gaulana* (smuggling) that must be done only at night to avoid being seen. Nor is it something that must necessarily be done during normal working hours on workdays, or an act of leisure on a Sunday afternoon.

Crossing at different times and at different points can be interpreted as an attempt to occupy time and space. We have already seen that the border is a temporal thing, and its establishment is related to a historical time. The same can be said with respect to territory. Thus crossing can be a symbolic form of overcoming historical time (days and nights; hours, months, seasons, and years). And given that the border tends to occupy territory longitudinally, crossing it at different points is a visualization of the desire to march backward in time and convert it once again into a muga.

The launching of seven fireworks rockets during the crossing is as much a symbol of the seven territories as it is an affirmation of liberty; the border barricades do not exceed one meter in height, while the rockets are lost in the heavens. Likewise, the woman giving voice to an irrintzi in Korrika 4 at the moment the dividing line was crossed reinforced the message of liberty as well as the strength or power of the voice; it is something associated with communication and the word that hangs in the air, and no one can stop it. Throughout Korrika, there are other occasions when an irrintzi is heard. It is a shout voiced at times of celebration, such as during popular festivals and on ritual occasions like funerals for members of the radical Left or at the end of demonstrations while "Eusko Gudariak" is sung. It resounds in the countryside when a person wants to catch the attention of someone who is physically distant. Barandiaran translates it as a shout or yell and narrates several legends in which both humans and spirits, but principally the latter (laminas among them),[6] gave voice to it, but it could only be answered by the spirits. If a human heard the irrintzi and answered it, he would be punished (Barandiaran 1972, 1:196–98).

The interaction that takes place in Korrika between people from both sides of the border is interpreted positively, as expressed by Daniel Landart, the writer from Iparralde who carried the testigo in kilometer 155 between Baskoitza and Hirriburu:

> I'm taking part in Korrika for the first time, because the objectives of liberty and independence are beautiful, but first of all we have to know our people well and the peoples of Zuberoa, Nafarroa Beherea, Lapurdi, and Euskadi as a whole. I propose the same to all Basques in the south for they are often reluctant to leave their district, we must cross the mugas more each time; it could be an important step toward unity. (*Egin*, June 2, 1985, p. 29)

While the ceremony of crossing the border aspires to erase political division, linguistic unity and ethnic identity are maintained and reinforced in these rituals.

In Korrika the word *muga* is used whenever reference is made to the geographic connection between the territories of southern Euskadi and those of northern Euskadi, and *border* is used when it is necessary to carry out some formalities to ensure the crossing or when problems arise. Negation is directed at erasing reality; from a symbolic interpretation, it would be something like the act of returning to put the mugarri in its place. Thus the caption that accompanies a photograph of the carrier of the testigo in Korrika 1 reads: "The mayor of Hendaia solemnly raises the testigo. The borders were not an obstacle to Korrika" (*Punto y Hora* 1982, no. 266). A photograph from Korrika 2 bore the caption: "The testigo of Euskara made 'Zazpiak Bat' a reality across the borders. What an omen!" (*Punto y Hora* 1982, no. 268, p. 18). In the first reference, border is counterpoint to muga, and in the second the border disappears, the muga remains behind, and Euskara is the element that transcends the territorial division.

The problems that present themselves during the crossing of the muga, such as tension, reveal the contradiction between the different meanings attributed to the muga. In Korrika 2, when the crossing began at Arnegi, a border town located between the two Nafarroas, the authorities of both sides faced off and announced that the border was closing at twelve midnight, although the Korrika was supposed to cross at three in the morning. Negotiations were fruitless, and the caravan had to stop; only the person carrying the testigo was allowed to cross: "Three young Nafarroans crossed the border on foot, and the carrier of the testigo handed it over from the barricade on the French side, and so the testigo continued along its path through Nafarroan lands toward Donostia." The one hundred people on the Spanish side of the border protested, and when the testigo was handed over they shouted: "Nafarroa Euskadi da" (Nafarroa is Euskadi); "Korrika bai mugarik ez" (Yes to Korrika, and no to the border); "Korrika, Korrika"; and "Txakurrak kanpora" (Out with the dogs). The people from Iparralde sang "Eusko Gudariak" with fists in the air (*Egin*, May 25, 1982, p. 1). The title of the newspaper article was "Problems at the Muga in Arnegi," and the author used the word *border* to discuss the conflict.

Another demonstration of the different ways of conceiving the territorial divisions happened in Korrika 2 when the civil governor prohibited the celebration of Korrika in Nafarroa a few days before its planned inauguration in Iruñea, an event I alluded to in chapter 2. One of the reasons given was that Korrika was to cross the borders of the province of Nafarroa, and that made it necessary to obtain permission from Madrid (*Egin*, May 19, 1982, p. 1). As we have seen, in the concept of territory expressed in Korrika, Nafarroa is *inside* Euskadi, while, for the governor, it was *outside*. Here is a demonstration of the differential meaning of *inside-outside* that stems from the social and political context from which one is acting. By making continual reference to *muga* and not to *border*, the territorial *outside* is pushed farther beyond the limits of the seven territories, and that was the reason for the protests incited by the prohibition.

The inclusion of the county of Trebiño and the Riojan locality of Nájera was of a different nature. The former currently belongs to the province of Burgos and therefore is outside the jurisdiction of the Comunidad Autónoma Vasca and the generalized concept of Euskadi. However, its incorporation into the route was intended to recognize the social movement among its inhabitants to become part of the territory of Araba. The basis for this dates from 1151, when the villa was founded by the Nafarroan king Sancho el Sabio, who called it "Villa de Treviño de Uda." At the beginning of the twelfth century Trebiño became part of Castille. The proximity of Gasteiz and greater contact with the Araban population and economy has led its inhabitants to solicit inclusion in Araba. In 1919, a referendum resulted in a negative vote for change; two referenda that took place in 1940 and 1958 favored the change but were not accepted by the central government in Madrid. Between 1980 and 1981 several motions on the part of the Ayuntamiento (area government) in favor of a new referendum were ignored in Madrid, where the referendum had to originate (*Punto y Hora* 1981, no. 211:13–16; 1983, no. 199:11–13).

In the third Korrika Trebiño was once again included on the map of the route, accompanied by the symbol of the ikurriña superimposed on the represented territory. In the fourth Korrika banners visible along the route through Trebiño read "Trebiño euskararen alde. Gu euskaldunak gara" (Trebiño for Euskara. We are Basques). As the runners passed by fields sown with wheat, beets, and potatoes, young boys in the crowd could be heard shouting "Trebiño ere euskararen alde" (Trebiño is also for Euskara). There were difficulties crossing the muga between Araba and Burgos. The Guardia Civil detained the race. The person in charge of the race at the time told the police, "Korrika cannot stop," and so the testigo continued while the rest of the runners were interrogated until they were given permission to follow. The photos on the first page of *Egin* the next day graphically demonstrated the contradiction between reality and the objectives of Korrika to reclaim Trebiño as a part of Euskalerria by presenting the carrier of the testigo crossing alone in front of two members of the Guardia Civil who would later stop the race.[7]

The incorporation of Nájera into the route of the fourth Korrika had a different motivation. On the day the official presentation of Korrika was made to the press in Donostia, a representative from Nájera came forward to make a case for the passage of Korrika through Nájera in the name of a popular committee created for the purpose. The request was based on Nájera's past importance as a Basque territory and as part of the Kingdom of Nafarroa, without any explicit claim for its inclusion in Euskadi, as was the case in Trebiño. Thus, on June 5, as Korrika passed through Viana at eight in the morning, historian Xabier Antoñana took up the relay carrying an exact replica of the testigo and started toward Nájera, accompanied by a small group, while Korrika followed the preplanned route toward Araba. In Nájera, I was told, the group moved toward the cathedral of Santa María la Real, and before the Roman sepulchre of Queen Blanca of Nafarroa the ex-mayor of Iruñea, Miguel Javier Urmeneta, deposited the reproduction of the testigo and a plaque with the inscription "Herri bat, hizkuntza bat" (One people, one language). After the "Himno de las Cortes de Navarra" was played and a prayer was offered for the recovery of Euskara, Urmeneta concluded the salute to the Korrika, symbol "of all the people of Euskalherria to the kings of Navarra." The context of the tribute made it a social statement of both the territory and the situation of Euskara in Nafarroa.

Korrika's broad capacity for expanding the limits of Euskara beyond the territorial concept of modern Euskalerria by using historical references was very well expressed on the poster written in Bizkaian that was carried in Korrika 4 during kilometer 1,468, between Getxo and Sopelana, by a sixty-year-old man who also carried the testigo:

Euskara is the ancient language of Europe. But we inhabitants have to speak it in order to achieve sovereignty for Euskalerria, our country, and for this sovereignty to endure.

The ancestral muga of the land of the people of Euskalerria used to be more extensive than it is today. It included old Rioja (Logroño), Soria, Burgos, Cantabria, Huesca, etc.

In Iparralde, it included the Llandes, all the area around Our Lady of Lourdes, etc. Euskara used to be spoken, the ancestral language. And today in Euskadi it is hidden and nearly lost.

The tramplers, the subjugators, were here then and they are here now. There is no union, there is abundant betrayal, deceit and argument. Euskadi and Euskara will be reborn and will be strong. They will need our efforts! Long live Free Euskadi!
(Translated from the original poster, Berango, June 6, 1985)

The reference to the "ancestral muga" incorporates a historical element because the populations mentioned appear on maps that show the Basque zone of the first through the sixth centuries; and the very term *euskaldun* evokes an even more distant time, similar to that evoked at the beginning of Korrika in the plaza of Atharratze. It constitutes, in turn, a complete sentence of the language-town-territory relationship.

Another form of incorporation, different from the previous ones, occurred in the fourth Korrika during its passage through Muskiz in Bizkaia (photo 11). In kilometer 1,314 Korrika stopped to wait for the runners who were coming from Castro-Urdiales. When they arrived, the crowd of some twenty-five to thirty people joined them, running the kilometer along with them and bidding them farewell on the following relay. The incorporation of the people from Castro-Urdiales carrying their own testigo with the flag of Castro was not by chance. Although it belongs to the province of Santander, Castro-Urdiales is geographically much closer to Bilbo and has better communications with that city than with the capital city, Santander, and its

11. Leaving Muskiz on the road to Santurtzi. The man wearing number 14 is the representative of Castro, and the number refers to the kilometers run up to the point when he joined the Korrika. The runners in striped shirts are a soccer team that joined in kilometer 1,312.

inhabitants are more familiar with the former. The crowds of people from Bizkaia who flock to Castro-Urdiales during the summertime contribute to this orientation, and this influx is important to the economy of the place. Moreover, many people leave Castro-Urdiales on a daily basis to go to work in Bilbo and its environs or in other places in Bizkaia. Even for sanitary assistance they turn to Cruces, the principal sanitary facility of Bizkaia. The local political group called Izquierda Castreña Unida (ICU, United Castro Left) has at different times supported proposals from the abertzale Left and has campaigned for the inclusion of Castro-Urdiales in Euskadi. If we keep in mind the historical limits of Euskara, it seems that at one time the modern territory of Castro-Urdiales also fell within the Basque-speaking zone.

We have seen the importance in traditional competitions of the points of departure and arrival. In Korrika, these points of reference mark the direction of the race and have their own symbolic content. The first two Korrikas began at the University of Oñati and the Plaza de los Fueros in Iruñea, respectively, and the next three departed from central locations in Iparralde such as the Plaza de San Andrés in Baiona and the plaza of Atharratze. The finish lines have been, chronologically, in Bilbo (Feria de Muestras), Donostia (Boulevard), Bilbo (Feria de Muestras), Iruñea (Plaza del Castillo), and Bilbo (Feria de Muestras). The choice of Oñati was closely linked to the cultural tradition of that Gipuzcoan village, which was founded in the eleventh century and had its own university from 1540 until 1901. Its monuments speak of a constant preoccupation with art, history, and culture. The dolmens found at its higher elevations—Oñati is situated at the foot of the mountains of Arantzazu—permit speculation about the ancestry of its settlement (Departamento de Cultura, Gobierno Vasco 1985:297–309). The monastery itself, erected in honor of the Virgin of Arantzazu, the patron saint of Gipuzkoa, and cared for by the Franciscan friars, is a meaningful place not only as a center of pilgrimage but also because of its relationship with significant aspects of the Basque cultural movement. Clandestine meetings were held there during the Franco era. Also during that time the sculptures of Oteiza were the cause of great controversy. Many intensive short courses in Euskara have been held in the monastery, and several of the Franciscans have made significant contributions to the development of the language. This combination of the accumulated knowledge of centuries, the enigma of its ancestry, and its proximity to Arantzazu gives Oñati a referential value. During the Franco era and in more recent years the monastery has played an important role. Oteiza's sculptures, the work of other artists and linguists, the organization of short courses in Euskara, and clandestine meetings converted Arantzazu into a center of both real and symbolic reference. This is similar to what occurred in the Monserrat monastery in relation to the development of Catalan culture and nationalism.

Moving on to another level, the most significant aspect in the selection of the routes in Iparralde and Hegoalde in the last three Korrikas is the contribution they have made to the configuration of the linguistic and territorial whole. "The act of leaving from Baiona is true to the intention of not giving Iparralde a merely testimonial treatment" (*Egin*, November 19, 1983, p. 1). People from the general organization recognize the importance of the binomial Atharratze-Iruñea for the support that the passing of Korrika could give to the situation of Euskara in Iparralde and in Nafarroa (Joxeromo, *Aizu*, June 30, 1985, p. [31]). The interviews conducted by the study team indicated general approval of the selection of the routes for the fourth Korrika, although the significance attributed to them varied.

It is tied to the idea of the goal of Korrika: to reclaim linguistic and territorial unity. Both Nafarroa and Iparralde are territories that find themselves more isolated, the act of having chosen them thus is a reflection of what they are attempting to reclaim: the territoriality of Euskadi.[8]

Another informant thought the routes selected were the perfect choice. Zuberoa is often seen as an abandoned province, and its inclusion "serves as recognition of and affection for the Zuberoans, and Iruñea . . . in its own right because it is the capital of Euskadi."[9]

Another aspect concerns the political interpretation of the route: "Iruñea was always a city of Euskalerria until our Basque government told us that we are only three territories, but we know that Iruñea is also a city of Euskalerria."[10]

The symbolic value of crossing the muga is also important: "One people. One political cause. We are a people divided in pieces, with the border in the middle, when we cross the border with Korrika we want to show that we are one nation with seven provinces again."[11] An interview with two local organizers of Korrika, who also carried the testigo, pointed out the existence of different views. The first offered this opinion: "Iparralde and Nafarroa are too spoiled, I don't say that some are not abandoned on the other side and others here. However, Araba is completely abandoned by the thinking heads of Bilbo and Donostia." His companion reaffirmed this and added:

> Considering that Araba is inside the Autonomous Community territorially and administratively, they forget about us. One fact is that in Araba only 2.35 percent are "euskaldunized." The next Korrika should end in Gasteiz. There's a reason why they say around here: "Araba, Euskadin zazpigarren alaba" [Araba is the seventh sister of Euskadi].[12]

Places central to the different capitals are chosen for the finish lines with the object of concentrating the greatest number of people and having the necessary space available for organizing festive events, but until the seventh Korrika in 1991 Gasteiz was not included, in spite of its being the seat of the Basque government—or perhaps because of it.

Within the different localities and municipalities, the organizers mark points of arrival and departure, giving an idea in turn of the importance of local divisions. Thus in Zalduondo, when Korrika left the center of town where the festival was celebrated, some twenty runners followed along the muga with Hasparrenal, the neighboring municipality, which includes the town of Araia mentioned earlier. Within the cities, distinctions are made between neighborhoods, and the people of each location assume a leading role. In Bilbo, upon arriving at the neighborhood of Santutxu, runners could see a banner hung from one side of the street to the other that said "Santutxu helmuga" (Santutxu finish line). In the third Korrika, the arrival at the muga in Izpegi was marked with a sign placed on the border that divides Euskadi through Nafarroa into north and south, and the spot where the testigo would be collected by the mayor of Errazu, accompanied by the youths of the town. In Elizondo it passed into the hands of the mayor, and each town of the Baztan region had its corresponding kilometer (*Egin*, December 3, 1983, p. 3). In Isaba the group of runners went first up to the muga that separates the valley of Salazar from that of Roncal, and they carried the testigo through the valley to Burgi, where the people from that town received it to carry it to Lumbier.

The distinctions between the two valleys are interesting. Although livestock is important in the economies of both Salazar and Roncal, the former surpasses the latter in extension, population, economic activity, and number of towns. Many treaties have been signed in the past between Salazar and the border valleys to settle the numerous disputes that have arisen over questions of pasture and water, the most famous being the "Tribute of the three cows," which involves the valley of Roncal. In turn, the demands of the administration of common properties have served as a unifying element within each valley (Gómez Piñeiro 1980 4:144, 256–59, 279–80). These factors have given rise to various elements of identity and differentiation that appear at different levels—between valleys, within towns, among the peoples of each community—and these elements are transferable to the dynamics of Korrika. When the time comes to recognize territorial divisions, no matter how small they seem, Korrika configures an image that encompasses the territorial integrity corresponding to Euskalerria.

Established points of departure and arrival within each locality help bring about Korrika's general objective of establishing the integrity of the territory through partial identification of the people with a small part of that territory. The signs that allude to the whole of Euskadi project a vision of what is expressed in a different way through the small routes that are covered step by step.

Longitudinal and Concentric Movement

I have mentioned how, in the act of Korrika, two different constant movements take place: one advancing from the beginning to the final goal, and the other a circular, enclosing movement. The principal objective of Korrika is to finish, and all through the race one hears continual references to the beginning and, especially, to the finish line. The phrase "Korrika does not stop" is repeated continuously, although the pace may change depending on the vagaries of the terrain, the speed the runners are able to maintain, or the receptions and activities that are prepared for its passing. It is interesting to have this image of uninterrupted movement superimposed on time, places, and political divisions, as expressed in the statement read at the start of the fourth Korrika: "Because we have one language and we are one people from Atharratze to Iruñea, 2,000 km, night and day for 9 days we will pass the testigo from hand to hand, from Zuberoa to Nafarroa throughout all Euskalerria." [13]

Korrika 3 posters frequently showed a green arrow with black letters on a fuchsia background, and the phrase "Baionatik–Bilbora 1983go abenduak 3tik 11ra" (From Baiona to Bilbo from the 3rd to the 11th of December 1983) was everywhere: on walls, on barricades, on doors, and on roads and highways as a clear exponent of Korrika's directionality. The specific symbol of Korrika 3 is a composition that expresses several things at once: the zigzag in which we see the embryo of the symbol for Korrika 4, a zigzag that is at the same time a lightning bolt with images of speed and energy and a highway with a dividing line. According to this image the race follows straight stretches in the direction of the arrow, heads down a long hill, and surrounds the main highway illuminated by the powerful headlights of the cars passing in both directions. Here directionality appears dominant, and within it, expressed in the arrow, is this other movement that indicates the variety of the route and the zigzag that carries out the physical and geographic expression of the conquest of territory.

The circular movement is in turn dual: the broader movement symbolically includes all of Euskalerria, and the less inclusive one incorporates the different localities into Korrika's passing. Thus the first corresponds to the general route that establishes the muga that delimits the territory in relation to the contiguous areas (France on one side and Spain on the other). The more specific movement marks the different localities: cities, towns, neighborhoods, and streets; it is what the broader route symbolizes for the whole territory (geographic integrity) carried out at a reduced level. The image evoked is that of a whirlpool that stretches the circular movement within the broader circle, strengthening the wrapping movement.

In traditional culture, the korrikalariak frequently covered routes that returned to the point of departure, enclosing a specific territory in their feat. This concept of closing a geographical area through the physical act of walking or running around it is deeply rooted in the *iñauteriak* (carnivals), especially those of Nafarroa, which are still celebrated today with some modernization. On Sunday, Monday, or, Tuesday of Carnaval it is the custom for the young boys to run through the town soliciting contributions for a dinner. Generally they receive eggs, ham, pork sausage, homeade bread, apples, hazelnuts, nuts, and, more recently, money, and they offer in exchange songs, dances, or music, principally accordion music. The route is organized in various ways in different towns. At times the boys are divided into two groups, as in Azkarate, where the younger ones make the rounds of the farmhouses, and the older ones visit houses where there is a young girl. In Leitza, the boys first meet at a tavern and from there go out in two groups to make their requests; the larger group visits the farmhouses of one neighborhood in the morning and the other group visits those of another, and in the afternoon several masked youths run through the town. In other places the entire group visits first the urban area and later the peripheral neighborhoods or farms. In Bearzun they visit half the farmhouses on Monday and the other half the next day.

The most important geographic locations in Carnaval are the points of departure and arrival. In Lanz it is the inn; in Eguaras, the house of an official; in Arano, the neighborhood of Goikoekin; in Aranza, the plaza; and in Leitza, the tavern. In Betelu, once the soliciting for funding is over, the *korrika dantza* (korrika dance) begins in the plaza and proceeds throughout the town. The meaning of these routes goes beyond mere solicitation. It is a time for the festival to shake ordinarily tranquil places out of their torpor, as reflected in Juan Garmendia Larrañaga's description of Aranaz: "At certain hours of the day you can hardly find a person crossing the street. Only the stubborn insistent ringing of the church clock from its airy tower reminds us of the inevitable passing of time in a conventional manner" (1984:17). In contrast, the music and dances set a happy tone that transforms the ordinary into the festive and the silent plaza or street into a meeting place. The physical action of surrounding the town, of running through the streets in an out-of-the-ordinary activity, is a form of isolating the everyday and imprinting it with a totally different character. The masks emphasize this inverted character of reality. In support of this interpretation is the exclusion of homes where people are in mourning. Thus in Bearzun, as the boys approached a certain house, silence would fall with the comment, "This house is in mourning" (ibid.:59); or they would make their request quietly (ibid.: 74). On the one hand, the boys recognized the mourners' presence and their need to participate in the soliciting, while, on the other hand, through silence, and in some cases by passing by at a distance, the boys respected the mourners' temporal distancing from the festive atmosphere by excluding them from the more raucous aspects of the festival.[14]

In Korrika we have this same characteristic of surrounding and enclosing a route by establishing its limits and reclaiming and isolating it, creating through it a preliminary space in which ordinary time disappears, daily activities are transformed, and the act of enclosing is endowed with consummate symbolism. The race transcends the reality that it encloses. It is, in my understanding, an example of the act of closing (*ertsi*) that Zulaika speaks of (1987:27–28). For that reason, in running through cities and towns, Korrika crosses streets, surrounds plazas, and integrates neighborhoods. In these runs through the cities and towns we can capture both what happens in the crowd and the context that produces it or the interaction that results—the elements that form the movement of Korrika. We shall see how the closure becomes real as Korrika passes through cities and towns of different territories: Baiona, Hernani, Bilbo, Gasteiz.

The arrival at Baiona on the first of June was announced by the sound of horns that attracted passers-by and brought people out of their shops and houses. As the race moved around and through the city, small groups, mainly adults with children, applauded, shouted "Aupa korrika," and carried stickers and posters. More people joined the crowd as the race passed through a park. The dog who seemed to be participating at his master's side because of the sticker he wore elicited more than one smile. The endpoint of the route was on a bridge; there another group was waiting while a band played in the background, and a banner appeared with the names of assassinated refugees from Atharratze. A French policeman followed the Korrika on a motorcycle while shouts of "Euskalerrian Euskaraz" were heard. Afterward, Korrika continued on toward Angelu and Biarritz, crossed the muga, and arrived in Gipuzkoa.

The fourth Korrika passed through Hernani (Gipuzkoa) at 11:00 P.M. on June 1. The townspeople had gathered in the most frequently used plazas: Zinko-Enea, Hildako Gudarien Emparantza, and Plaza Berri. Korrika's arrival at those locations was considered the official arrival since they are in the heart of the town. Similar crowds appeared in Donostia when Korrika arrived at the Boulevard, and, later, when it arrived at Arenal in Bilbo.

Korrika's route through Bilbo includes the great variety presented by that industrial city. It runs through streets that bear different names than those they had during the Franco era, such as Sabino Arana Avenue instead of José Antonio Avenue, and Autonomía Street instead of Gregorio Balparda Street.[15] It passes through areas where the young people meet and completely fill the bars and taverns in Licenciado Pozas Street; it crosses the Gran Vía, the principal artery of the city, to arrive at Arenal, the finish line for every political and labor demonstration of the last few years and the central location of the August festival; it is there that one finds the greatest concentration of people on the route. The route circles the Old Quarter of the city and continues through neighborhoods densely inhabited by a mainly emigrant population: Santutxu, Otxarkoaga, Txurdinaga, Uribarri, a result of the accelerated development of the 1950s and 1960s. In the Arenal, a huge banner in memory of the tenth anniversary of the death of Aresti was visible in Korrika 4.

In this twenty-six-kilometer stretch we saw signs that different groups had taken possession of the route. When a group from AEK took the testigo in kilometer 1,367 in front of the Basurto hospital, one could see painted on the ground next to them "Borrokan hospitalea" (The hospital struggle), coinciding with a banner that said "Hospitalen borroka eta korrikaren alde" (The hospital in struggle and support for Korrika). Later, prisoners were symbolically included through banners with their names and photos carried by men and women; likewise the labor causes of the workers of the Aranzazu hotel chain were included: "Langileak gara, Hemen bizi gara, Hemen borrokatzen dugu" (We are workers, we live in Euskadi, we fight in Euskadi), and this was synchronized with the handing out of brochures explaining their claims. As the race approached the Santi kilometer, political slogans were heard: "Up with militant ETA," "Yes to Korrika and to amnesty as well," and "We are not all here, the prisoners are missing." In Santutxu the shout of "No police, thank you" expressed the neighborhood's rejection of the permanent presence of the police.[16] The same message appeared on a banner in the Txurdinaga neighborhood.

The enclosure of the city is complete when Korrika enters through Basauri and continues on to Getxo after passing through the Bilbo neighborhoods of Deusto and San Ignacio. Deusto is a conglomerate that has developed in the last twenty years and could be classified as middle class. Students who attend the various colleges of the public and private universities are present,[17] as well as people from offices and businesses. It is likewise a place to have fun and a meeting place for people from inside and outside the area who flock to the restaurants, bars, pubs, and movie houses located there.

Passage through Gasteiz, another Basque capital, consisted of a twenty-nine-kilometer route run on the morning and afternoon of June 8. The route included the different zones of the city by covering the periphery in the morning and the downtown in the afternoon. During the morning run there were two moments when two of the peripheral neighborhoods were completely "closed." In Abetxuko (kilometer 1,798) a number of Basque youths ran as representatives of the local ikastola, followed by some cyclists. Children who ran holding their parents' hands predominated, and as we passed we saw new construction, big buildings with many floors; their unfinished entrances gave the impression that in this neighborhood urbanization had stopped in mid-stride. There were no green areas, and the whole reflected a sense of impersonality.

Children carried the testigo on that cold and foggy morning. Participation was encouraged with a loudspeaker: "Hemen gaude euskararen alde" (We are here for Euskara). There was applause when a girl of seven with a very new pink jogging suit and a happy expression collected the testigo. The crowd advanced, filling the whole avenue, to the merry rhythm of the music, which was momentarily interrupted by an announcement that after Korrika passed there would be puppet shows and games for the children in the Plaza Nueva.[18] Later the loudspeaker invited those watching the race to join in Korrika "in order to warm up." On the right, a painted sign said "More municipal funds for employment, L K I."[19] It began to rain and some-one shouted: "This is good, this is good," to which a young boy replied in jest, "The rain will ruin my permanent wave." The majority of the crowd seemed to have entered into a long-distance dialogue with the Basque gov-ernment,[20] a dialogue we could hear only one side of: "Ertzainaren dirua euskara ikasteko" (Ertzaina[21] money for learning Euskara). At that moment a group of boys waved good-bye and left the crowd that filed toward the town of Berrostegieta.

In the afternoon Korrika entered the southeastern part of town in an ex-aggerated zigzag and traversed the downtown area of Gasteiz. At the begin-ning of the stretch many of the inhabitants followed the passage of Korrika from their balconies while in the street cries of "Araba is also for Euskara" were heard, along with a rhythmic "Korrika, Korrika, Korrika, tralaralara" mixed with "Euskalerrian euskaraz." A representative of the communica-tions media took the testigo, and later it was passed among adult members of the crowd. A group of young people was waiting with an A E K banner. It was cold. Banners lined the route: "Korrika, our strike, no to discrimination" (alluding to the protest in the Plaza de la Virgen Blanca mentioned in chap-ter 3). Every now and then one could hear "Get out, get out, get out . . ."[22] The people sang, jumped, and followed along in rhythm with the chant: "Ito, ito, ito euskara eta kitto" (Euskara and nothing else).[23]

As the race passed before the Basque Parliament, while people on the sidewalks had their hands in their pockets or arms crossed to protect them from the cold, the crowd of runners chanted "Independentzia" to rhyth-mic clapping. Later they jeered at a police wagon that was moving away in the opposite direction. A banner entered the race, and a boy who was running with a child in his arms passed the child to his female companion and stepped forward to help support the banner. The young woman passed the child on to another boy and moved over to help with the banner. This happened in the space of a few minutes. Meanwhile the child applauded. As we passed through the neighborhood of Zaramaga, slogans painted on the walls indicated its public-spirited character: "For a public and participatory culture"; "No to extraditions, no to deportations";[24] "Democrats before, assassins now."[25] Rhythmic applause was heard along with the shout "A E K." People stood on balconies hung with drying clothes. It was 9:15 P.M. and the atmosphere of music, jumping, and dancing brought to mind the bands of celebrants that race through the city during the festivals of the White Virgin at the beginning of August. Another brass band joined in and the festival continued. On the sidewalks people with strollers full of kids and people in chairs watched the passage of Korrika; it was incorporated into the leisure activities of a Saturday evening. Someone cried, "Viva España," but the shout was lost in the rhythmic clapping and shouts of "A E K." As we passed through the Plaza de los Fueros[26] we saw painted on the surrounding barricades: "Hunger strike. A E K-solidarity," indicating that we were approaching the Plaza de la Virgen Blanca, symbolic center of the city, and at that moment the location of the seven hunger strikers.

The conquest of the center of a city would take place even more clearly later in Iruñea, where Korrika, in addition to reaching its goal, reinforced the symbolic conquest of that city with its arrival at the Plaza del Castillo. The plaza summarizes the life of the city: official buildings, residences, hotels, businesses, societies, cafés, and bars. It is the preferred meeting place for the inhabitants on workdays and Sunday mornings. The porticoes that surrounded the plaza protect it from cold and from heat. During the Sanfermín festival it is the gathering point for many from every part of the city; groups pass through to go and come from the encierro, brass bands gather, music explodes as the afternoon draws on, and during both day and night the people walk, jump, sit, and fall down depending on the time and the state of their spirits. With the arrival of Korrika, the plaza is similarly closed off to traffic and the testigo is carried to the kiosk for the reading of the final message, which concludes the morning run through the neighborhoods, streets, and plazas. Once more the city has been taken, its space surrounded, in the way Korrika has done at other times in other towns, plazas, and neighborhoods.

Conclusions

A key part of the Korrika ritual is the symbolic distinction made of territory, in the way it is traversed, and the meaning we can attribute to direction and inclusion. We have seen how in Korrika the shaping of Euskalerria's territorial integrity is achieved through a recurrent series of mechanisms, some involving longitudinal or concentric physical movement and others having an evocative and symbolic nature. The former maintains a consistent advance toward the completion of the goal. Thus progression is achieved in time, minute by minute, hour by hour, day by day, and advances in space, kilometer by kilometer, through the measured expanse of the territory of Euskalerria. The latter encloses or isolates whatever happens at any given moment in each locality, and what it contains is strongly rooted in the everyday reality of each city and each town. What it evokes, through the power of its symbols, transforms the ordinary into something extraordinary. References to a historical past at certain moments, or a joining with traditional elements and values at others, makes that moment and place a liminary state, somewhat different from the moment before the arrival of Korrika, and different from the moment after its passing. The act of closure allows for the establishment of the inside-outside with characteristics of inclusion-exclusion at different levels. In these two movements the placement of the mugarri establishes limits that mark both territory and the language of Euskara. In some cases the mugarri is placed again in its original location when the limits expand beyond the current political borders, as would be the case with Nájera and Trebiño, in an attempt to recover territory from the past. In other cases, foreign signs are eliminated (barricades and police checkpoints), such as at the Spanish-French border, and the mugarri are recognized as markers of the traditional mugak between territories. And finally, at times new mugarri are established in the spaces, visualized in the graphic images of Korrika's propaganda as a way of shaping Euskalerria.

If as Zulaika says (1987:27) "to limit a world, to perceive the difference between denotative and connotative meaning of formal closure, is to transcend it," we think that in Korrika, in the act of placing mugarri, what is being done is to enclose a territory, both in direction and inclusion, and to enclose a language, Euskara, within those same limits. With that, for as long as the ritual lasts, it transcends the clearly defined political and linguistic realities that affect the everyday life of the inhabitants of Euskalerria; for the inhabitants of Iparralde, it is their inclusion in the organization of the French government, and for the inhabitants of Hegoalde, it is belonging to the Spanish state. Within Euskadi, it overcomes the fact that Nafarroa remains outside the Comunidad Autonoma Vasca and, for a few moments, Trebiño, Castro-Urdiales, and Nájera once again become Basque territories. And throughout the entire territory linguistic unity becomes a reality.

Chapter Five

The Dynamics of Action

Korrika is an action charged with physical and symbolic energy. An analysis of its components can lead to understanding both its attraction and the opposition and rejection it evokes. Korrika demonstrates an integrating capacity that, on the one hand, incorporates a variety of social causes, and, on the other, points out the humorous side of public expression. Its capacity for expansion is expressed through strategies for multiplying participation in the ritual, such as the use of the evocative power of people, places, and symbols, and the versatility attributed to the concept of a people.

Integrating Capacity

RITUALIZATION OF DIVERSITY THROUGH SOCIAL CAUSES

Korrika's passage through different territories and through different locales within each territory provides an opportunity for collecting information on the economic, linguistic, historical, political, geographical, and social variety that exists in Euskalerria, as well as the opportunity for interpreting these differences from within. One way of transmitting this plurality is through the expression of socially important causes by different groups that demonstrate the conditions of each zone through the problems that affect it. In this, Korrika demonstrates its capacity for capturing new problems that can be conveyed because they belong to the people.

PASSING THROUGH IPARRALDE

From the beginning of Korrika 4 in Atharratze the problems affecting Iparralde were indicated through banners, through the role of the Unemployment Committee, and through the festive humor of the representatives in the plaza, all of which emphasized urgent problems such as unemployment, growing emigration, and lack of support for the preservation of the region's artistic and cultural patrimony. These problems reflect the historical development of Iparralde during the twentieth century, which has been marked by a growing imbalance between the coastal areas and those of the in-

TABLE 5

The Population of Iparralde during the Twentieth Century

	1911	1936	1954	1968	1975
Lapurdi	99,910	118,260	140,040	156,048	175,055
Benafarroa Beherea	—	70,024	40,039	37,011	35,522
Zuberoa	—	18,895	17,609	10,690	16,397
Totals	—	207,179	197,688	203,749	226,974

Source: F. J. Gómez Piñeiro, *Geografía de Euskal Herria,* vol. 5: *Laburdi, Benabarra, Zuberoa* (San Sebastián: Luis Haranburu, 1980), p. 114.

terior; that is, between Lapurdi and the territories of Benafarroa Beherea and Zuberoa. As table 5 shows, Lapurdi reflects a dynamic of constant growth. Although its population growth has slowed notably since the 1970s, in 1975 it contained 77.1 percent of the total population. In contrast, Benafarroa Beherea and Zuberoa have experienced continual decline (Gómez Piñeiro et al. 1980:114–17).

I should note that the demographic increase is in inverse proportion to the size of the territory. In Lapurdi, the smallest cantons, less than one hundred square kilometers in area, are located along the coastal strip. In Benafarroa Beherea and Zuberoa the cantons are larger, with Atharratze the largest in Zuberoa, followed by Donapaleu and Baigorri in Benafarroa Beherea. However, Atharratze is experiencing a notable population decline.

The 1975 population census indicated 230,556 inhabitants and a density of 77.83 inhabitants per square kilometer; the canton of North Baiona was the most densely populated. The rest of the territory is much less densely populated, but all the cantons of Lapurdi have more inhabitants than those of Zuberoa and Benafarroa Behera except for Donapaleu and Maule (ibid.:18).

This demographic inequality can be explained on the basis of the availability of manpower in industry and the hotel business generated on the Lapurdin coast, as well as by the exodus that the rural cantons of the other two provinces experience. Traditionally, Iparralde has been a provider of manpower. Its people emigrated to America and to France in search of opportunities that their own agrarian structure and weak industrialization could not offer.[1] The tendency has been to move toward the coast and to other areas in the French state.

Progressive change has occurred in the economy of the coastal zone. In 1936 the greater part of that sector was oriented toward livestock herding, but currently the industrial and service sectors predominate. Industrial activity is centered mainly in Baiona. Commerce is important along the entire coast of Lapurdi, and the hotels, residences, and spas attract a great number of tourists, especially in the summer. There are also quite a few second homes along the coast. Fishing is important in Donibane-Lohizune-Ziburu, which is the eighth largest fishing port in France and is first in tuna fishing (ibid.:264–75).

The cantons of Bidache and Hazparne in the interior of Lapurdi have experienced the demographic decline characteristic of Benafarroa Beherea and Zuberoa. The young people, especially women, have left for Baiona, Burdeos, and, in some cases, Paris. In these two cantons, especially in Hazparne, the decline has slowed somewhat owing to small leather and shoe factories and services that have opened in Hasparren. The rural areas clearly depend on livestock; tourism is not very well developed there in comparison with the coast (ibid.:276–80).

In Benafarroa Beherea the population declined by 13.5 percent between 1936 and 1954; during the period 1954–75, the decline was 2 percent; only between 1968 and 1975 was there an increase (of 4.5 percent) owing to the presence of the sectors and services in the neighboring zones of Hazparne, Donapaleu, and Maule-Laextarre. Agriculture is generally prominent in these areas, in the form of corn cultivation and sheepherding. The sheep's milk is used to produce cheeses of very high quality. Industrial activity is reduced to leather processing and shoemaking in Donapaleu, where commercial activity generated by the Lur Berri agricultural cooperative is notable in turn. The rest of the communities have only small textile and food industries (ibid.:280–85).

Turning to the mountainous zones of Benafarroa Beherea and Zuberoa, the three mountain cantons showed the most accelerated decline after the 1970s, owing to high emigration rates and intensified by a negative relative growth rate. Female emigration played a definitive role in the sharp decline in birth rates between 1954 and 1975. The hotels along the coast attracted a great number of women, who first went temporarily but later stayed on. This resulted in a large number of bachelors back in the mountains and contributed to the increase in the age of the population because of the imbalance between the number of births and the number of deaths (ibid.:123–24).

Both Benafarroa Beherea and Zuberoa sheepherders practice transhumance. In the former (Cize and Baigorri) the transhumance routes are longer and extend into Lapurdi and Zuberoa; the routes of the latter do not exceed the valleys' limits (ibid.:159).

In the northern hilly part of Zuberoa that belongs to the canton of Maule-Laextarre there was a loss of 1.8 percent of the population in the period from

1936 to 1954, but new industries in Maule led to an increase of 1.9 percent between 1954 and 1957 and 1968 and 1975. Agricultural activity still predominates in this canton, including the cultivation of corn, meadowlands, and horticulture near the urban nuclei such as Maule. As in Benafarroa Beherea, industrial activity in Zuberoa is very scarce, with the exception of Maule-Laextarre with its leather, shoe, and espadrille industries and some mechanical and canning factories (ibid.:286–89).

Along with the economic slogans I alluded to in chapter 1, all along the Korrika route through Iparralde one could also hear linguistic slogans relating to two categories: schooling in Euskara and the presence of the language in the media, especially on the radio. Children take a leading role in the school causes, although the presence of their parents revealed that the latter are the promoters and sponsors. Thus in kilometer 132 on the route from Kanbo to Azparne the testigo was carried by a group of seven (five boys and two girls) who also carried a banner with the slogan "Ikastola geure eskola" (The ikastola, our school). Later, on kilometer 205 near the muga, there was an abundance of banners with the theme "Ikastola Herri eskola" (The ikastola, school of the people) as well as shouts of "Euskalerrian euskaraz" (In Euskara in Euskalerria) and "Euskaraz bizi behar dut" (I need to live in Euskara). The media's role was demonstrated before the race reached Maule when a representative of Zuberoko botza (the Voice of Zuberoa) took the testigo, and it was emphasized by a banner with that name and cries of "Euskaraz irratia" (Euskara on the radio).

Until we approached the muga there were few political slogans or banners carrying statements about amnesty, extradition, and prisoners. This appears to be related to the ambivalent situation in which the people live with respect to the presence of refugees from Hegoalde and their degree of identification with their cause. It also indicates the different focus on the Basque problem on the part of the French and Spanish governments and the differences in the demonstrations of feeling and nationalistic action on both sides of the muga. Although banners with the names of the people who had been assassinated had been visible since Atharratze, it was more a testimonial presence, unaccompanied by slogans or other banners, that was seen in Hegoalde. There were some shouts that made reference to amnesty, but in general, the most important concerns expressed were unemployment and schooling.

The ritual of the muga that I described in chapter 3 can be seen as a reclaiming of territory, but it occurs in precisely those locations where there is a large contingent of residents and refugees from Hegoalde. Nationalist militance has been much stronger in the south. Contact with the refugees from the other side of the muga during the Franco era led to the beginning of Basque nationalism in Iparralde, and it can now be said to be on the increase. However, the violent events of the last few years, including assassinations of refugees and numerous assassination attempts, have led the French government to develop a policy of supporting extraditions and have created a certain ambivalence in the population, an ambivalence that affects public demonstrations in a negative way, in contrast with what happened in Hegoalde; all this is reflected in Korrika.

The conscientious objectors who took the testigo in Maule protested against military service through banners that alluded to the army, and they used the parody of masks, but there were no nationalist allusions as such, while in the south, where similar circumstances exist, allusions to the repressive Spanish military service were much more common.

Nor did the team note the presence of women's associations such as those we had seen in other territories.

ON THE SOUTH SIDE OF THE MUGA

Once the Korrika reached Gipuzkoa the social causes most emphasized were language, politics, and unemployment. The first two constituted the leitmotif of the passage through that territory. The language was reclaimed for all of Euskalerria through shouted slogans and banners; the concept of language was united with that of territory in "One people, one language"; citizens asked for free schooling in Euskara through "One network of Basque public schools," beginning with preschool, as in "Haurtzako-ikastola" (Preschool-ikastola).[2] The slogan shouted in the Donostia neighborhood of Bidebieta, "Bidebietan bide bat euskaraz" (In Bidebieta only one path, Euskara), is a play on words because Bidebieta means "the two roads," referring to its location, while affirming that there is "only one," the language Euskara.

Other signs referred to language policy, protesting because the Basque government was giving preferential treatment to HABE at the expense of AEK. From the crossing of the muga onward, there were signs of solidarity with the hunger strikers in Gasteiz; other signs forthrightly indicated support for AEK and denounced HABE's economic advantages. On kilometer 231, before we arrived in Rentería, we encountered a banner that said "Life for HABE, nothing but words for AEK" and "Less talk, more money. Hernani's AEK," demonstrating the value of words with content and the lack of respect for empty words without commitment. Symbolically it would be comparable to the act of placing a mugarri with no agreement to express what the placement means. In Donostia a banner that said "Euskararen Plangintza orain. Euskarazko Kulturaren Batzarra" (Plan for Basque now. Cultural Assembly of Euskara) came into view at the very moment when the representative from Euskalerrian Euskaraz took the testigo. Newspapers published photos of the same banner that had appeared in Iparralde about the importance of Euskara on the radio: "Basque Radio—Radio of the People."

Solidarity with the strikers in Gasteiz was constant. Political claims and causes were especially notable in the kilometers where members of Gestoras pro Amnistía and militants or elected officials of Herri Batasuna ran their relays. In addition to references to territory and the presence of absent participants—the dead, the prisoners, and the exiles—shouts were heard in support of the alternative Koordinadora Abertzale Sozialista (KAS), militant ETA, and independence; against extraditions; and in favor of amnesty. Integration by means of language was also supported: "Ni kanpotarra naiz izatez, baina Euskadin bizi naiz, horregatik euskara ikasten ari naiz Korrikan" (I am a foreigner but I live in Euskadi, that is why I am learning Euskara and running). Here the use of the word *Korrikan* has a double meaning, although both meanings reinforce the concept of action. On the one hand, it can be interpreted as saying that the person is learning Euskara "on the run" (quickly), and, on the other hand, that he is doing it with Korrika, that is, with AEK. The message was reinforced by the presence of people who ran carrying the ikurriña and the Extremeña, Andaluza, and Asturiana flags as well as the Republican flag.[3]

The unemployment problem was accentuated in Hernani and Donostia. In the former, a woman representing the coordinator of unemployment carried the testigo. During one kilometer in Donostia runners shouted, "Yes to Euskara and to work as well." Following the example set in Atharratze, a member of the Unemployment Committee carried the testigo through the central zone of La Concha, and the same was done in other localities. A statement distributed in Euskara and Spanish entitled "Korrika and Unemployment" provided information on the acute unemployment situation. The committee's position was that access to the teaching of Euskara should be free, the responsibility of all political institutions.

Other groups appeared all along the route, including antinuclear committees, whose presence was most keenly felt in Donostia when the father of Gladys del Estal took the testigo in the Egia neighborhood and people shouted: "Destroy Lemoiz" and "We remember Gladys."[4] A group of women from Egia carried a banner linking themselves to her memory.

On the route through Araba banners with slogans about the language and especially those related to the motivations of the hunger strikers in Gasteiz were most notable. On the whole the runners shouted fewer slogans than in other territories. The most heated moment occurred during the passage through Gasteiz, where political and labor causes were promoted. In Araban Rioja the slogans were few and limited to Euskara. Those that expressed the language-territory relationship dominated, mentioning places such as "Lantxiegon euskaraz" (Euskara in Lantxiego) and other areas such as Kuartango, Izarra, Maeztu, Agurain, and, more generally, "Gora Araba euskalduna" (Up with Euskara-speaking Araba). In the locations where there were ikastolas, such as Lantxiego and Gasteiz, children carried the testigo. Because of the regressive situation of Euskara in Araba, their presence was a demonstration of strength for the future, for only then will the implantation of Euskara in that territory become a reality in the children. A few political slogans in favor of ETA and independence were heard, the most notable ones related to language policy; these confronted not only the members of AEK and HABE but also the different sectors within the Basque cultural Left. The labor slogans centered on the problem of the workers in the Aranzazu hotel chain who, in a written statement distributed through the streets as Korrika passed, came out in favor of Euskara and denounced accusations that they were foreigners "with no link or roots in our little country, leaning toward places outside of Euskalerria," and that they were "irresponsibly destroying jobs, bringing Euskadi to ruin." They answered those charges by saying:

> Undoubtedly in the Aranzazu chain, as in other businesses, there are workers from other communities who are not Basque. In spite of this, the general feeling is one of total identification with the problems of Euskadi, given that we consider ourselves Basques and we have set down roots here. (Statement from the workers of the Aranzazu hotel chain)

The passage through Bizkaia was characterized by the participation of many of the groups already mentioned and by a more aggressive external political demonstration than we saw in the other territories, expressed in slogans either chanted in chorus or carried on banners. Thus, "A lot of police, not much fun"; "Civil guard, evil throttling"; and "Ertzantza, police, pigs all the same." "The police torture and assassinate" was shouted on kilometer 1,252 while the race passed near a barracks; "No to the dogs [policemen], yes to Euskara"; "You fascists are the terrorists"; "PSOE, GAL, the same thing."[5] In Lekeitio we saw a banner signed by Herriko Alder Sozialista Iraultzalea (HASI): "Izar gorria biztutzera zoaz herriaren askatasun bidean. Tortura egiten da. Euskadi 1985" (You are going to ignite a red star on the road to the people's freedom. In Euskadi they torture people. Euskadi 1985).[6] The tributes to Brouard and Galdeano, to which I will return later in this chapter, constituted the high points of the race from a political point of view. An allusion to international political events was made in kilometer 1,391 when, along with cries of "Gora ETA," one could hear "Nicaragua Sandinista."

Although it had its political references, the tribute to Aresti was more an expression of support for the language and the culture than for politics, although there were those who believed that Herri Batasuna was involved in the tribute. Solidarity with the hunger strikers in Gasteiz was expressed in a banner that appeared in Orduña on kilometer 1,224. All along the route we heard general slogans similar to those heard from the beginning of Korrika. School demonstrations took place in both Basque-speaking and non-Basque-speaking zones, but always in places where there were ikastolas. During kilometer 1,354 in Barakaldo, a twelve-year-old boy ran the relay followed by a banner carried by children: "Eskola guztietan—eredua nahi dutenentzat Miranda Ikastola Publikoa" (In all the schools for everyone who wants an example, Miranda public school). In Euskara-speaking towns where the ikastolas participated, more concrete expressions of the local situation took place, as in Zaratamo with the white banner with red letters carried by eight-year-old boys and girls: "Zaratamokoak ere Eskola publikoren alde" (The people of Zaratamo in favor of public school); and in Lekeitio: "Ez diguzue kenduko gure hizkuntza, Lekeitio" (Don't take away our language). In Ermua people from Free Radio Pottoka took the testigo and carried a banner that read "Pottoka Korrika euskararen alde" (the Pottoka Korrika on behalf of Euskara). *Pottoka* has two main meanings. On the one hand, it is a term of endearment similar to *potxola* (dear), and on the other, it is the name of a native horse that runs wild in Iparralde; the latter meaning allows a play on words giving the impression that the radio "runs," or gallops, in Korrika. During a good portion of that stretch the radio people recorded interviews with the runners without breaking stride.

The unemployment problem surfaced on several occasions. What happened in Barakaldo could very well represent the strongest moment of support for the unemployed that occurred in Korrika 4. Moments before the arrival of Korrika in the plaza in front of the Ayuntamiento where the unemployed and representatives of unions, political parties, and unemployment committees had locked themselves in, edicts were placed in front of the building in support of their claims. Upon Korrika's arrival rockets were launched, and, unexpectedly, the race stopped in front of the Ayuntamiento while the testigo fulfilled a symbolic act. One of the people locked inside the building came out on the balcony, lifted the testigo in both hands, and began jumping up and down. The runners clapped and shouted various slogans in support: "Yes to Euskara and to work"; "There's no lack of money for the wooden hearted"; "In Euskara in Euskalerria"; "Get out"; "No to the dogs, yes to Euskara"; "No to NATO and the police, yes to Euskara." Each group displayed their banners, but "Work for everyone" stood out. Then the testigo came down and Korrika continued along its route.[7] Later

*12. Boy from an ikastola carrying the testigo on which the ikurriña and the
inscription "Askatasuna" (freedom) can be seen.*

we met another group from the Aranzazu hotel chain who presented their
claims with a banner: "We are workers. We live here, we fight here." Two
more banners appeared in kilometer 1,390: "One job for every worker" and
"Against the PSOE's savage reconversion."[8] At other times along the route
the commissions of the unemployed carried the testigo.

The ecologists, who had already appeared in earlier kilometers, carried a
banner on kilometer 1,445: "Yes to Euskara, and yes to ecology."

The principal characteristic of the passage through Nafarroa was the socially significant presence of the ikurriña in conjunction with slogans and
banners. When we arrived in Nafarroa, someone placed a small ikurriña in
the testigo (see photo 12), an act that has become part of the Korrika tradition and part of its "magic." Nobody can say exactly when it is done, but
it has happened every year since the first Korrika. Later, something written
appeared on the testigo, and then stickers alluding to the political prisoners,
such as "We are not all here" and other emblems of amnesty. A comment
I heard indicated that it occurred "mysteriously." Also in Nafarroa, certain
contrasts became evident with relation to the testigo; on the one hand, there
was a certain ritualization—for example, kissing the testigo at the moment
one takes it in the relay, carrying it high in the air, and looking at it while one
runs. In contrast, one heard comments such as "Pass me the stick" among

members of a group of friends running together (photo 13). On the road to Corella, without anyone realizing that it had happened, the testigo showed up open and without a message inside. The thirty-year-old man who had been carrying it went back a few steps, picked up the fallen message, kissed it, plugged it in, and continued on, lifting the testigo high in the air.

The ikurriña is almost constantly present during Korrika. In kilometer 450, when we left Leitza, four could be seen in the crowd of runners. A few kilometers later, before the race arrived in Ezkurra, a nine-year-old boy accompanied the testigo with an ikurriña in his hand. When the race passed through Berroeta in kilometer 506, going down a steep hill at the entrance to the town, people were passing the ikurriña and the flag of Nafarroa from one balcony to another. Among the group from Cascante, the person carrying the testigo in kilometer 851 wore the ikurriña as a neckerchief, as one would wear a red scarf during the festival of Sanfermín. The slogan "Ikurriña yes, Spanish flag no" was heard in Peralta; while passing through Andosilla, where the flag appeared through the window of a car accompanying the crowd of runners; in Tafalla; and on the road between Valtierra and Cadreita, where four people supported an ikurriña as they ran. On the road to Lerin someone passed the runners on a bicycle with an ikurriña over his shoulders that he passed on to a runner in kilometer 1,001. Before arriving in Lizarra, at kilometer 1,030 at about four in the morning, a group of twelve people who were waiting for the race to pass waved two ikurriñas high in the air. When we entered that town, there was excitement in spite of the hour, and slogans in support of Euskara echoed through the streets.

The largest demonstrations of political activism occurred in Tafalla and Iruñea, which were, in turn, places where the most numerous groups from the abertzale Left were gathered. The slogans referred to prisoners, extraditions, amnesty, independence, and support for militant ETA. In Iruñea the presence of Catalan, Corsican, Gallegan, and German representatives lent an international tone to kilometer 2,060. A banner that read "Als paisos Catalans en Catala!! Grups de Defensa de la Llengua" (Cataluña in Catalan![9] Group in Defense of the Language) likewise incorporated their causes into Korrika.

General slogans about the language were heard all along the route and predominated over the political slogans. In Nafarroa more than in any other territory the language itself became a subversive statement because of its minority situation and the politics that surround it, even when it is no longer mentioned. Slogans related to specific valleys were often heard, such as "In Baztan the language is Euskara," more a statement of the past than of the present, as we will see later; "In Baztan we are for Euskara"; "Ulzama in favor of Euskara"; "Euskara in the Roncal"; and, even in Erribera, "Ziuntrenigo on the side of Euskara." In Iruñea we heard slogans from the most general—"Nafarroa in favor of Euskara"; "In Euskara, in Iruñea"—to the more specific ones heard in the neighborhoods, such as: "Txantrea in favor of Euskara";[10] "On the side of Basque, S. Juan Hauzoa"; and "Administration workers in favor of Euskara." Likewise public space was reclaimed with the cry of "Nahi dugu, behar dugu, euskaraz kaleratu" (We want to, we need to, take Euskara into the streets) and the banner "Administration in Euskara."

Solidarity with the hunger strikers also appeared in this territory, in Leitza, with a banner that read "Gora greba—dizkriminaziorik Ez" (Up with the strike—No to discrimination).

In contrast with Iparralde, the school issue appeared only timidly, reflecting the situation of Euskara in Nafarroa. In Tutera a very small boy carried the testigo followed by six children with a banner that read "Local area for the ikastola"; and later, in Iruñea, a young man carried the testigo in the name of the ikastola of Sanfermín, and the banner "Students of Sanfermín ikastola running for Euskara" was present. Slogans in support of a Basque university showed up as the Korrika passed through the Opus Dei campus of the University of Navarra: "Euskal Unibertsitatea"; "Opus kanpora" (Out with Opus).[11]

INCORPORATION OF THE FESTIVAL

An important characteristic of Korrika is its festive air. Many months of serious work go into this event, and thousands of people divide the responsibilities, but along with this reality the planning of the festive part of the race is always present in the organizational process. The first four runnings began and ended with parties. The 1980 Korrika in Oñati began with a fireworks display at ten o'clock at night accompanied by the tolling of bells for a full minute, and the bell tolling was repeated in many places in Euskalerria as the Korrika passed. This served to reinforce the festive character tied to the celebration of the popular *verbena* (evening party held in the open) in many locations. In many towns the korrikalariak were welcomed with brass bands, verbenas, theatrical presentations, competitions, masks, mime groups, and dance groups; and the big papier-mâché heads, or *cabezudos*, and giants on stilts appeared to the delight of the children. Where the passing of Korrika coincided with the celebration of local festivals, the festival was tied to the welcome for Korrika. And all the runnings of Korrika have ended with crowded festivities.

The first ending celebration was held in the Feria de Muestras in Bilbo on December 7, 1980, and it included all the characteristics of a Basque festival: music, typical food, booths, mimes, a circus, giants and cabezudos, singers, musical groups, bertsolariak, and, of course, the obligatory presence of the

Gargantua of Bilbo. The refreshments included Gipuzkoan cider, Riojan wine, homemade *patxaran*, [12] chorizo, and even dishes prepared by the great masters of Basque cooking.

In spite of the governor's initial refusal to let the race be held in Iruñea, the beginning of Korrika 2 took place in the Plaza de los Fueros in the presence of brass bands and dancers and more than five thousand people. It was symbolic that historian José María Jimeno Jurío initiated the race by passing under the festive "tunnel" of the sticks and arcs of the dancers of the Ayuntamiento. All the towns along the route were decorated for a celebration, such as Rentería, where the display of joy began on the Sunday morning when Korrika 2 was supposed to pass through with performances by Basque dance groups and bands; the same thing occurred in the final act of Korrika 2 in Donostia, where, behind the testigo, brass bands and choruses mixed with the crowd, signaling that it was time for the party to begin for everyone.

This festive air took form on the announcement poster for the Korrika in Iruñea. On the poster, the cabezudos that surround the central figure of the girl carrying the testigo form part of the world of fantasy, evocative of the races on festival days through the streets and squares of Iruñea and other towns as well. The connection is easy to make: the happy music of the *txistu*, [13] the bands, the people that flood the streets on both sides of the Estafeta on a San Fermín festival morning while the balconies are populated with people eager to see the costumed group of twenty-five people pass by, among them zaldikos, kilikis, cabezudos, and giants, all keeping time with the music as they step, leap, run, and turn. Among them, causing an uproar among the children, are five cabezudos who chase them and strike them with their air-filled balloons, imposing a festive disorder. For the little ones, the giants are threatening; even seated on their fathers' shoulders, they hardly try to touch them as they dance with stares fixed at the end of the street or on the second-floor balconies; they are alien sights to the astonished children. The children are less afraid of the cabezudos, and they approach them with a combination of fear and attraction, ready to run at the first sign of movement. They dare to touch them, to slap them, and run quickly back again to avoid being hit with an air balloon.

On the poster, each cabezudo appears with its own personality: the "Japanese" man and woman with dark hair painted on the surface of their heads; between them the "grandmother," who cannot quite be seen, wearing her hair in a bun; to the right of the Korrika girl is the "mayor," the only one with a beard and moving eyes; and finally the thickly moustached "councilman." In the parade, the "mayor" will go first, followed by the "grandmother," the "Japanese man," the "Japanese woman," and the "councilman." [14]

The cabezudos are grotesque; the large head and burlesque expression on a normal body is a satire of the ordinary. Their presence on the poster evokes this and more with their staring eyes and their bodies that appear immobile, but only until the festival begins. The festive message of the poster is within everyone's grasp.

The lower part of the poster announces the activities that are to take place during the last three days of the Korrika. It is a summary of elements representative of different points in Euskalerria from the world of song, music, and dance, as well as all that associated with the street or the square, such as the bertsolariak, the parades, the verbenas, and the *txoznak* (refreshment stands). There are plenty of representatives of rural sports and the arts, cinema, and theater. All this is waiting for the people in Iruñea if they will only go there. Here again we have the emphasis on the directionality of Korrika toward the end: toward Iruñea. Korrika has a goal, just as it had a beginning in Atharratze, and everything leads to that goal. This appears throughout Korrika. The closed space that we examined in chapter 4, the space in which ordinary activities are suspended, where time is reduced to the days or the moments of the passage of Korrika—that space is something that can be touched, something that becomes a reality, making it possible for "new time" to have a beginning and an end within an atemporal situation in a liminal space: the circle is complete.

RECLAIMING AND GENERATING THE FESTIVAL

Let us analyze the passage of Korrika 4, "Atharratzetik–Iruñera," as the poster says, from Atharratze to Iruñea. The comical festive element is always present at the beginning of Korrika, as we saw in the first chapter when we discovered dance, music, and parody. These components will remain constant throughout the more than two thousand kilometers the race will cover, adding local elements and incorporating new aspects along the way. Music is heard many times along the route, as it was when Korrika crossed a silent, unpopulated landscape at two-thirty in the morning after having passed Donapaule, and in Baiona, and later in Hendaia, close to the muga.

In Gipuzkoa the festive atmosphere was present from the crossing of the muga and increased at various moments as Korrika passed through Hondarribia and Rentería, where a band was waiting in the plaza to encourage the passage of the korrikalariak. In Donostia, supporters of the feminist and antinuclear movements of the Egia neighborhood played music in the background, and the same thing happened on the Boulevard with the change in relay runners at kilometer 252 when a festive protest march began. The march ended in front of the HABE offices, and the music, leaping, and shouting were accentuated by a moment of silence there. When we passed through the new Amara zone we heard the *txalaparta*,[15] whose rhythmic sounds reminded us of the ancestral past that is evoked throughout the race.

In Araba the festive atmosphere was strongly felt in Gasteiz on the route through the city, in spite of the aspect of a social protest it took on at many times. When we passed through the streets and squares, especially in the center of the city, the people danced with their arms in the air while shouting, "Korrika, Korrika, tralaralarala . . . Korrika, Korrika tralaralarala."[16] There were times when the rhythm of the music and the people's clapping turned that part of the city into a party.

The passage of Korrika through Bizkaia produced moments of great excitement, as in Orduña, where we arrived after one in the morning. The political slogans "Up with ETA," "Keep on until victory," and others related to Euskara had band music as a backdrop, as well as the applause of the people clustered about the town square and the slow, undulating movement of a large green giraffe that moved about the square delighting both children and adults; the atmosphere of the verbena that had been organized to prepare the welcome for Korrika was still in the air. The party continued in the next town, Llaudio, where Korrika was welcomed with the txistu, music played over the loudspeakers, and people bouncing about in the square. In Bilbo, people sometimes appeared in disguises or walking on stilts, but most of the excitement took place in neighborhoods like Santutxu, where the neighborhood band announced and welcomed the arrival, and in Deusto, where the fireworks bull was lit between the clatter of the rockets and the music. In Elizondo a brass band was waiting in the center of town, and people shouted their support of Euskara: "Baztan in favor of Euskara." In Lumbier there was general participation, and in the plaza where a three-year-old child took the testigo, everyone was dancing and applauding to the music of a brass band. Later, two men danced an aurresku while another held up the ikurriña, and they followed with a song: "Let's sing, let's sing. Nafarroa for Euskara. Let's sing." We heard music again in Tafalla, but along the final route through Iruñea the city literally converted itself into a festival. Outside the city, a truck joined the caravan and encouraged the runners with music from a brass band. Later, in Burlada and Billaba, Korrika was received with music; at times the musicians ran alongside, carrying their instruments. In our passage through Ciudadela, the festive atmosphere was combined with shouted political slogans. The culmination was the arrival at the Plaza del Castillo, which was packed with people. The kiosk was adorned with red, blue, and green ribbons. There were people on stilts and three giants dressed in typical costumes. The cabezudos crisscrossed the plaza while the band could be heard between notes from a txistu. But the txalaparta was the protagonist of the scene. From its location on the kiosk, and through the loudspeakers, its sound inundated the square. The crowd of runners was approaching slowly,

13. *Laughter and group relays were characteristic of the passage through Erribera from Buñuel to Cortés in Korrika 4.*

the people linked arm in arm, in rows. The bertsolari welcomed them from the kiosk and the giants showed their approval with gigantic applause. As on the three previous occasions, a festival marked the end of Korrika.

Capacity for Expansion

THE DIFFERENT LEVELS OF PERSONALIZATION AND THEIR POWER

One of the images that appears most frequently in the publicity for Korrika portrays the massive support from groups that participate in and advance the event in the different localities through which the race is to pass. One of the posters from Korrika 3 best expresses this statement. The visual impression one receives from it is that Korrika is advancing and seems on the verge of running over the viewer. It is taken from a photo that caught the avalanche of people passing through Bilbo in the third Korrika, a photo that can barely contain all the people in the front row (see photo 8). It is a vision of united power, of masculine indarra, transmitted through the compactness of the group and their interlaced arms. The figure of the running child carrying the testigo, absorbed in his task, oblivious to those coming up behind him but obviously conscious of the importance of his role, accentuates the collective impact by its contrast. We guess that the photo represents the moment of arrival at some important town and that the pace of Korrika has slowed to accommodate the crowd that has incorporated itself into the run. The message of the importance attributed to popular participation is in the poster's slogan: "Euskararen Alternatiba Herritarra A E K" (A E K is the people's alternative), and the phrase "Euskara eta kitto" (Euskara and that's that) corresponds to the slogan of the third Korrika.

Massive participation is interpreted as a sign of progress when one can say, "But clearly, if . . . 200,000 people set out to run like crazy from point to point in Euskal Herria, as was the case in Korrika-1, because they wanted to recover the Basque language, there is no doubt that giant steps forward are being taken." After all, "a 1,822-kilometer stride is not within anyone's reach, God knows it's a giant step" (A E K 1983). All these references have a strong dynamic content, and their language urges haste and progress. They not only walk but take "giant steps." They don't just run, they run "like crazy." This is doing, effort, intensity, and movement. A verse of the Korrika hymn says:

> Ez dugu nahi Euskadirik
> Euskaraz izan ezik
> esan baietz eta korri
> ez gero, orain baizik.

We do not want an Euskadi if it's not in the Basque language. Say yes and run, not later, but now.

And at the same time Korrika is not a pointless walk. It has concrete goals with stages and finish lines, and there is also a pragmatism that links the action to obtaining concrete goals through it.

A power is produced as people join the crowd of runners. Energy is captured, and it is gathered up by the caravan as the people are gathered together. The music, an increase in the number of shouted slogans, and a rhythm that generates tension are accompanied by a decrease in speed, and all that multiplies the effect beyond the true number of people participating. Add to this passing underneath a bridge or through a tunnel where shouted slogans are amplified and echo with thundering results, and the energy that is produced and incited by the race can actually be felt (photo 14). At times the power is generated from the runners themselves when they begin to chant slogans or sing to give themselves encouragement along the route. For example, on the road to Zumaia (Gipuzkoa) in the fourth Korrika, at a moment of special effort they sang, "Aldapa gora Korrika aldapa bera" (Up-

14. Korrika does not stop in spite of the night and the cold.

hill Korrika and downhill). Later, before beginning to climb the Orio hill, they said, "Eman martxa" (Keep going). The personification of this power was demonstrated through the rhythmic shout: "Ika, ika, ika, hemen dator Korrika" (Ika, ika, ika, here comes the Korrika). *Ika* can be interpreted as an onomatopoeic sound with no other meaning or as a form of direct intimate address: "You, you, you, here comes Korrika." At other times there would be a request for music from the runners, and the response was songs, mainly in Euskara, or lively music from one of the organization cars. One article said that "the meeting of two generations, the euskaldunberris from the ika- stola and the euskaldunzaharras, gave more power to Korrika" (*Navarra Hoy,* June 4, 1985).

Indarra seems to be generated through generational continuity and the actuality of a language that responds to the needs of new generations. At other times it is the people watching the passage of Korrika who commu- nicate their energy, as when they salute Korrika's arrival at a location with applause, new slogans, and expressions of "Aupa Korrika" (It's arriving, it's arriving, it's already here), or when they add their voices to those of the runners who are shouting slogans. Gestures demonstrating their support, such as applause, or hugging the person from whom they take the testigo, or forming a row with linked arms, or jumping up and down, or lifting children onto their shoulders so that they can follow the passage of Korrika, along with music, firecrackers, banners that appear upon the group's arrival, people in costume, and the presence of giants and cabezudos, all have a revitalizing effect on the race. Let's take a paragraph from the field journal that reflects the race as it passed through Llaudio in Bizkaia:

> It is kilometer 1,261 where a twenty-five-year-old-woman takes up the testigo. People start to join the crowd of runners. Shouts of "Ika, Ika, Ika, hemen dago Korrika." We pass by the Aceros de Llodio factory where people are working. Rhythmic applause. We begin to notice the excitement of the moment, music on the loudspeaker. Shouts of "Free the prisoners, onward with Euskara." The runners come to the passage. A change has taken place during these moments and a man is lifting the testigo overhead. We hear horns. At this moment we see how the fourth Korrika is formed in its whole dimension. Once again the banner "Amnesty" appears, now carried by a group of young people, mainly boys, in contrast with the group of young women who carried it in Amurrio, the previous town. They are singing "Korrika, Korrika, ohe, ohe." [17] Again, "Ika, ika, ika badator Korrika." It is beautiful to see it advancing through the night. Trees on the right and lights. A banner appears, "Herri bat, hizkuntza bat" in black with white letters and above the white the emblem of the Gestoras.[18] In front, two banners with photographs of prisoners that stand out above the runners.

The incorporation of causes advocated by groups from outside Euskadi through their participation in Korrika is considered reinforcement and enters into the planning of Korrika. Thus on the final route of Korrika in Iruñea, delegations from Corsica, Cataluña, and Germany took the testigo; the latter, representing the Greens, were received with applause.

Handicapped persons who enter Korrika are featured in the newspapers and are applauded for their efforts. There were some outstanding moments of this type in Korrika 4. While the race was passing through Lasarte, a forty-year-old man in a wheelchair took relay 284 and carried the testigo overhead; he was very emotional, and the people received him with applause (photo 15). Thirteen kilometers later, in Orio, another did the same and kept up a good pace. In Ondarroa a blind man, seventy-five years old, took the testigo, accompanied by a woman who led him by the arm. In Agurain in the middle of the night, five people participated in wheelchairs, and it was

15. *Extraordinary participation is met with applause. Pennants with the word "Amnistía" and photos of prisoners are visible above the runners (Korrika 4).*

almost impossible for the other runners to keep up with them. In every case, the people showed their admiration.

Another image reproduced in Korrika posters is tied to the vision of movement, so important in the projection of Korrika, and reflected in the design of the symbol of Korrika 4. Its use of fuchsia, yellow, black, and white produces an immediate impact. At first glance one sees the symbol of the lightning bolt in relation with the word *Korrika*. On closer examination the lightning bolt can be identified with the number indicating the fourth running of Korrika. The effect is a piercing one, like the instant lightning strikes on a stormy day, somewhat fleeting, past before we realize it was there.

The lightning bolt is respected for its destructive power (photo 16). Barandiaran speaks of the relationship between the Basque word for "lightning bolt," *oneztarri*, and a certain belief. The word, which joins *oneztu* (lightning) and *harri* (stone), comes from the belief that the bolt of lightning is a stone thrown from the storm cloud. When it falls to earth that stone penetrates to the depth of seven states; later, it rises again, one state every year, until it reaches the surface; from that moment it possesses the power to protect the house where it is found against evil spirits (Barandiaran 1972, 1:186).

It is clear from this and other beliefs that the people attribute extraordinary power to the lightning bolt, and this is likewise reflected in the diverse

16. *Symbol of the fourth Korrika.*

measures they take to protect themselves from its destructive effects, such as placing thistle flowers and branches of ash and thorn on doors and in fields, throwing blessed water and salt out the window, ringing church bells, reciting prayers and spells, and having masses said (ibid.:186). The bolt is feared because of its great power, and the spirit that throws the bolts is known by different names in different places: Aidegaxto in Lapurdi and Ortzia in Dohosti (Saint Esteban; ibid.:18). In Zegama and other towns in Goiherri (a region of Gipuzkoa) people believe that Mari launches destructive storms, either from the cave of Aketegi on Mount Aizkorri or from the cave of Murumendi on Mount Itsasondo (ibid.:163, 186–87).

Thus, the symbol of the lightning bolt used to distinguish Korrika 4 accentuates the speed of the race. Korrika is dressed in symbolic power from the extraordinary energy of nature and from the context of the Basque environment; it is energy that can be translated, according to Barandiaran, by *berezko* (that which exists because of itself): "a thing or phenomenon produced *by its own virtue*, spontaneously, independent of any outside agent" (ibid.:63). In Korrika the power of the lightning bolt can be interpreted in two ways. Supporters of Korrika believe the power of Korrika is projected and received as positive, some say mysterious, energy as long as Korrika advances, thus the continual emphasis that Korrika does not stop. For those who do not support the race, that same energy is perceived as generating conflict, and the obstacles they throw in Korrika's path—prohibitions, difficulties, detours— are aimed at stopping what they see as destructive power.

The same idea that Korrika cannot stop is reflected in cartoons. In most of the vignettes in the publication *Korrika Komikorrika*, a collaboration of at least nine cartoonists, the characters who participate in the race always appear in motion, unstoppable day or night, whether passing through towns or cities. They overcome fatigue and interruptions by the Spanish or French police; and even different animals—a snail, a tortoise, a rat, a rooster, a flock of sheep—participate in the race. At other times it is said, "The comic has also been running in Korrika since yesterday."

THE USE OF EVOCATIVE POWER

Part of the power of Korrika lies in its capacity for using the evocative power of places, actions, people, and symbols with the goal of amplifying the effect of the race's principal message. We have learned about the selection of locations for the points of departure and the finish line and how the organizers keep in mind what each place represents, and what each evokes and incites among Korrika's participants, spectators, and sympathizers. Through evoking other times, places, people, and actions Korrika incorporates the near or distant past into the present, into the real moment in which we live.

That is how the symbolic and emotional power of the moment are effectively amplified.

The most powerful evocation is the "presence of absence," by means of which Korrika revives the memory of significant people who were associated in life with the Basque cultural or political cause. Also incorporated is the presence of those who for political motives are in exile or in jail, or who are considered "disappeared." In the first cases, tributes carried out through Korrika are important because of their public projection and their amplifying effect. Through these tributes the Korrika tradition is generated, and from that tradition likewise arise the heroes who are incorporated through the actualization of memory.

At the end of the second Korrika, in the Feria de Muestras in Bilbo, before the final message was read, a minute of silence was observed in memory of three people: Ricardo Arregui, the founder of AEK; the teacher Xabier Peña; and the child Xabier Exeberri, to whom I referred earlier and who was expressly mentioned in AEK's final message (*Punto y Hora* 1980, no. 205, p. 9–11). Also mentioned were the importance of the time, dedication, energy, and enthusiasm that Arregui and Peña had given to the promotion of Euskara and the active participation of Xabier Exeberri in the first Korrika. The tradition of Korrika had institutionalized the memory of Xabier in its passage through Etxarri-Aranaz. The final message likewise contained a positive reference to the continuity of the educational efforts on behalf of Euskara and a sentence of support for those who carry it on in the present.

Tributes acquired a special emphasis in the fourth Korrika. Homage was paid to Pierre Lafitte in Iparralde as the race passed through Ustaritz, to Gabriel Aresti and Santi Brouard in Bilbo, to Xabier Galdeano in Getxo, and to Gladys del Estal in Donostia and Tutera. From a general viewpoint these people have some characteristics in common, but the localities and specific circumstances pertaining to their memories are unique.

Lafitte is "unanimously recognized as the patriarch of Basque letters in the French Basque Country, he who was able to receive the torch from the hands of the previous generation and pass it on to the next" (*Iker* 1983, no. 2, p. 11). His memory evokes his work as a professor of Euskara "during many years in the seminary, and as such, the founder of a school of disciples, grammarian, lexicographer, literary historian, critic, text editor, and journalist" (ibid.:12). A tribute to Lafitte was held in the plaza in Ustaritz, where an aurresku was danced in his honor and a plaque was erected in his memory. The fleetingness of the moment was in sharp contrast to Lafitte's lasting legacy.

The tribute to Aresti coincided with the tenth anniversary of his death. His wife and daughters participated in Korrika, and it was his wife, Meli, who took the testigo in kilometer 1,370 and passed it in turn to Teresa Aldamiz, the widow of Santi Brouard. Photographs of both moments were printed on the first page of *Egin* (June 7, 1985). The tribute to Aresti opposite the Museum of Fine Arts in Bilbo emphasized his contribution as a poet to the development of the new literature in Euskara, which in turn proposed support for Euskara Batua; the example of himself as an *euskaldunberri* for other people learning Euskara;[19] and his contribution to the demythification of the difficulties of Euskara, "demonstrating that it was not impossible to learn, on the one hand, and, on the other, demonstrating that a writer can change his maternal language and take a chosen tongue as his literary language, carrying it to its highest degree."[20] What ties Aresti to Lafitte is his dedication to the survival and development of the language through literary creation. In other aspects they offer striking contrasts: age, place of birth, life-style, political stance, characteristics of their literary works, and the audience they addressed.

In the tributes to Brouard and Galdeano, and to a lesser extent in the tribute to Gladys, the political significance of their deaths predominated, and the tributes constituted acts of resistance through the slogans that were shouted. I have already described the memorial to Brouard during the passage through Bilbo on June 6. On the following day, in the early hours of the morning, a crowd of some two thousand people received the testigo opposite Algorta Station and headed for Txiki y Otaegi Plaza.[21] There the testigo passed from the hands of representatives of the school of bertsolaris to the daughters of Xabier Galdeano amid strong applause and shouts of "We will not forget you, Xabier." Sometimes the two girls carried the testigo together, and at other times one of them carried the testigo and the other a poster with a photo of Xabier. Public attention was captured by the fact that Xabier's dog, Gogor, also ran in the Korrika. Xabier was remembered as a journalist, a father, a friend, and a popular character; and Brouard was remembered as a dedicated professional, a family man, a friend to children, and above all a political leader and ideologist.

The tribute to Gladys was shorter and more related to the antinuclear cause, and it took place at two separate times. The first was when Korrika passed through Tutera on the bridge where she was shot and killed by the Guardia Civil. The crowd of runners stopped for a moment at the very spot, where flowers from the tribute held the previous Sunday still lay. There they shouted, "We remember you, Gladys" and "Nuclear power no, amnesty yes." The second tribute occurred in Donostia in the neighborhood of Egia. Although the ideology of Korrika emphasizes that Korrika does not stop, in all the tributes except Galdeano's, Korrika paused for a few moments in those places that retained a territorial reference with the targets of the tributes: in Etxarri-Aranaz, on the spot where Xabier Exeberri was run down by a car and where a monolith had been erected; in Ustaritz, in the plaza where Lafitte took the testigo in Korrika 3 and where a commemorative plaque had been placed; in Bilbo, in the park, where a tree was planted in memory of Aresti, and in the Alameda de Recalde in the "house of Santi"; and in Tutera, on the bridge.

Within the importance given to the "presence of absence" it is clear that at various moments of the race prisoners, the disappeared, and the assassinated were incorporated without stopping Korrika but rather by emphasizing their inclusion into the movement of the race. When the race passed through Tolosa in Korrika 3, the participants brought forth the memory of the disappeared, who "reappeared" on posters (photo 17). In Korrika 4 that memory was constant. The poster with the names of twenty-two assassinated refugees, which left Atharratze on May 31, remained through the greater part of the Korrika. At its head the poster carried the words "Assassinated refugees are also in Korrika," and, at the bottom, "We are running behind you." At the times the poster appeared, it actualized the power of presence. At other times of the race the presence was localized, as on the route from Hondarribia to Oiarzun, where individual posters appeared with photographs of prisoners from the area, something that would be repeated at other locations along the route (photo 18). At other times one could hear direct references, such as "We remember you Peru" or references to others who were absent. In Donostia, as the race passed under the bridge on the road to Ondarreta, the runners chanted in unison, "Your mother is waiting, your father is waiting, your wife and friends are waiting," affecting the emotions of those present with the pain of those who wait, along with the memory of other loved ones.

Another form of transmitting evocative power is realized through the choice of those who carry the testigo. It is not by chance that the organizers choose people from different professions and political ideologies, athletes, bertsolariak, people from the media, artists, politicians, and members of parliament to carry the testigo. I have already spoken of the importance of the insertion of Korrika into local contexts. Thus, in each place the organizers try to play with what each person or group evokes; that is, with the capacity for symbolic representation that in turn is related to the evocation of differentiating elements: language, culture, territory, and their interrelationships. Thus the criteria for selecting bearers of the testigo are very broad, but no one who has made statements against the Basque language and culture is chosen. That does not mean that everyone in favor of Euskara will be accepted. There are other considerations, especially after the first Korrika. The implications or political interpretation that could be made of their presence in support of organizations such as A E K are also taken into account.

17. *The personalization of absence. The poster gives the names of ETA exiles who have been assassinated. Included are the date of death, first and last names, and place of death.*

18. Korrika 4 passing through the center of Rentería, symbolically incorporating political prisoners through photographs; each photo carries a name and corresponding number.

For someone from outside Euskalerria who attended the race, all the people and groups who participate would be simply runners with names and numbers on their backs. For those familiar with the history of the daily events within a specific sociopolitical framework, however, the runners' presence speaks of the power of symbolism, of the meaning and power of the evocative. That is what gives Korrika its effectiveness. Not that it is unique among its genre; rather it links the experiences, memories, and emotions of a large number of people. It captures elements that flutter in the air like pennants and transmits part of a cultural legacy. It isn't that all these elements affect onlookers and participants at the same time; nor do they all attract the same people with the same force, but rather that when seen in conjunction these cultural elements can be analyzed under this prism.

In the same way, when I spoke of territory I emphasized how the language can go beyond political differences, as was the case when the mayor of Hendaia carried the testigo and when it was carried by representatives from different political parties. Thus one could see a PNV mayor in the first Korrika (Jon Castañares from Bilbo) pass the testigo to Ortzi, a member of Herri Batasuna; and later it might be taken up by someone from Euskadiko

Ezkerra or from the Communist party (EPK). For that reason, when Telesforo Monzón carried the testigo in Korrika 1, and in his absence in Korrika 2 when his widow, María Josefa Ganuza, carried it, the moments went beyond the popular representativeness of each person to give way to the interpretation of everything that situation evoked: their positions on the language and the territory, where the importance of linguistic unity was stressed. María Josefa represented Monzón and his positions on the language and the territory, and her presence emphasized the fact that he was absent and carried the emotion of the moment. Anthropologist José Miguel de Barandiaran's act of carrying the testigo in Korrika 1 at the age of ninety-one affirmed that the responsibility for euskaldunización has no age barriers, and at the same time it brought to mind his works, his exile, his entire life dedicated to the study, knowledge, and development of Euskara and Basque culture. It seemed to say: "It is not just something of today, it is also of yesterday, and it is a long struggle toward tomorrow." It was the symbolic support of the continuity of the language and culture to which I alluded in chapter 1.

The presence of bertsolariak such as Xanpun in Iparralde and Enbeita in Bizkaia carrying the testigo has the power to evoke the history of the language transmitted orally. It brings out the close, intimate, popular elements of that activity. It evokes the context of the plaza, competitions in the cider houses, the *txapelketak*,[22] the language associated predominantly with festive space and masculinity. Finally, the presence of bertsolariak evokes one of the maximum expressions of linguistic capability that harmoniously combines rhythm, technique, and improvisation.

This evocative power of an individual presence is also fostered in collective participation when a group carries the testigo (photo 19). On the one hand, the collective effort is emphasized, meaning that the causes of Euskara imply effort from everyone. Sometimes the groups in Korrika 4 were players from La Real, a soccer team in Donostia, or athletes from a rowing team, or members of the Coral Iradier.[23] Other groups were neighborhood associations, professors and alumni of HABE, or newspaper or factory workers. But some of the groups also exhibited an evocative dimension that has its own meaning in the Basque context. For example, the presence of players from La Real brought to mind their donated work, preparing future players through youth clubs; people from HABE in Korrika 2 brought to mind their support of Euskara over and above differences in the politics of teaching the language; and something similar could be said of all the different groups that participated collectively, from city councils to children from different ikastolas to hospital workers.

There are times when one person's presence generates a whole week of massive participation, as when Iñaki Landa carried the testigo in Gasteiz

19. *Past Trebiño and on the road to Bernedo in Araba, the scene of the fourth Korrika illustrates the message that "we must all carry" the language.*

in Korrika 2 as a representative of the *blusas.*[24] The presence of Iñaki, the "Celedón" of the Blanca festivities, initiated a crowded demonstration that celebrated his appearance on August 4. The festivities began with the descent of a life-sized doll representing the mythical person called Celedón. When it reached a balcony on the plaza, Iñaki Landa, dressed as Celedón—blue pants, blue-and-white-striped blouse, a big cigar in his mouth, and a large open umbrella in his right hand—made his way through the thousands of people who filled the plaza until he reached the central balcony. From there he saluted the people and opened an uninterrupted week of celebrations led by groups of blusas. Within that context, the presence of Celedón in Korrika presented the popular support of Euskara with a greater impact than would have occurred if it had been demonstrated through chanted slogans and posters.

There are times during Korrika when the effect produced has an extraordinary quality to it, something phantasmagoric, almost magical. In the third Korrika, on a cold December night, I was impressed when in one relay four strong young men appeared dressed in abarcas, blue nankeen trousers, white shirts, and berets carrying a large ikurriña among them. At other times the light of torches pushed back the night, as in Korrika 4 when at two-thirty in the morning "a loud file of people with torches lined the seashore from Zarautz to Zumaia" (*Egin*, June 3, 1985, p. 9). There was the sudden appearance in Alsasu of the *momotxorrak* (carnival characters) with their ancestral dress and the rhythmic clanging of their cowbells as they ran.[25] Other sounds also live in my memory: bells ringing when Korrika left, passed through, or arrived; the chilling sound of the irrintzi when we passed the muga; the echo of shouted slogans in the silence of a Nafarroan valley or when we passed under a bridge or overpass in the industrial areas. The same slogans were adapted to the need to change the rhythm in order to express the importance of the moment, as when nearing the plaza of a town or the downtown area of a city, or at the point that marked the end of the race. Thus we heard "In—de—pen—den—tzia, in-de-pen-den-tzia, independentzia" (independence) accompanied by rhythmic applause; or "Korrika . . . bat, bi . . . Korrika iru" (Korrika one, two, Korrika three) jumping through a change of rhythm. The rhythm of the passage and the impression of the group's arrival always achieves an intensified effect.

THE CONCEPT OF "A PEOPLE" AND ITS EXPANSIVE MESSAGE
The success of Korrika lies in the power transmitted by its messages, the popular leadership role being one of the most important. Through Korrika there arises an abstract generalization of a group that has been operating in time, avoiding specificity or reference to a historical epoch, as one of the posters from Korrika 4 confirms:

A people who thousands of years ago set their roots down here and here they continue. A people who, in the course of their history, gave life to the seven regions of Euskal Herria. A people who do not believe themselves superior or inferior to any other, but who have their own obviously different personality. This people of shepherds, rural society and fishermen, shaped since ancient times by their way of living in valleys, on mountains, and by the sea, have with time converted themselves into a vast conglomerate of industrial dominance. (*Deia*, May 9, 1985, p. 22)

Atemporality is one of the Basque people's characteristics. It goes beyond history and is based on an ancestral past that demonstrates the power of permanence tied to the land, to the image of a tree whose roots are inside the earth: "It set down its roots here, and here it continues." And at the same time these people have been delimiting and establishing their territory. The statement made by the existence of the muga that delimits the seven territories remains clear. Economic differences may have been erased in the passage to an industrial society, but the image that predominates is rural, bucolic, and romantic.

This atemporality presents and emphasizes continuity in reference to varied surroundings, on the one hand, and, on the other hand, the changes the Basques have been subjected to as a people. These changes are related to industrialization, to the creation of jobs that have attracted foreign workers:

> It has not ceased to be the same for that reason. On the contrary, it maintains both its specific personality as well as its decisive will expressed collectively well intact. A collectivity that has grown with the incorporation of many thousands of immigrants who, already integrated in the Basque community, are today participants in its political and cultural project. (Ibid.)

This concept of a people remains intact despite the complexity of the changes they have experienced down through the centuries, especially as a result of the industrial revolution. What is more, the Basques are people with a unitarian political plan, a plan that is not specified but that through context is the plan of the entire collective. Problems of industrialization were overcome by the plan, but the political frameworks of France and Spain present new problems:

> On one hand, the people feel uncomfortable within the administrative frameworks imposed by the old states that choke off their desire to be a nation. On the other hand, they find themselves faced with grave problems posed by postindustrial society: renewed situations of exploitation, unemployment, weapons factors, ecological imbalances, imbalances between towns. . . . Problems the people respond to in a thousand ways, in their desires and plans for a better society. (Ibid.)

Conclusions

The dynamics of Korrika are intended to generate a mass adherence to its objectives and goals. Its underlying concept is that of a people anchored in an ancestral past but with an ongoing continuity in history, thanks to their posture of resistance at certain times, in certain circumstances, and against certain powers that wanted to subjugate them. Euskara is one of the characteristics of their permanence. The changes caused by the move from a subsistence economy to a market economy have been incorporated into this concept of a people, emphasizing their receptivity to technology and their capacity to integrate the outsiders who have come among them in response to the demands for manual labor. There is no reference in this concept to the dominant class, even by inference, that must have been present in this process of industrial development and whose role has been widely documented historically and socially. The Basque vision is an egalitarian vision in which enemies are principally thought of as being from outside Euskalerria and are often identified with the Spanish and French states where the Basques as a whole have been politically inserted.

These people, of whom it is said that "both their specific personality and their free will to perceive themselves collectively remain intact" (*Deia*, May 9, 1985, p. 22), are the people who present themselves as the protagonists of Korrika, and they do so symbolically through the crowds of runners and the massive mobilizations that await their passage, and those who support Korrika with their presence. That is why it is so necessary to achieve the image of a massive adhesion of the people. One of the organizers of Korrika commented: "For me, when they say Korrika is coming, it is the people who are coming, because it is a popular demonstration on behalf of Euskara, a form of reclamation of the national identity." That is why it is so important to put into action all the mechanisms that can reinforce, invigorate, and extend that impression of participation by the people.

There are times when Korrika seems charged with an innate energy, something similar to *berezko*, something magical, unexplainable, outside the normal control of actions; something situated in reality but at the same time outside reality. At other times the presence of indarra is evident in the act of running, the shouting of slogans, the singing of songs, and the extraordinary manifestations of strength. In the dominant image, this indarra is projected more as a masculine indarra than as a human indarra in general. Participants say that the magical quality cannot be explained, and often it is expressed as "the magic of Korrika," while indarra is visible, is referred to throughout the race, and is highly valued.

The organizers try to accentuate the breadth of participation through the evocative power that amplifies and magnifies both the past and the presence of the persons and symbols which produce that power. On the other hand, it is the actualization of the integrating capacity of Korrika that incorporates the aspirations of such different groups, many of them representative of alternative life-styles and movements: feminists, ecologists, conscientious objectors, and alternative radio projects, who ordinarily have no institutionalized public forum. Likewise Korrika provides a place for groups to demonstrate their political, linguistic, and labor-related causes. From this perspective Korrika has certain subversive characteristics that we will examine in the following chapter. If we accept that Korrika creates a liminal space, it would be in this space where the utopian concept of a people is realized, a people with roots in their ancestral past who face the present and the future, reaffirming the integration of differences and the expression of various aspirations that always exist within the general political, cultural, and social plan proposed in Korrika.

Chapter Six

Diversity and Contrasts

Presented by Euskalerria

In the earlier chapters we saw Korrika's importance in providing the territory with signals that proclaim it as Euskalerria as well as the mechanisms that are used to establish its limits. We have seen how Korrika passes through Euskalerria, changing and lengthening its routes each time, but always with the objective of traversing the seven territories, including the capitals, cities, and towns, without neglecting those places that are most representative and have the greatest symbolic weight. In this way, the message of the unity of the seven territories becomes a reality for as long as the event lasts. All the participants and places along the way are incorporated, either graphically on posters and in photographs or in written and verbal references that record what happened. Included in these records is the invocation of certain moments that will later be related as part of the "tradition of Korrika."

In this chapter we will consider how the great diversity of Euskalerria and the contrasts presented within its space become a part of Korrika. The symbolic resolution treated in the final chapter will be offered through this incorporation.

The route of Korrika continually emphasizes climatic variations, orographic difficulties, and the distances between locations. The daily cycle becomes evident—dawn, noon, sundown, and nighttime—because Korrika does not stop. It traverses open country and population centers; it covers the flatlands and overcomes the difficulties of the seaports. It borders the coast, runs along the sea, and turns inward into the interior. Climatic differences—cold, heat, rain, sun, fog, and clear skies—form part of the Korrika experience. Finally, Korrika captures the contrasts between the zones where Spanish is spoken and those where Euskara is spoken.

The Incorporation of Differences:
Mountains, Plains, and Coastline

Of the seven territories, Nafarroa presents the broadest spectrum of geographic diversity in Euskalerria. The mountainous zone, extending for 4,719
square kilometers, is the most extensive and the least populated area in
Nafarroa. Within it, 50 percent of the population is concentrated in 1,652
square kilometers in the valleys of Iruñea, Aoiz, and Lumbier. In the Pyreneen and Cantabrian valleys, 3,067 square kilometers in area, there were
hardly more than 45,000 inhabitants in 1975, providing a population density of 14.9 inhabitants per square kilometer (Gómez Piñeiro 1980, 4:248).
There is generally an abundance of rain, and the geology and terrain are
heterogeneous.

In the Pyreneen valleys, herding and forestry are still the major economic
activities. Cultivated lands lie on the valley floors, and among the crops corn
and high-quality potatoes sold as seed potatoes predominate. These crops
coexist with large areas of harvested fields and, at higher elevations, sub-
alpine meadows. In the valleys of Roncal and Salazar raising sheep for meat
and wool has largely been replaced by potato cultivation. The towns situated
at the north end of the Roncal and Salazar valleys—Luzaide, Orreaga, and
Burgete—were once characterized by the movement of the herds. The flocks
have been coming down from the mountains at the end of September since
the remote past, moving toward middle Navarra and Erribera to spend the
winter and returning in June, occupying first the lower parts of the valleys
and slowly ascending to the higher regions (ibid., 4:144, 154, 157–58). Today
the few sheep that are raised are not herded to the Bardenas but rather to
Benafarroa Beherea or Zuberoa, where they are normally pastured through
private contracts. The owners of the pastures demand five out of every seven
lambs born during their stay (from November to April) and all the milk from
that period. Dairy products (homemade cheese or yogurt) are sold at fairs
or regional markets in Etxarri-Aranaz, Santesteban, Lesaka, Vera, Elizondo,
Irurzun, and Iruñea.[1]

In the Cantabrian valleys the temperatures are more moderate than in
the southern valleys. Prominent vegetation includes oak trees at the lower
elevations and beech trees higher up. There are abundant rivers, the most
important being the Bidasoa, which serves as a muga between Lapurdi and
Gipuzkoa. The most important valleys are Cinco Villas and Baztan. The
former is important for its border location, its physiognomy, and its population centers—Vera, Lesaka, Etxalar, Aranaz, and Yanci (in order of greatest to
least importance in population and industrial development). Both Vera and

Etxalar, because of their border location, have Guardia Civil barracks, and in all five the plaza constitutes the center of town (Gómez Piñeiro 1980, 4:84, 280–81, 255; Caro Baroja 1982, 2:79, 82–83, 130–31, 144, 156–58, 160–61).

Baztan features fourteen towns with a total of 8,545 inhabitants. Elizondo is the capital. The economy revolves around agriculture and animal husbandry. Corn, potatoes, and animal fodder are the predominant crops. The municipalities of Zugarramurdi and Urdax, although also in the valley of Baztan, are independent. The population has declined by more than 25 percent with respect to the 1950 census (Gómez Piñeiro 1980, 4:241–52, 255, 280–81).

Erribera, in southern Nafarroa, offers a contrast of rich irrigated lands and poor dry ones, a situation that has given rise to unequal economic development in the area. The rich land represents 45 percent of the Nafarroan agricultural surface area. The population is concentrated in large towns that apear like smudges in the midst of extensive plains. The most important towns are San Adrián, Lodosa, and Peralta in western Erribera, and the market city of Tutera in Tudelana, where there is also varied industrial activity: food, metallurgy, ceramics, construction, paper, textiles, and graphic arts. The population has increased here, primarily in Tutera but also in Castejón, Corella, Cintruénigo, and Cortes (ibid., 4:272–75).

In the eastern part of the middle zone of Nafarroa, contrasts appear between mountains with their little villages and plains with big towns. Just as in the mountain valleys, there was a demographic decline between 1955 and 1980, with the exception of Tafalla and Sangüesa, which have recent industrial installations: a paper factory, metallurgy, food canning, and shoemaking. Economic activity revolves around agriculture centered on wheat, vineyards, and olives, and in some valleys there is animal husbandry and a lumber industry. Tafalla is the principal nucleus and the center of communications with Iruñea, Gasteiz, and Zaragoza. The western middle zone, or Tierra Estella, presents a conglomeration of valleys, plains, and mountains, dominated by the River Ega. Its economy is based on agriculture: cereals, olives, vineyards, legumes, and potatoes, and the lumber industry. Lizarra, which was established in 1090 by King Sancho Ramírez, is the center of the region and has been important as a crossroads and marketplace since the period of pilgrimages on the Camino de Santiago (ibid., 4:266–72).

The valleys of Barranca and Burunda are located among the Aralar, Andia, and Urbasa mountains. Barranca and Burunda have certain factors in common with the Cantabrian and southern valleys, such as animal husbandry, corn as a main crop, the small size of worked fields (between 1 and 5 hectares), and industrial activity centered on metallurgy, chemistry, paper making, and food production. They differ in that Barranca and Burunda experienced a population growth of more than 30 percent between 1955 and 1980, and they have pioneered in the industrial development of Nafarroa. The livestock, forestry, and industrial activities of Barranca are principally located in Irurzun and Etxarri-Aranaz. In the Burunda Valley, Alsasu is the most important industrial site, followed by Olazagutia, and Alsasu is also a communications hub for trains and highways (ibid., 4:252–55).

On its pass through Nafarroa, Korrika first crosses the mountainous zones and then zigzags through the different regions: through Erribera, where it travels through many towns, covering numerous kilometers as a result of the distances between them; through the middle zone, Barasoain, and Tafalla; continuing through the valleys of Barranca and Burunda; and ending in Iruñea, the end of Nafarroan territory. In the Pyrenees zones, close to the border, there is the constant presence of the Guardia Civil, which follows the race and causes animosity; their presence diminishes in other areas.

The fact that Korrika physically covers the territory has made general and local organizers, runners, and observers aware of the influence that local characteristics have on the configuration of Korrika's route. Through data from the team's field journals we will examine the local peculiarities that have given Korrika the power and size to take on the whole of Euskalerria on its passage through mountains and valleys while remaining rooted in the everyday life of its inhabitants in many of the places through which it passes.

Dawn, we are surprised upon entering Zubiri in kilometer 571 where a group of 18 people wait and join in immediately while music plays. The sixty-five-year-old town baker comes out to see Korrika, and the young runners shout loudly upon entering the town, "Hika, hika, hika, here comes Korrika." In kilometer 574 a young man runs the relay, smiling as he climbs uphill. We go through a door. The towns are small and somewhat scattered. We enter Agorreta, and one of the runners salutes an acquaintance who appears on a balcony. When we arrive in Erro, twenty people accompany the testigo. A baserritarra [inhabitant of a farmhouse] appears to watch Korrika pass and smiles. The korrikalariak recognize people in the town who appear at windows and greet them. It is seven in the morning. Later on, we pass through Linzoain, a very small agricultural town where hardly anybody appears. When we enter Biskarret in kilometer 585 the cistern truck is collecting milk in the square; the livestock tenders greet the people they know who are running in Korrika. Later it begins to rain and the difficulty of the climb toward Mezkiriz becomes apparent. At the entrance to Espinal a worker appears, and others also appear throughout the town, but nobody joins in. Descending through Burgete toward Garralda, Korrika has to compete with six horses that run on a parallel course in the field, and someone says, "Korrika even makes the animals run."

In kilometer 993 Korrika entered western Erribera when it passed through Peralta, and in the following kilometer, when it entered Marcilla, Korrika moved into Erribera Tudelana. This crossing back and forth among different regions within a territory happened quite a few times during the race. In kilometer 998 the race returned to the west, and in kilometer 1,052, when it entered Los Arcos, it passed into the middle zone. The participation between Peralta and Lizarra was small due to the distances between the towns and the political and linguistic characteristics of the area. The abertzale Left is in the minority there, the movement for euskaldunización is less effective, and the language disappeared some time ago. Neither was a competitive spirit observed between the runners of the towns as we saw happen in Araba between Araia and Zalduondo. Interest lay more in being able to cover the route, and whether or not the runners' numbers corresponded to the number of the kilometer in that stretch had little importance. When the runners passed through Peralta groups applauded in the plaza. In Marcilla the person carrying the testigo was accompanied by eight runners. In Andosilla Korrika recieved a lot of applause, but no one joined the race. On that stretch only five young people ran. Each wore the number of a different kilometer, which meant that they were distributing the route, and each ran several kilometers. In Lerin a group of eight or ten people waited, and in Lizarra, Korrika was welcomed a little after four o'clock in the morning with applause, music, ikurriñas, young people of both sexes mixed with men between forty and fifty years of age, and shouts of "Nafarroa on the side of Euskara" and "Euskara in Euskalerria." In kilometer 834 a twenty-year-old man carried the testigo, saying that he had left his job harvesting asparagus to come and run. At that moment our noses as well as our eyes were witness to the peculiarities of the zone and the countryside: fields with a strong odor of manure, others with recently cut corn, and, more abundantly, asparagus fields where people were bent over the earth. We saw wild rabbits, and someone said that there were a lot of them in that area. We heard shots coming from North American aviation training exercises on the firing range at Bardenas, an activity that has encountered strong opposition from local groups. People commented on their difficulties in covering the kilometers: the hour was bad, the distances were too long, many of the young people were busy harvesting asparagus, and too few people were trying to learn Euskara. One of the organizers said,

It is so difficult to organize Korrika here, you have to underscore the people's morale. The ones who run, it's not that they're learning Euskara but rather that they agree with what Korrika means. There are times when, because of the combination of the language with politics, . . . the situation becomes difficult.

We have viewed Nafarroa as an example of how ecological, demographic, economic, and linguistic differences are incorporated through the running of Korrika. Now let us follow the race through Gipuzkoa and Bizkaia to see how the coastline and sea are incorporated.

The sea has played an important role in Euskalerria's history and technological and economic development (Caro Baroja 1985). Fishing is still important to the economy (it occupies sixth place in its export potential), in spite of restrictive quotas imposed by the European Community in the last few years. There are some seven hundred vessels dedicated to shallow-water and deep-sea fishing, and some ten thousand people work as crewmen. In addition, many participate in the fishing industry on land (Caja Laboral Popular, *Atlas de Euskal Herria,* p. 89).

An important part of Korrika's route takes it along the coast, first through Lapurdi in Iparralde and later through Gipuzkoa and Bizkaia, where at two spots, Pasaia and Santurtzi, the race passes next to the sea. A few kilometers after leaving Donostia Korrika begins to follow the coast: Orio, Zarautz, Zumaia, Getaria, Motriku, Ondarru. In this passage along the coast, off the main highway, Korrika covers the fishing villages step by step and places mugarri all along the Cantabrian coast. The contrast with the interior is captured in a newspaper title that refers to the route of June 7: "After bordering the sea, the testigo returns to dry land" (*Egin,* June 8, 1985, p. 33).

When Korrika 4 arrived in Zarautz in Gipuzkoa at two-thirty in the morning, "a loud file of people with torches skirted the seashore from Zarautz to Zumaia: in Mutriku they waited for Korrika at dawn with music after an animated all-night vigil" (*Egin,* June 3, 1985, p. 9). (This was the first time Mutriku was included in the route.)

On the route through Bizkaia, Korrika 4 approached the coastline and ran through the fishing village of Elantxobe and the towns of Natxitua, Ea, and Ispaster, arriving in Lekeitio at nine-thirty in the morning of the seventh. Six hundred people ran the urban route through Lekeitio and continued on toward Ondarru (photo 20), a prominent fishing village whose welcome was considerable. The significance of fishing in those towns is complemented by the strong presence of Euskara, manifested in Lekeitio and Ondarru in the importance of their ikastolas and literacy groups. On this maritime route the outstanding moments occurred when Korrika ran next to the sea. These areas are considered "hot spots" similar to crossing the muga.

20. A sense of humor helps on the hills between Lekeitio and Ondarru in Korrika 4.

Another hot spot for Korrika on its passage through Gipuzkoa will be Pasajes where the testigo carrying the message written by Pierre Lafitte will cross the bay of Pasajes where a new concentration [of people] will take place. (*Egin*, June 1, 1985, 34)

Upon arrival at Pasaia de San Pedro, the testigo crossed the river in a boat as far as Lezo, where four hundred people were waiting, and a woman took up the relay in kilometer 240.

Days later, in Bizkaia, Korrika first ran through the port of Santurtzi, where groups of friends waiting in *la txitxarra* (a gathering place) encouraged the korrikalariak as they passed by. The route traversed the park and arrived at the port, where the testigo was carried on kilometer 1,334 by a rower from the Itxaso Ama rowing club, the club to which the fishing boat *Sotera* belongs.[2] As on other competitive occasions a large number of people accompanied the boat and the members of the crew, adding on this occasion shouted slogans of "Euskara in Euskalerria," "Amnesty for all," "Korrika, Korrika," and "Free the prisoners." The boat made its way from Santurtzi to Portugalete followed by people who took an overland route. At the end of the stretch, the testigo passed from the boat that had transported it to the rowers of the boat *Jarrillera* from Portugalete, which belongs to the rowing club of the same name.[3]

Euskara: Beyond Variations and Circumstances

The spatial distribution of Euskara presents a series of characteristics, including dialect and subdialect variations differences in the intensity of the language, and its actual presence or absence. Eight dialects are distinguished in Euskalerria: Bizkaino, Gipuzkoano, Northern and Southern Goi-nafarrera (High-Navarrese), Lapurdin, Zuberoan, Eastern and Western Behe-nafarrera (Low-Navarrese); within each there exists a series of subdialects, for a total of twenty-five subdialectical variations. Thus within the Bizkaino dialect there is the version spoken east of Markina and that spoken west of Markina, with variations in turn in Gernika, Bermeo, Plencia, Arratia, Orozko, Arrigorriaga, and Otxandio.

Dialectal divisions establish separations distinct from the territorial *mugak* mentioned in chapter 3 that are incorporated into and transcended by Korrika. Thus the Gipuzkoano dialect includes zones in Nafarroa such as Burunda and Etxarri-Aranaz. Also, the division between Iparralde and Hegoalde is erased when one considers the extension of the Lapurdin dialect spoken in Urdax and Zugarramurdi into Nafarroa, while these towns remain a part of Benafarroa. At other times, as is the case in Nafarroa, one finds two dialects within a single territory: Northern and Southern Goi-nafarrera. Thus, linguistic variations establish their own limits; subdialects often coincide with ecological divisions, as occurs in the Pyrenees valleys, and at other times the same ecological zone presents various linguistic differences.

Korrika's passage through different parts of the Nafarroan mountains reveals the unequal status of Euskara in the area. Korrika 4 crossed the muga and entered Nafarroa. Leitza was the first important town, and there the testigo was taken up by the mayor-elect, Jesús María Zabaleta, who ran kilometer 445, the first kilometer in Nafarroan territory. On the way to Elizondo the largest concentrations of people were in Leitza and Donesteban. In Leitza, a town of 2,606 inhabitants where the Inza variety of Northern Goi-nafarrera is spoken, 2,230 people speak Euskara (Yrizar 1981, 1:197). A group of 20 people was waiting there, and later a crowd of some 100 people joined the race, shouting "Korrika, Korrika" as they ran. Students and teachers of the ikastola took the testigo in the center of town, which was filled by a huge crowd in spite of the heat. Groups of people were in the streets—couples with children, women, and youngsters—shouting "Euskara in Euskalerria" and applauding. People of all ages participated, although young people seemed to predominate. The organizers announced that the funds raised from the first twenty-four kilometers surpassed 500,000 pesetas, and 20,000 pesetas had been contributed for each kilometer. The welcome festivities featured events such as an appearance by Titiriteros de Sebastopol (a theatrical group) in the town square (*Navarra Hoy*, June 3, 1985). In Donesteban, where a different variation of the Leitza dialect is spoken, approximately 20 percent of the population speak Euskara (180 of 892 inhabitants; Yrizar 1981, 1:195), and in Legasa the percentage is much less. The team's field journals describe Korrika's passage through Legasa in the valley of Bertiz-Arana at 9:00 P. M. on June 2:

> A group of some twenty-five awaiting the testigo. We enter the heart of the town, there are very few people, all adults. One woman applauds, the majority are men of about sixty years old, they give no sign, they are in the doorways of their houses or on benches. The town is very small and the majority of the people are on the bridge where we entered and where we leave again for the highway.

In Elizondo about a hundred runners joined in, and in the center of town, where the testigo was passed in front of the town hall, the group increased to about two hundred while the music of a popular band played and people shouted, "Baztan is also for Euskara." We saw people over fifty-five among the runners. In Elizondo they speak the same dialect as in Leitza but with Elizondo variations, and of the 2,496 inhabitants, 1,600 speak Euskara (ibid., 1:194).

On the uphill stretch between Olagüe and Egozkue someone commented that Euskara has been lost in that region but that there are some euskaldun-berris. In that zone the Guardia Civil were present all along the road. Passing by Espinal, a strong welcome took place in Garralda, where schoolchildren participated. As in the previous zones, these areas have lost Euskara.

In the valley of Salazar, where the people speak Eastern Behe-nafarrera, there was an outstanding reception in Otzagi, a lovely town in the Nafarroan Pyrenees with 839 inhabitants and 100 Euskara speakers, all of the latter in the adult generation of sixty-five to seventy years of age (ibid., 1:211). We were welcomed by *dantzari txiki* (young dancers) in the midst of great excitement in the streets. We heard an irrintzi, and on kilometer 626 Teófilo, a local elder, held the testigo high and "guided the race and above all cheered on the participants. At 70 years of age, he found words of encouragement for all those who had to do more than 30 kilometers in relays from Otxagi to Erronkari" (*Egin*, June 4, 1985, p. 22). The dancers joined Korrika, and their red-corded white costumes added a festive note to the crowd of runners.

In Roncal, where different varieties of the Zuberoa dialect are spoken, the language has disappeared in Urzainki, Ustarroz, Bidangoz, Burgi, and Garde (ibid., 1:206–7). Although Pedro de Yrizar believes that it is also lost in Isaba, people there told us that some very old people still speak the language, and we heard a young person say, "My *aitona* [grandfather] spoke it but he went to Aragón to work and lost it." In Isaba the mayor carried the testigo accompanied by a group of about twenty-five people, most of them young, many of whom were learning Euskara. That same group organized the relays all the way to Burgi, a town where, according to what we heard, "no one wanted to run." In Urzainki the runners shouted "Euskara in the Roncal," but one of the organizers noted that "no one was seen," and the people who were in charge of the route between Urzainki and Navascues (fifteen kilometers) were all from Navascues. In that town, where Korrika passed through at five in the afternoon, the runners said that "practically the whole town was there." People in their early twenties had come from Iruñea to run in Navascues, demonstrating with that action the importance of Korrika's local connection, something I have emphasized throughout this volume.

With respect to the presence and utilization of Euskara, the valleys of Barranca and Burunda show a more continuous presence than the Pyreneen, Cantabrian, and Southern valleys. In Barranca there are zones that are predominantly Basque speaking, such as Arbizu, Lakunza, Arruazu, and Iraneta. In Burunda, Urdiain stands out as an area that speaks the Burunda variety of the Gipuzkoano dialect (ibid., 1:190, 196). Support for the language is evident through support for Korrika.

From Alsasu (kilometer 1,998) to Yabar (kilometer 2,019) there was active and heavy participation through people joining the runners, the applause of those who waited for them, music, posters, ikurriñas, and shouted slogans. In Alsasu the momotxorroak took the testigo, and the experience with all its contrasts was recorded in the field journal:

> Impressive is the sight of the ancestral costumes of these characters from the iñauteriak (carnival) traversing the town surrounded by the crowd of runners. They pass the testigo among themselves and later to a young man who represents the group. The noise of the drum, the sound of the cowbells produced by the rhythmic passing of the momotxorroak mixes with shouts of "Up with ETA," "Korrika," "Amnesty." It is 5:30 in the morning and we see the first light of day.

Many people were waiting for the race in Lakunza, where the Huarte Arakil variety of Northern Goi-nafarrera is spoken, and the one who took the testigo shouted, "Gora Euskadi Askatuta" (Long live free Euskadi). The shouted slogans and the rhythm of the group of more than a hundred people made it seem as if the whole town was running. We saw a banner with the slogan "AEK boarding school: We are one people and we have one language" carried by a group of twelve who were taking an intensive course in Batua organized by AEK in the town.

Through these vignettes one can appreciate how Korrika accumulates the particulars of the places through which it passes and reflects in turn certain general characteristics of Euskara's situation. It is not possible to establish a correlation between a positive response to Korrika and a high index of knowledge of Euskara, but certainly in those places where Euskara continues as a living language there is a positive response to Korrika. Even in some places where the language is disappearing, the people support Euskara through Korrika, at least on a symbolic level; thus, Korrika in turn becomes an element of reaffirmation of Basque identity. With that action they support a territorial concept that transcends current political divisions. Korrika passes through places where the language has disappeared, as in Roncal and Baztan. In other places, not even a historical memory of Euskara remains. But everywhere the emphasis is on recovery. In addition to considerable dedication, in many cases the task of resurrecting Euskara requires identification with sectors of the abertzale Left and Basque cultural movements. The passage of Korrika gathers together dialectal variations, even when people express themselves in Batua; at times the variations correspond to geographic divisions that result from the terrain of the valleys, and at other times they do not.

Looking at the passage of Korrika through the zones of Nafarroa as a whole, one can see that even in the areas where Euskara disappeared in the last century, it has been taken up as a social cause; its representation may be minor, but to evaluate this one must keep local circumstances in mind. When a gau eskola or an ikastola exists in a town, its presence serves to bring together the people with an interest in the language. Although the elders support the cause, the young people are the ones who participate most. The differences among the various areas are colored by the difficulties of the mountain terrain. Thus the newspapers give more space to the stages of the race in the Nafarroan Pyrenees, which are considered to be the hardest slopes in Korrika, and the relays are organized on the basis of active participation by local teams.

The valleys of Ulzama and Erro first, and those of Erronkari and Salazar next, competed yesterday with two peaks on the road—the Alto de Laza and Las Coronas—the first serious orographic difficulties on Korrika's course that put into effect yesterday a new mode of relays to enable the involvement of localities that are tens of kilometers apart. Several teams of runners belonging to the cuadrillas of Otxagabia, Erronkar and Nabaskoitz participated. Those teams used their own cars to keep a portion of their runners in reserve, while the rest accompanied the testigo. (*Egin*, June 4, 1985, p. 22)

Teams likewise appeared from various villages to cover the lonely distances of Erribera. Covering so much territory integrated the different regions and their peculiar characteristics.

Dialectal borders are also crossed in Gipuzkoa and Bizkaia. On the route between Hernani (kilometer 268) and Berastegi (kilometer 444) on the muga with Nafarroa, we passed through distinct variations of the Gipuzkoan dialect (Azkoitia, Zegama), and when passing through Elgoibar we sampled a variation of Bizkaino. It was also obvious from the beginning of the race in Atharratze that dialectal variations from Iparralde were included; they were expressed on banners and written in the text of the message read by Amaia Fontán and in the Lafitte text inserted into the testigo. However, throughout the race, and all through the preparatory campaign, the unity of Euskara was proclaimed in the slogan "Herri bat hizkuntza bat," and it was done in Batua. The slogan was generic, and it included all the dialectal and subdialectal variations within the term *Euskara*. The same thing was emphasized through publicity, slogans, and posters when they referred to the institutions—the Basque government, AEK, HABE, and Euskaltzaindia—that had demonstrated their position with respect to Batua as the most appropriate means for the preservation, transmission, and development of the language.

The Rural-Urban Dichotomy

In Korrika the rural-urban counterpoint is experienced at times as part of the race's strategy of collecting diversity and differences. Some of the posters and other Korrika publicity play with the idyllic and evocative aspect of the country. On the principal poster for Korrika 4, against a background of cold, dark shades, there appears the stark silhouette of an open hand, cut off from the background by a splash of intense red. These colors bring to mind other posters used in previous Korrikas and in Gestoras pro Amnistía campaigns to call attention to political prisoners, but this poster is different from the other Korrika posters with regard to the utilization of color, design, and theme.

Compared with the aggressive impact of this combination of colors, the countryside in the background, with its silhouetted baserri, suggests a certain lyricism. The denuded trees indicate the season, and the pines accentuate the sad tone of the landscape. Superimposing the different fields establishes several levels of meaning in the message. The bucolic countryside with its single baserri remains in shadow; the slogan "Euskal Herria herri bat hizkuntza bat" (Euskalerria, one people, one language) occupies the foreground; the hand is in the middle ground, acting as a transformational element since the light outlines the silhouettes of the pine trees in the background as if it were dawn. Two elements—one physical (the baserri) and the other linguistic—express the message of Euskalerria. The repetition of *bat* (one) in the message ties in with the uniqueness of the baserri, which, as Zulaika (1988:125–26) states, has come to symbolize Basque culture.

The hand lends strength to the message. Through the hand, perceptions and associations with humanity are generated in a generic sense, and there is a suggestion of transformational power. The hand is open toward the person contemplating the poster. The testigo, the symbol of Euskara that is passed from hand to hand during the Korrika, represents the association with the language and therefore the synthesizing character of the message, the nexus of the union between the countryside in the background and the slogan. The poster to which I am referring appeared on the frontispiece of a triptych in full color announcing Korrika; on the facing page appeared a hand carrying the testigo, wrapped in the ikurriña. This hand, held high, was taken from a larger drawing of a fourteen-year-old boy wearing a green jogging suit and carrying the testigo in his left hand at chest height. The drawing appeared on the cover of the magazine *Aizu,* announcing the third Korrika with the phrase "It's coming, it's coming . . . the third worldwide Korrika!" Thus the message of the hand with the rural background as the heritage of the past is likewise expressed in the young hand that carries the message throughout the diversity that is Euskalerria.

The graphic representation of the urban in contrast with the bucolic is present on another Korrika 4 poster. While on the poster described above the bucolic quality of the rural world dominates and human presence is merely symbolic by means of the hand, here the real beehive buildings and people running are the leading figures on the poster. The baserri has been transformed into a neighborhood just like those found in different spots throughout Euskalerria: Otxarkoaga and Santutxu in Bilbo, Rentería in Gipuzkoa, Txantrea in Iruñea. While the baserri speaks of isolation, of the ideal people, the buildings on the second poster suggest to us in every opening, on every floor, a world in tumult, people contemplating the passage of Korrika through windows or from their apartments, or running in the street sheathed in clothing to protect them from the cold. In contrast, the blue of the poster's background communicates an unreal hue in a country where sunny days are few and cloudless blue skies are even rarer; it does not imply a winter day, as the runners' clothing suggests.

Elements of Inclusion-Exclusion and the
Contrasts on Which They Are Based

Korrika emphasizes the *inside-outside* dichotomy, and the different levels of classification of the players demonstrate their multivocality. This is reflected in the following article, which appeared in a small newspaper published during Korrika 2:

> It is easier to learn Basque than English, for example. . . . At least for the inhabitants of Euskal Herria. Just as it is easier to learn to ski in Baqueira Beret than in Puerto de Santa María, or it is more comfortable for a citizen of Munitibar to learn to play handball than cricket.
>
> The question lies not in comparing the intrinsic difficulty of one language or the other: we would surely lose ourselves in arguments if we did that.
>
> Learning English to speak it supposes the necessity, dear reader, of spending a rather long stay in Great Britain, or if you want to make it more difficult, in the Malvinas Islands, where they have been speaking Thatcher's language for the last few days. (AEK 1983)

This article establishes contrasts between two political entities: Great Britain and Euskalerria, with two pairs of differentiating characteristics for each one: cricket and English as opposed to handball and Euskara. Here the *inside* is the place where one can learn Euskara, and it is presented with all its nearby, intimate characteristics—characteristics that tie it to the people and have powerful evocative content.

Another level of the *inside-outside* of the article takes place in the context of what previously was considered *inside*, that is, in the geographic context of Euskalerria. Here *inside* means home; that is, the place where Euskara is normally transmitted or the places where it is formally learned, as through the euskaltegi and the barnategi. Efforts on the inside should be aimed at sending euskara *outside*. This idea is captured on the posters that frequently appear on Basque streets, such as "Euskara, really, in our city halls" and "Anywhere, any time, in Euskara." The way to establish Euskara is, first, to gain support through strong popular demonstrations such as Korrika, and, second, by means of teaching and learning it. A slogan from Korrika 2—"We only lack 1,822 kilometers to recover Euskara"—accompanied by a photograph taken of the mass participation in kilometer 1,557 explains that only *outside*, in the streets, can the language be revived, and that is linked to the 1,822 kilometers symbolic, as we have seen, of all Euskalerria.

In all these levels of differentiation with their specific complex of meanings, the language appears as the key element and is always linked to great activity. The effort of running is symbolically valued when each kilometer is translated into a number of Euskara speakers. Thus it is shaped in the publicity: "One may think that this is something that should not be measured in kilometers, but rather in the number of Basque speakers" (ibid.).

Euskara is a living thing, but it moves from *inside* (from the classroom) to the *outside* (to incorporation into ordinary speech) when those who learn it are integrated with those who already know it. It is interesting that in this manner the pamphlet's authors are insisting on a process of integration that breaks with other types of barriers—as, for example, with that of being born or not being born in Euskalerria. They say, "without moving from here, in 500 hours, A E K offers you the possibility of becoming a Basque. People who stood the test can tell you about it now, but in Basque" (ibid.). When language is seen as a defining element, we confer upon it the power to integrate those who speak it into a life experience that also appears different, and this process takes place not by the ordinary transmission of language from parents to children in the process of socialization but rather by breaking communication barriers. Knowledge of the language, the authors say, will allow you to communicate with many persons you could not have spoken to when you did not know the language, even though they were nearby. "In contrast, Euskara is so nearby that only when you learn it will you realize that there are quite a few more Euskara speakers than there appeared to be" (ibid.). This sentence emphasizes the closeness once more, but also the element of the unknown, of what can be discovered.

People's Reactions as Korrika Passes

Let us now revisit some locations as spectators of the passage of Korrika and hear the evaluations made by some of the participants, including comparisons with previous runnings. In the evaluation of the race's success in any place one must keep in mind the number of people, the state of the language, the active presence of forces from the abertzale Left, and difficulties of climate and terrain. We cannot evaluate participation in two cities such as Donostia and Iruñea in the same way, since the latter lies outside the Comunidad Autónoma Vasca and has, moreover, a small number of Euskara speakers. The same could be said if we compared two rural towns such as

Larrabezu in Bizkaia and Cascante in Erribera. The number of participants in
Cascante would have to be evaluated more qualitatively, while in Larrabezu,
in contrast, we should consider the relationship between the participants and
the total population: Larrabezu has a very high number of Euskara speakers,
a notable presence of the abertzale Left, and a marked history of militancy
in favor of the Basque language and culture.

Korrika 4 began in Zuberoa, and two locations played leading roles: Atharratze and Maule. While the preparations for the start were being made in
the first town, the final touches were being put on the fronton in the second
town for the festival that was going to take place on May 31 to celebrate
Korrika's arrival. Many people who came from Hegoalde to be present at the
beginning of Korrika stopped in Maule, and there they exchanged their first
impressions and comments on the event. Thus one could see A E K people
from Gipuzkoa and Bizkaia having a beer with their companions from Iparralde. They would return to Maule a few hours later, when the testigo
arrived at kilometer 14, signaling Korrika's entrance into that town.

In spite of the fact that it was 9:15 P. M. , it was still daylight, and a large
group was waiting to receive Korrika in Maule. Some twelve-year-old girls
took the testigo and passed it among themselves. It was an exciting jour-
ney. The people chorused loudly, "Euskara in Euskalerria!" and applauded.
The road went on for quite a while, and we climbed a pronounced hill.
Many young women were running in the crowd. The relay in the following
kilometer was taken by a boy, and he was accompanied by more youths.
Although Maule is a tranquil city, small groups did come out to welcome
Korrika. At kilometer 16 a group of boys passed the testigo to a representative of the conscientious objectors, who came in costume, one as a soldier,
another as a prisoner, and still another as a priest; they carried posters op-
posing the army and military service. The one who carried the testigo ran
arm in arm with his companions. In the center of the plaza there was a group
of dantzari. A little later, someone shouted one of the few political slogans
we heard in Iparralde: "Free the prisoners. Send the prisoners home," and
it continued during the rest of the route through Maule.

The swing through Benafarroa included kilometers 38 through 103 and
had its most important expression in the passage through Donapaule at midnight. In spite of the hour, Korrika received a warm welcome. We counted
more than a hundred people, including children and many young people.
The residents added a number of their cars to the race, forming a caravan.
Cowbells were ringing somewhere in the distance, and two girls were carrying cowbells attached to their backs, letting them ring into the night. On
kilometer 66, at two-thirty in the morning, a popular band joined in and
encouraged the runners from a truck while the race crossed an unpopulated,

quiet area. It was hot, and the night was clear. On kilometer 69 costumed Zanpanzaharrak[4] joined the race, and one of them took the testigo. They evoked ancient history with their costumes, and the sound of their cowbells filled the night. A noticeable din announced that we were approaching Doni-bane Garazi, and there a good number of people joined the race, among them a young man covered with Korrika posters and a sign that read "Korrika erotika."

Some of the places we passed in Lapurdi contributed the most emotional moments of the run through Iparralde, especially Ustaritz, where the residents paid homage to Lafitte, and Baiona. In some cases people simply watched us pass without expression or comment. Others said *agur* (goodbye). In some towns people came out of their shops or out of the hairdresser's, like the woman who appeared in a doorway with her hair in curlers.

Evaluating the race in general, the number of people in the crowd of runners was constant, although in some places it increased little by little, especially between Baiona and the muga. On many kilometers the people simply watched, contemplating our passage as if watching something alien, coming out of their shops and houses without applauding or showing any great interest. Thus in Donibane, on kilometer 198, while the runners were very excited and shouted slogans continuously, the people in the shops and in the street stopped to observe, but no one seemed prepared to welcome Korrika.

Still carrying the emotion of crossing the muga (described in chapter 3), Korrika entered Hernani punctually at 11:00 P.M. on Saturday, June 1, where the greatest concentration of people was in Zinko-Enea at the center of town. Nine people carried the testigo, representing a broad spectrum of institutions and groups: two from the labor committees from the Aristegi and Orbegozo factories; one from *Egin*, whose print shop and offices are in Hernani; one from the theater group Tanttaka, representing cultural groups; the mayor, who belonged to the HB coalition; someone expressing the politics of the Gestora; someone from AEK; a woman running in the name of the coordinator of unemployment; another running for Basque public schools; and a representative of the ecologists. In earlier Korrikas, events such as two korrika txikiak had been organized for students from the ikastolas, and a meal was served in which some two hundred people took part and eighty place settings were left vacant. In contrast, in the third Korrika, with the same number of place settings, many people were turned away. Some people blamed the previous lack of attendance on bad timing (the event took place at 8:00 P.M.), but the majority said, "we must throughly examine the reason for such low attendance, since it is clear that it had nothing to do with the menu, but rather the more or less militant plan."[5] The slogans shouted in Hernani were mostly for Euskara, along with some more politically oriented ones, such as "Independence," "Long live militant ETA," and "Amnesty for all" along the routes where the Gestoras or the mayor carried the testigo. Someone commented that the slogans of the patrons of each kilometer were more respected than in previous runnings, owing, perhaps, to the fact that people ran where they felt an identification with what the carrier of the testigo represented; very few ran the whole route.

Total participation in Hernani numbered about three thousand people, with about three hundred at the peak moment of the race. The lack of participation was explained in several ways: "Korrika arrived quickly in Hernani; it began yesterday and the people did not have time to get excited" and "there wasn't sufficient excitement with txarangas and so on before its arrival." These reasons are not very convincing, since on the day Korrika was to arrive a caravan of cars drove through the town announcing its arrival, and shortly beforehand different theater groups moved through the streets, encouraging people to participate.[6]

In Rentería the team recorded the following random sampling of comments about what could be considered good participation: a young couple, both twenty-six years of age: "Well, we're not from Rentería, we're from Alza, and we thought that it wouldn't get the approbation there, in Alza, that it had here, and that's why we came." Alza is a few kilometers away from Rentería and has a predominantly emigrant population. In fact, participation there was minor, although I do not wish to establish a correlation between emigrant populations and rejection of Korrika. In places such as Rentería, Santurtzi, Barakaldo, and the Txurdinaga and Santutxu neighborhoods of Bilbo, the opposite occurred. More important factors are probably the presence of a nucleus of people who support Euskara and the presence of political forces from the abertzale Left that transcend differences between autochthonous and emigrant populations.

Continuing with the observations from Rentería, we heard the following from a forty-year-old man: "Fabulous, it's the popular sentiment of the people toward Euskara." The comments of a group of women in their fifties were, "Oh, it seemed phenomenal to me." "Very nice, very exciting." "Since it is ours, it's stupendous to me." A man in his sixties: "Stupendous, stupendous, there is nothing like it, for me, especially the photographs of the prisoners; that is something. . . . Too bad I'm old and I cannot run but . . . I walked about half a kilometer, if I could . . . I would have run more."

From a group of young people, about twenty-one years old: "Korrika is not just one problem, there are several problems in this town, we have seen that there are more problems encapsulated under different slogans. In previous years, only the Euskara problem came out, this year there was more: the prisoners. . . ." A handicapped participant stated: "Very positive, in favor of Euskara, Euskadi, in favor of everything. As far as was possible, it was rather good, I was content although the wheel of my chair broke down a little, but we did what we could." A forty-six-year-old man: "It was phenomenal, more people than last year, at least in this area of Rentería. I went as far as Oiarzun, and from there I came to Rentería and stopped." The evaluation of some ten-year-old boys was: "Yes, we liked it. We ran one other year and we liked it a lot."

Finally, the opinions of members of an A E K board:

"I think it was fine, similar to other years. In spite of the boycott that happened over it, official and all."

"A letter appeared over it last week or two weeks ago: the P N V sent a note to its members saying not to support Korrika."

"The collection of signatures was a damn mess. We have been running every year, moreover we have to run by obligation . . . this thing about being a Basque prof . . ."[7]

Returning to the race, the arrival of Korrika in Ordizia on June 2 at ten-thirty in the morning is described in the field journals:

The txaranga continues to play popular music and the people begin shouting "Korrika, Korrika." . . . The organizers, the runners, and the members of the committee exchange greetings. We had calculated that there would be 175 people. In spite of the happy atmosphere, there is a certain apathy in the town. There is no applause as we pass, except that of a few people. Several informants point out to us that because it is Sunday and very hot, it is possible that many people have gone to the mountains or the beach. Also they emphasize the lesser interest in Korrika demonstrated in some political sectors that had supported it strongly in previous years.

Other people who had been in Lazkao and had participated on previous occasions explained the lesser enthusiasm of this year thus: "On the one hand, the lack of interest in people previously committed, and the excessive control in the hands of very specific groups; and, on the other hand, the withdrawal of certain political powers." The day and the hour were less important in the view of these people.[8] The general evaluation of the fourth Korrika's passage through the Gipuzkoan region of Gohierri was positive, in spite of apparently less enthusiasm than in previous runnings. Some people thought there should have been more emphasis on certain political and social problems: amnesty, unemployment, the regulation of employment. Others felt that different slogans, not only "Korrika," should have been shouted. We also heard negative comments about the PNV's failure to support Korrika.

In Barakaldo, where labor problems are severe, responses about the effectiveness of Korrika were varied. The older people who responded to questions about Korrika ranged from those who did not know how to answer because they were not familiar with its significance to those who were unable to participate actively but supported the action of the young people. Among the young people there was total support.[9] In Santurtzi the comments heard in the different neighborhoods emphasized the atmosphere created by Korrika's passing. The progressively increasing participation of people in the race was evaluated positively. The only negative aspect mentioned was the swift pace that left children and older people behind.

In the Araban town of Agurain, Korrika was scheduled to arrive around two in the morning on June 8. "Toward two o'clock the organizers arrived in the town saying that Korrika would arrive a little early; the news traveled from mouth to mouth, causing great nervousness because no one knew when they would have to run." Korrika's arrival in Agurain is described in our field journal:

> The testigo is first taken up by a dance group two kilometers from the town, and they pass it to a group of young people, and these in turn pass it to the Manu Yanke mountaineering club inside the town. Here the brass band Aguraindarrak takes it and runs the kilometer playing their instruments; participation on this kilometer is massive. Gestoras banners appear, one alluding to a prisoner from the town currently in Herrera de la Mancha.[10] It is accompanied by shouts of "Free Xabi" and "Agurain is also on the side of Euskara."

On that day and the following days participation received a positive evaluation and was considered "superior to that of previous years owing in large measure to a better route since in previous runnings they had to climb a mountain pass in the early hours of the morning." Moreover, this time people who were heading for Zalduondo and Iruñea to run stopped and joined the race.[11]

In other towns of Araba the response was positive as well. The people of Peñacerrada ran the seventeen kilometers between numbers 1,828 and 1,844. The testigo was carried in turn by young people, the fifty-year-old mayor, and, closer to the town, by children. When they entered the nucleus of the town, there were eighteen people in the crowd of runners carrying an ikurriña and shouting, "Korrika, Korrika." In the center of town were many children and a rather large group of adults. The testigo was carried by a two-year-old girl who was in turn carried on the young people's shoulders (photo 19). They made a complete tour of the town and the little girl went along, laughing happily. The people applauded from their houses. The girl continued to carry the testigo, and the crowd took turns carrying her on their shoulders until they left the town. At kilometer 1,844 the testigo was handed over to the people from the neighboring town of Pipaon.

When we passed through Pipaon a wedding feast was being held in the town square, and the newlyweds took up the testigo. The people cheered, and we could feel the emotion of the moment. Later, a young man in dance costume took the relay. Farther on, when we passed through Villaverde, a small agricultural town, women, men, and children were waiting and ap-plauding. They shouted, "Korrika, Korrika, Korrika," and the youngest ones joined the race.

The people's opinions of Korrika as it passed through Erribera revealed local variations. In Ribaforada the area organizer said that they had had prob-lems finding runners. In Ablitas the people noted more participants than in earlier Korrikas and a more enthusiastic atmosphere. In Cascante the town's militant group, all but one of whom were twenty years old, joined the run-ners (five men and four women). We saw practically no one in the town of Cintruénigo. In Corella the people paid little attention; they watched, noth-ing more, although there was great excitement in the crowd of runners. In Tutera the Plaza Nueva filled with people who waited for us in groups at six in the afternoon on Tuesday, June 4. The atmosphere grew more and more festive. The waiting groups commented on possibilities: "Will they arrive late? . . . What if they run through such-and-such a street. . . . Let's take a jug of wine, just in case." The people approached the post to buy a sticker or a metal plate and to ask if anyone knew anything about where Korrika was now. Committee members and their friends chatted about the sale of stickers, the greater participation than the year before, and the excitement of it all. The hour was approaching, and groups of young people were pre-pared to run and accompany the children from the local ikastola who would collect the testigo in the plaza. They wore cardboard posters on their backs and chests. Some *gaita* (bagpipe) players passed by in a car announcing the advance of the group. When the testigo arrived, everyone applauded. The boys from the ikastola unfolded a banner asking for expanded facilities. One of them took the testigo; the applause increased and they left the plaza at the other end. Then the people stopped cheering and gathered in groups to discuss what had happened. The plaza emptied little by little.

In the following moments, with flushed but smiling faces, those who had run entered the bars as soon as they could, where the first comments they made referred to the act of running: "Ho . . . man, I thought I wouldn't make it. . . . I didn't cover even half a kilometer. Well, I was typical. . . ."[12]

And they realized that the act of Korrika does not mean only a contribution of money or a simple public demonstration. Rather, it consists of a symbolic act on behalf of Euskara that materializes in a real, individual, physical effort.

At nine-thirty at night Korrika entered Villafranca, where we were told there existed a strong Basque sentiment. The *dulzaina* (flute) players from Tutera arrived, and men waited in the street with ikurriñas. There were twenty-five people in the crowd of runners, and people joined in until the number reached forty: middle-aged women wearing shirtdresses, espadrilles, and jackets tied at the waist; young people; and children. An older man lifted his left fist on high, and the shout of "Viva Korrika" echoed to the cheers of those on the street and on the balconies.

In Etxarri-Aranaz it was Sunday, June 9, at six in the morning. "The town is covered and stopped up by fog, it's rather cool, and we are watching the day break little by little." People began to gather at the town hall and at the first of the six kilometers that corresponded to the town. We heard: "It's really cold" and "It's a bad hour, too early." The people were dressed in sport clothes. There was no festive atmosphere, and the few people gathered seemed to be waiting only to run and fulfill an objective. When the caravan arrived, there were fifty runners, with a larger proportion of men and a few children. At one time near the second kilometer there was an attempt to start a chant of "Korrika," but after five repetitions it faded away, and the rest was run in silence. When we arrived at the town hall, the mayor took the testigo and seven more people joined in. The Guardia Civil traveled in separate jeeps before and after, "protecting Korrika." Once the six kilometers were over, the people dispersed; they returned to town and most of them went back to bed.

The comments of the few people who stayed to talk were about the low level of participation: that it was due to the hour, and that some of them had gone the day before to Iruñea to participate in the end of that route.[13]

Conclusions

The route through Nafarroa demonstrates the diversity extant in Euskalerria insofar as ecological variety has had, and continues to have, a place in linguistic development or regression. Nafarroa is a good example of ecological and linguistic differences. In spite of the fact that Nafarroa is outside the

Comunidad Autónoma Vasca, the Korrika route was created to take in all its differences. This political reality in Euskalerria has created a situation in which the continuation and organization of Korrika are difficult. At the same time the fact that Korrika continues demonstrates the presence of scattered nuclei of people who consider Euskara to be a differentiating element at either a real or a symbolic level. The same ecological context, whether in the harsh mountain passes or in Erribera with its great distances and scarcity of settlements, furnishes opportunities to establish distinct evaluations of the routes through those areas. Overcoming the harshness of these routes requires an external projection of indarra; the need to base organization on the importance of groups and their function furnishes exceptional and valuable characteristics. It is in turn one more element of the connection of Korrika with local situations that evoke strong ties.

The delineation of territory treated in chapters 3 and 4 was completed in the route Korrika took by sea from Lapurdi to Bizkaia. With that action the race incorporated a whole tradition, a history, and an economy that was and is vital to the Basque economy. The act of enclosing the territory includes past deeds of Basque sailors, economic fishing activity, commerce, sports associated with the sea, and international repercussions from the last few years as a result of the new fishing rules of the European Community.

Korrika recognizes dialectal varieties and at the same time implants the importance of and the need for Batua. It gives popular strength to a position that has seen its share of conflict at different moments.

Also present is the act of transcending the historical discontinuity of the language that first appeared in the plaza in Atharratze. Korrika passes through areas where Euskara is receding, through places where it has disappeared and lives on only in the memory of the people, and through other places where Euskara has no history and is seen as a new language. In this case it is treated merely on a referential, symbolic level and is wielded as the defining element of Basque identity, especially in towns in Erribera, Nafarroa.

The different responses to Korrika, whether positive or negative, and in many cases silence itself, permit an evaluation of the event as a whole. The organizers provide an overall view, and they emphasize elements that amplify and reproduce the reality of Korrika because of their massive, extraordinary, or spectacular nature. Another value that could be attributed to Korrika is the utilization of its growing success, without recourse to analysis and the demonstration of debilitating elements that continue to appear and are included in the evaluations made by people interviewed in the street. Everything that projects the success of Korrika is used because it contributes to the reinforcement of the groups and movements behind the race.

The analysis of inside versus outside allowed us to view the relativity of situations, to give strength to elements that, in isolation, do not have the importance that they acquire through the provocatively contrasting contextualization they present, based on the evocation of political and cultural meanings that have a popular interpretation.

In the act of running through it, the territory's relationship with Euskara is reclaimed. By placing the mugarri, the language also is put into place. This act of placing the mugarriak suggests an affirmation of Euskara's existence and a protest against its abandonment on the part of larger political forces. In places where the language is becoming extinct, such as different areas of the Nafarroan mountains, placing the mugarri is a way of fighting generational discontinuity. In Araba, Nafarroan Erribera, and the Bizkaian Encartaciones, it constitutes an act of recovery of a language present at another time in history that people hope will be present again through the euskaldunberris and those dedicated to the task of spreading it and learning it.

Chapter Seven

Korrika as a Metaphor for Basque Unity

The global experience of Korrika is a collective secular ritual in which the actors respond to a series of stimuli of diverse origins that generate popular interpretation. It presents a symbiosis between collective preoccupations with identification-differentiation (which in this case are centered principally on the binomial language-territory) and the political processes of structuring and restructuring nationalisms that pulls these preoccupations together and makes them possible. The ritual process creates a space and a liminal period in which a temporal space is constructed within a determined time frame, which permits the external creation of a political, linguistic, and cultural concept of a utopian society. Within this time frame, the discontinuities and contradictions that affect language and territory are overcome.

Korrika occurs in a concrete space and time (day, month, season, and year), but it has characteristics, images, and symbols that give it meaning beyond those realities. This transcendence is carried out through the symbolic exit from the current territory, with its concrete territorial limitations, in two ways: by means of graphic references that transform reality and by putting into motion the evocative power of other tangible physical realities. Although Korrika takes place in the here and now, references to a nonhistorical time—especially ancestral references such as those in the initial scene in the plaza at Atharratze—weaken the importance of scientific tests for demonstrating the continuity of the language in time and space. Discontinuous temporal reality is transcended through powerful, atemporal symbolic continuity.

We have seen how territoriality can appear clearly marked through action in the form of individual and collective participation, as well as through symbolic and social dimensions. Territoriality is understood to be the definition of a geographic space. To the Basque people, their territory includes the seven territories, and they refer to it as Euskalerria throughout the Korrika. The emphasis on territory includes the global experience and the local registration kilometer by kilometer. The conjunction of the two enables different ways of integrating and identifying individuals and groups.

The contradiction that exists between the feeling of unity transmitted continually in Korrika and the reality of territorial politics is presented in this specific reclamation of territory in the form of the difficulties caused by these differences, difficulties that are logistical in some cases and political in others. Transcendence of political divisions is produced by denying the existence of the border and simultaneously emphasizing the significance and meaning of the muga. The palpable existence of the border is transcended in Korrika through several strategies. One strategy consists of creating powerful images that diminish or erase the existence of the artificial division by proclaiming territorial totality either with words or in graphic form. Another strategy consists of ritualizing the crossing of the border, affirming through symbols the necessity of turning border into muga. As in the legends about the suffering of people who moved mugarriak, protests on both sides of the valleys demonstrate the fact that peace will be achieved only when the mugarriak are reinstated and the border disappears. The power of the symbolism of territorial totality transmits the demarcation of borders that suppress current political divisions and the abolition of existing borders by incorporating new social causes and projects. Symbols make it possible to express the concept of a close-knit, intimate people, a concept that applies to all levels of Basque society. The versatility with which the concept is applied and its lack of definition allows social and ethnic differences to disappear in the allusions created in the race, and it acts as an integrating element for those who were born outside Euskalerria, those who speak different dialects, and those who communicate in Castilian. In this way, the power of the ritual generates the experience of a new society in Korrika.

In Korrika there is a constant tension caused by the task of representing an entire people who possess roots lost in antiquity. Constant references are made to ancestral qualities, historical permanence, and continuity, references that affirm the Basques' existence as well as conveying the experience of actions that make those references possible. The problem of the patrimony of Euskara appears tied to this. Concerns include defining to whom Euskara belongs, maintaining a vigil for it, transmitting it, and teaching it. This is made obvious through the AEK-HABE conflict. The former organization proclaims its right to teach Euskara on the basis of criteria of precedence and heroism. AEK began its operation under the difficult circumstances of the Franco era when such activities were clandestine, costly, and subversive. AEK claims that its system reaches everybody, that no economic or linguistic discrimination exists, and that its function is self-motivating and participatory. Members of AEK defend themselves by saying that their methods are based on the importance of social and linguistic contexts in learning a language. In contrast, HABE bases its position on the legitimacy granted to it by the government and its obligations as a democratic institution, as well as on the conviction that the organization possesses a high degree of professionalism. With that HABE legitimizes its demands for regularity, selectivity, control, requirements for degrees, and the increase of fees. It is interesting that AEK, a private institution, presents itself as the more public, the more popular, and the more representative.

In Korrika the power of tradition and effort coincide through evoking and producing effects that cannot be measured. Intangibility is a weapon, as are references to magic and frequent utilization of the evocative power of places, people, symbols, and actions. What are the mechanisms that cause the ritualization of Korrika to connect so strongly with such a broad group?

In Korrika there has been a process of selection in which aspects that tie the people together are promoted, re-created, and lived, and these factors make possible a variety of interpretations that have the capacity to evoke a broad popular response. Thus certain questions hang in the air: Why are some selected and not others from among all the possible characteristics? What criteria are enacted in the selection of those elements?

One criterion could be the attempt to emphasize meanings that allow the people to feel, immediately and profoundly, all that unchains and broadens associations and all that, setting diversity aside, can create adhesion. A second criterion could have to do with the capacity for linking with nearby realities and generating a spontaneous response. In order to do this, the connection established with determinate forms of behavior is important. Thus we find the importance given to group behavior, cuadrillas, associations, and clubs as organizational bases. The dynamic they evoke makes the people take part, since these groups reinforce activities that recruit people as volunteers. The utilization of social nets depends on positive experiences for the maintenance of communication and identity, as occurred during the Franco era. At the same time, groups can exert social pressure, since belonging to the group and not participating would be seen in a bad light. In the same way, joining in or supporting Korrika would be very difficult indeed once the group, association, or party to which one belongs has prohibited it or advised against it. This assigns value to nonparticipation by PNV members in the second Korrika, since the PNV told its members not to take part; and, in contrast, it increases the meaning of the act for those who did participate either in groups or individually. Also, in the face of a deficiency or difficulty, there is an almost basic need for "action" that implies physical movement. It can represent a cultural form of resolving an intangible concern through the visible and experiential act of movement. The act of running provides a sensation of being involved in the resolution of the problem. When this occurs in a group, as in Korrika, it has the power to prolong the enthusiasm of the moment and carry forward to concrete actions that transcend the moment in which they were generated.

The third selection criterion could be whatever carried us to the distant and ancestral and meanwhile generated the fantastic and utopian. That magical character, that uncontrollable force, is a powerful element in Korrika. It allows reference to something intangible, something outside ordinary control that acts in spite of our not being in agreement with it. At given moments this magic exercises its power through its very distance. Moreover, one withdraws and ceases to analyze what appears to be inexplicable. That is what happened with the disappearance of the message in the first Korrika. Thus we include extraordinary participation, the unexpected, and the phantasmagoric within this category of "magic." That is how the legend is created. Events of a religious dimension take place at certain moments in Korrika, but in a secular context. This is the religious idea of overcoming time, overcoming the moment in which we live, in which we are immersed, with something transcendental imbued with distant animist and ancestral connotations.

There is one last point I should emphasize in the analysis of the elements that generate popular adhesion to Korrika: its capacity for presenting different historical visions, both near and far. In spite of the short history of Korrika, it is possible to obtain different visions of its process. One vision is based on the quick glance provided by the passage of Korrika in each of its runnings. Our analysis of the fourth Korrika allowed us to capture the synchronous and comparative perspective. This interpretation can be transformed in turn into a diachronic one through the analysis of the temporal progression measured in Korrika by minutes, and through the intensity with which we live it. The symbolic responsibility that Korrika entails acquires a relevance comparable to the passage of a much longer period. This is visible in the description of the tributes and in the moments of exit and arrival at important places. The continuity with which Korrika was celebrated in such a short time (1980–91) and the structural repetition of its organization has allowed the development of a tradition that is respected and gathers strength each time it is mentioned. At the same time, the cumulative capacity Korrika demonstrated from the first to the seventh runnings makes it possible to establish certain generalizations about the process.

We can recognize a greater economic contribution and a greater deployment of means in the organization that translate into an increase in funding and in donations received. Some of this is demonstrated in the progressive importance given to graphics and in the quality and number of posters and the greater media publicity.

Changes in participation have occurred in relation to a greater politicalization of the race. Although I have spoken of "mass participation" in each Korrika and the organizers place a positive value on the number of people who participate, in reality total participation has declined, although in some locations it has remained stable or has even increased. If we compare the first race with the seventh, we must say that participation has declined. In general this decline took place after the second Korrika when the PNV withdrew its support. At the same time, Korrika has been identified more and more with the positions of the abertzale Left, and within that group with those of Herri Batasuna. The ritual of Korrika exposes the differences that have been appearing between the two nationalist plans, not only with respect to Euskara but in the understanding of Basque politics. We perceive this through observation and through the opinions of the people interviewed in different locations. In the first Korrika Euskara was the unifying force. In the second, Euskara was separated from that which could be implied as support for other nationalist political powers.

Compared with Korrika 7, Korrika 1 placed a much greater importance on the individual participants who carried the testigo. Today, priority is given to group participation and the cause the groups represent. There are several reasons for this change: groups have greater visibility, they allow a greater number of people to establish a relationship with the Korrika movement, they have a multiplying effect by carrying more weight, and they generate greater economic contributions. This is evident in the way the organizers contact groups and associations for the sale of kilometers. This change does not nullify the individual's role, and in those cases where the person enjoys great social prestige, his or her participation can be even more important than that of a group.

The notion of Korrika as strictly a linguistic cause has given way to the inclusion of other types of demonstrations. Residents of Iparralde emphasize economic problems and resulting depopulation, which have had a negative impact on the conservation and development of the language. After the second Korrika there was a progressive increase in political and economic statements, some related to the differences of opinion over linguistic policy and others of a more opportunistic character that make use of the immediacy of the moment. Levels of influence vary; some statements reflect a large part of the Basque collective, others a territory, and others apply only locally.

The change in routes meant an increase in kilometers from Korrika 1 to Korrika 4. The tendency has been to incorporate new territories, to grant the requests of locales that ask Korrika to pass through them. On the one hand, the number of groups carrying the testigo has increased, and, on the other, a greater individualization has taken place, especially through the tributes to specific people. These tributes have led to the progressive development of a tradition in which the memories of people who have acquired the status of cultural heroes within Korrika live on: the Basque scholars Ricardo Arregui and Xabier Peña, the child Xabier Exeberri, the politician Santi Brouard, and the linguist Pierre Lafitte. The memory of others is brought to life through their contributions to Basque language and culture. People with political significance are also incorporated, although there is a tendency to place more emphasis on their cultural contributions, as in the case of Telesforo Monzón. Apart from what these tributes represent at the moment they are celebrated, they have become institutionalized as an important ingredient of Korrika, as the tributes to Gladys del Estal, Exeberri, and Brouard show. Memorializing is a demonstration of the ways in which certain persons, events, and places acquire importance stemming from the validation attributed to them by a group, in this case the nucleus of people to whom I alluded in the Introduction.

The individual or collective refusal to participate in Korrika says something about the event and goes beyond the race itself. There are people who do not participate because the abertzale Left is associated with Korrika, and this has become more and more important throughout the seven runnings. Korrika is an act of commitment because it obliges those who support it to define themselves, to publicly state their position. Korrika is a two-edged sword from which those who do not participate cannot escape.

Taking Korrika as a microcosm, we see the past, present, and future in this one event. We see the beginning in Atharratze, we experience the present continually in the seconds during which each locale experiences its passing, and the future is continually emphasized with the perspective of reaching the goal, the final location.

In Korrika, processes containing diachronic elements are visualized. In the plaza of Atharratze we see the ancestral past and the present. In passing the testigo, linguistic continuity down through the generations is visualized. In the route through the territory, linguistic gaps become obvious, the fruit of the process of regression-advance that has been taking place for several centuries. The passage of the testigo between men and women represents the social identification of public-private spaces on the basis of the existence and acceptance of the criterion of sexual differences. There are moments when reference to the past serves to affirm causes of the present, as when the ancient possessions where Euskara was once spoken are reclaimed. The dynamic aspect of the language, and the fact that its existence is tied to the task of re-creating it through constant usage, is implicit in the continual affirmation that "Korrika does not stop." Korrika presents itself as the energy of the people who carry the language—who transmit it, respect it, and pass it down through time (in the historical sense), through territory (in the people who occupy concrete space), through different ways of life connected with ecological and economic diversity (when experiencing the variety of the territories), through natural transmission (in the generations), through private space (in women and children), through public space (in official organs), and through the media (which play a leading role in spreading information). Euskara claims to have adapted to the passing of centuries and to serve at home, in the street, at school, on the radio, in the press, and on television. Dialectal and subdialectal linguistic demonstrations are incorporated, but the need for one unified language is proclaimed: *Batua*.

There are moments when the past is brought into the present in a contemporary context, such as the moment in the plaza of Atharratze when the past became the present in the public space of the plaza. Comprehension of the action was verified through the positive response of the people who filled the plaza. At other times the present is rejected. The border crossing proclaimed the border's divisive character and filled the event with political interpretations. Crossing the border affirmed the contrary; that is, the existence of an ethnic unity and a shared history in spite of the divisive lines. While Korrika evokes the archaic, the traditional, the ancestral, and the idyllic, all of this is at the same time projected toward the future and is taken as justification for the survival of the language, its continuity, and its unifying power in the future. Thus Basque traditions take on political hues in Korrika because the race is intimately associated with social causes and subversive elements. But Korrika is also an integrating force in many ways: persons or groups who aspire to an identity with Basque culture have the opportunity to participate in it and experience it, to be seen doing so, and to reinforce that timely belonging. The most diverse social causes are integrated, always in relation to opposition to the political forces responsible for the situation Korrika is trying to transcend.

All these activities are carried out on the basis of the existence of numerous expressions of reality that appear in Korrika and have powerful mechanisms of identification and resolution. They generate, in turn, different versions of a popular interpretation. However, in spite of all these utopian, futuristic elements, we must accept that society as put forth in Korrika continues to appear real to many people. Moreover, in my opinion, if Korrika should disappear, it would leave a space out of which would arise another type of action with different ways of transmitting the same idea; but in any new elaboration, reference would still be made to the ancestral past and the projection of a not-too-distant future goal, all acting as a vehicle of Utopia.

Notes

1. The Segundos Cursos de Verano were organized by the University of the Basque Country from August 22 to September 7, 1983. The paper ("Korrika: A Basque Symbolic Act") was presented as part of the course titled "Ethnicity."

METHODOLOGY

1. The team was composed of Begoña Aretxaga, Txemi Apaolaza, and me as director. Other people participated in the gathering of data as noted in note 3 below. The study recounted here was in turn part of a general project, "Identidad étnica y procesos migratorios en el Estado español: Andalucía, Cataluña, Euskadi, Galicia," in which four teams participated. Those teams were associated with the Universities of Sevilla, Barcelona (in Tarragona), the Basque Country, the Universidad Autónoma de Madrid, and the University of La Laguna (in the Canary Islands) under the general coordination of Ubaldo Martínez Veiga. The research was carried out in 1985 and was financed by the Ministry of Education and Science Advisory Commission for Scientific and Technical Research.

2. For detailed information about the plan of the Euskadi project see del Valle (1985). For a general vision of some of the theoretical and methodological results see del Valle, Apaolaza, and Ramos (1990). Other publications from the project are Apaolaza (1985–87) and Aretxaga (1988).

3. Mobile team: Mari Carmen Diez, Carmen Larrañaga, and Teresa del Valle (coordinator). Fixed team: Carmen Pérez (coordinator), Txemi Apaolaza (coordinator for Araba), Astrid Arkotxa, Luis M. Astigarraga, José Ramón Basterra, Monserrat Carreras, Maider Etxaide, José Luis Fuika, Ana Isabel Gandarias, Rosa María Gañán, Julio González, Maite Lopetegi, Eguzkiñe Muguire, Julene Olea, Lourdes Paneigo, Agustín Ramos, Antxon Sánchez, Ione Usabiaga, and Txelo Yurramendi.

INTRODUCTION

1. For a book in English that summarizes the situation in Euskadi during the Franco dictatorship see Clark (1980). To appreciate the complexity presented

by the birth of ETA see Clark (1984), Douglass (1985), Zulaika (1988), and Heiberg (1989).

2. With this I do not allude to the Basque case, where a flow of information and collaboration exists between native and foreign anthropologists.

3. From here on, I will use the term *Euskalerria* to refer to the geographic and cultural entity that includes the seven territories. I will use *Euskadi* as a political term that includes the four territories of Araba, Bizkaia, Gipuzkoa, and Nafarroa. (In some citations, this term is used to refer to the seven territories.) *Comunidad Autónoma Vasca*, the Autonomous Basque Community, includes Araba, Bizkaia, and Gipuzkoa.

4. These three names refer to different institutions that teach Euskara. In the *ikastola*, primary and secondary education are totally in Euskara. The *euskaltegi* is directed at the adult public and offers day classes at all levels with flexible schedules, in villages as well as cities. The *barnategiak* provide intensive courses in a boarding-school atmosphere; course length varies from fifteen days to a year. During the summer months school activities intensify in order to cater to students and teachers who wish to take advantage of their vacations for such studies. Generally these schools are established in Euskara-speaking areas so that the students can experience the living language at the same time.

5. *Abertzale* refers to people who feel a Basque identity.

CHAPTER ONE. THE IMPORTANCE OF CONTINUITY AND ITS DIFFERENT INTERPRETATIONS

1. Atharratze, in Zuberoa, is an area of 14,199 square kilometers that had 818 inhabitants in 1975. Just as in other areas of Zuberoa, agriculture and the sheep industry and its derivatives constitute the principal economic activities (Gómez Piñeiro et al. 1980:289).

2. The caves have been the object of important archaeological studies that have contributed to knowledge about the way of life of their inhabitants.

3. Euskaltzaindia was founded in 1918. Today it is the official organ of Euskalerria "for the preservation, cultivation, fixation, and unification of the Basque language" (Euskaltzaindia 1984:43).

4. The assembly was held in the monastery of the same name and convened by Euskaltzaindia on the occasion of the fiftieth anniversary of the founding of the academy (Euskaltzaindia 1984:58).

5. The arguments against Batua and the positions in favor of the dialects, especially Bizkainoa, are found in Basterretxea "Oskillaso" (1984), Lasa Apalategui (1973), and Aguirre (1985). Positions on Batua are found in *El libro blanco del euskara*, by Euskaltzaindia, the title of which inspired Oskillaso's book and the contrasting visions of both sides in the round table of the Segunda Semana de Antropología (Second Week of Anthropology).

6. The English translation of "Euskal Herria Euskaldunuk" (the Basque Coun-

try and Euskara speakers) does not convey the full force of the implied meaning: the unity of territory and language.

7. The *encierro txiki* (children's running of the bulls) has been prohibited since 1986 due to its danger, and although the decision was very controversial, the event is no longer held.

8. Interview with J. R. T., ten years old, carrier of the testigo, Zurbaran (Bilbo), June 6, 1985.

9. A great tradition in Euskalerria; a *bertsolari* is a person who improvises in verse. Although there have been female bertsolariak, men dominate the genre. Performances take place in informal contexts such as cider shops, taverns, and in town squares during festivals. The term *plaza-gizon* (a man of the plaza) alludes to the centrality and relevance of the figure. Bertsolariak also participate in both ritual and funeral activities, and they have a special place in Korrika.

10. In this first part about the role of women, I received contributions from Laura Mintegi, Karmele Esnal, and Carmen Larrañaga, obtained in interviews and conversations on the subject.

11. A kind of yell used to locate people in open country. Barandiaran (1972, 1:196–98) translates it as a cry or shout and narrates several legends in which spirits let their presence be felt through the irrintzi. Today it is commonly heard in ritual contexts such as political funerals of the radical Left, as mentioned by Aretxaga (1988), and at the end of demonstrations while the song "Eusko Gudariak" (Basque soldiers) is sung.

12. Interview with K. M., one of the local people responsible for Korrika, Rentería, June 1, 1985.

13. Ibid.

14. Women and men helped in the organization of Korrika activities in Bizkaia as follows. Women were organizers in the towns of Hego Uribe, Txori Herri, Uribe Rutroe, Lea Artibai (2), Busturialdea, Arratia, and Ofxandio. Men were organizers in Enkarteria, Meatzeta, Ibar Eskerra, Bilbo, Uribe Butroe, Uribe Kosta, San Inazio, Durangoaldea, and others.

15. This refers to a position against Spain's permanent membership in NATO. Later, in a referendum held on March 12, 1986, Euskadi along with Cataluña and the Canary Islands would vote no, but the total result from the entire state was favorable.

16. A women's group within Herri Batasuna.

CHAPTER TWO. THE CREATION OF KORRIKA

1. Translation of the letter from Ricardo Arregui to José María Satrustegui, January 17, 1966, published in *Egin* in its original version.

2. The group known as Bai Euskarari was formed with the goal of organizing events aimed at gathering financial support for the work of Euskaltzaindia and for Euskara in general. Members of this group had a common interest in the de-

velopment of the Basque language and culture. Among the events they carried out were Kantaldi in San Mamés in 1978; two football games—one, Euskadi against Ireland at San Mamés (1979), and the other against Belgium in the Atotxa stadium in Donostia—with the box-office receipts from the first game destined for the ikastolas of Hegoalde and those of the second for SEASKA (an organization of the ikastolas of Iparralde); the Eusko Eskolak campaign (1979); the Eusko-Prentsa campaign (1980); an homage to the famous soccer player Iribar in 1980, the funds from which went to support a technical dictionary in Euskara (Bai Euskarari, private archive).

3. *Kilometroak* as a popular activity consists of organizing a walk of several kilometers once a year in some location in Gipuzkoa. It lasts one entire day and is usually on a holiday or weekend. Stalls and activities are arranged along the length of the walk. These include expositions of traditional arts and crafts, cultural information services, sports, and traditional competitions, games, and dances. Something like kilometroak is organized in the other territories in southern Euskadi: Nafarroa oinez (Nafarroa on foot), Araban euskaraz (Basque in Araba), and Ibilaldia (March) in Bizkaia. In northern Euskadi, Herri urrats (Popular steps) is celebrated. The monies earned are destined for the local ikastolas (del Valle et al. 1985:436–37). Thus, when Ibilaldia was celebrated in Bermeo, the money was turned over to the ikastola there. The basic difference with respect to Korrika is in the local character of these events and in their objectives, which are directed at supporting the local ikastolas. One participates by walking instead of running, and no symbol is carried. For more information on these events see Euskal Kulturaren urtekaria (1984).

4. Interview with B. A., president of the AEK of Gipuzkoa, Donostia, May 17, 1983.

5. Interviews held in Bilbo in September 1986 with members of Bai Euskarari helped me understand the circumstances of the birth of Korrika. Those members were Bittor Artola, Enrique Ibabe, and Alberto Elorriaga, as well as AEK members Joseba Campo and Urtsa Errasti.

6. Interview with B. A., May 17, 1983.

7. For this section the following sources were used: Villán and Población (1980:40–41); information booklet by AEK published for the second Korrika; Euskal Kulturaren urtekaria (1984:176–77). Moreover, I had direct contact with AEK teachers and students, principally from Gipuzkoa and Bizkaia. I participated as a student in an intensive course in a boarding-school atmosphere organized by AEK of Bizkaia, in Lekeitio, from October 15, 1984, to February 15, 1985. During that time I had additional contacts with several groups that were holding courses in other locations in Bizkaia and Nafarroa.

8. Interview with a group of unemployéd participants in the fourth Korrika, Bilbo, June 6, 1985.

9. Three mimeographed pages published by AEK on the occasion of the second Korrika.

10. Interview with S., director of the euskaltegi in Santurtzi, June 10, 1985.

11. Interview with a female teacher from AEK on the occasion of the second Korrika.

12. Interview with I. S. from AEK in Bilbo, June 4, 1985.

13. Interview with E. B., female coordinator of AEK in Bilbo, June 13, 1985.

14. Interview with J. M. and M., Isaba, June 2, 1985.

15. Interview with A. R., Tutera, June 4, 1985.

16. Interview with J. B., twenty-five years old, Iruñea, June 9, 1985.

17. Field journal, Kanpezu, June 8, 1985.

18. This appears in the documents worked out for the planning of Korrikas 3 and 4. AEK, Korrika 3. Finantziaketarako aurreproiektoa (no date); AEK (1984).

19. AEK (1984).

20. Ibid.

21. Ibid.

22. A cuisine that has arisen in the last few years that combines elements of traditional cooking with new ways of combining the same ingredients or using new ingredients. It has been institutionalized as such and its creators and products enjoy great prestige both inside and outside Euskadi.

23. Oriundo from Bizkaia is an important bertsolari; he is likewise a columnist and a writer.

24. An organization of ikastolas in Iparralde.

25. This group has achieved great popularity both inside and outside Euskadi, and they have made several recordings.

26. For the lists of people attending see *Egin*, May 19, 1985, p. 28.

27. References: *Egin*, May 23, 1985, p. 20; *Egin*, May 24, 1985, p. 21.

28. *Egin*, November 25, 1983, p. 27.

29. "Eusko Jaurlaritza-Kultur Saila A.E.K.-ren Eskaera Udaletan."

30. Ibid. I received information on HABE from an interview with its director, Joxe Joan de Txabarri, in September 1986.

31. A translation of the letter into Spanish was published in *Punto y Hora* 1981, no. 212, pp. 37–39.

32. AEK (1987).

33. Highest decision-making body of the PNV (Basque Nationalist party).

34. ETB (Basque television channel) and TVE (Spanish television channel).

35. For statements from the different political parties see *Egin*, May 20, 1982, p. 3.

36. Cited in "Los organizadores de la korrika 2 en Navarra siguen haciendo gestiones para lograr su autorización," *Egin*, May 21, 1982, p. 20.

37. Ibid.

CHAPTER THREE. THE SIGNIFICANCE OF TERRITORIAL BOUNDARIES

1. Initials of Euskadi ta Askatasuna, a predominantly activist Basque nationalist organization. ETA was created in 1959 when the group EGI-EKIN broke from the Partido Nacionalista Vasco. It developed during the Franco dictatorship and continues today.

2. The DYA (Asociación de Ayuda en Carretera) is a private organization founded in Bizkaia to lend service to motorists; it operates in the Comunidad Autónoma. The DYA participated voluntarily in Korrika, contributing its services and technical personnel.

3. A trikititxa is a musical group that performs principally at fiestas and popular events. It consists of an accordion and a small tambourine.

4. A term used to designate the president of the Basque government.

CHAPTER FOUR. THE RITUALIZATION OF TERRITORIAL INTEGRITY

1. On the theme of indarra in general see Douglass and Bilbao (1975:407–10), Ott (1982, 1991), Zulaika (1987:96–106); del Valle et al. (1985:178–90) discuss indarra applied to women.

2. The president of the Herriko Alderdi Sozialista Iraultzalea (HASI; Popular Socialist Revolutionary party), which belongs to the Herri Batasuna coalition. In addition he was well known as a pediatrician, his profession when he was assassinated. The death of Brouard, on the ninth anniversary of the death of Franco, was repulsive to the various political powers. Tributes in Bilbo and the funeral and burial in his native village, Lekeitio, were occasions for important, tension-filled demonstrations on behalf of the abertzale Left, and Herri Batasuna played the leading role.

3. Interview with Urtsa Errasti, Bilbo, March 19, 1985.

4. Quotations taken from the Zalduondo field journal.

5. Apaolaza (1985–87:157).

6. Spirits with a human shape that generally present themselves as females. They have the feet of a chick, duck, or goat. For more information see Barandiaran (1972, 1:138–44).

7. See the photo in *Egin*, June 9, 1985, p. 1.

8. Interview with J. A., age twenty-four, AEK organizer, Bilbo, June 4, 1985.

9. Interview with I. A., Donostia, June 1, 1985.

10. Interview with P. C., employee of the Ayuntamiento, Ordizia, June 2, 1985.

11. Interview with M. C., teacher in an ikastola, Ordizia, June 2, 1985.

12. Interview with J. A. M. and J. G. de A., Kanpezu, June 1985.

13. Original manuscript of the message read by Amaia Fontán on June 1, 1985, at the beginning of Korrika.

14. For the carnival dates I relied on Garmendia Larrañaga (1984:17–18, 22, 30, 35–36, 50, 56, 58–59, 63, 71, 73, 100, 138, 154, 165, 168, and 171).

15. Sabino Arana Avenue, named in honor of the founder of the Partido Nacionalista Vasco, replaced the street name honoring José Antonio Primo de Rivera, founder of the Spanish Falange, the only party allowed during the Franco years. The change of names indicates the end of the Franco dictatorship.

Gregorio Balparda was a historian and politician born in Bilbo (1874–1936). His best-known work is *Historia crítica de Vizcaya y de sus fueros*, published in three volumes between 1924 and 1945. His works and his political activities were intended to demonstrate his position against Basque nationalism (B. E. L. 1971:621–22). On the basis of this antinationalist posture his recognition by naming the Bilbo street after him during the Franco years is understandable, as is the replacement of his name years later.

16. The decision of the military government of Madrid to install barracks and police stations in the different cities and towns met with strong opposition from the local population; for example, the neighborhood of Egia in Donostia, the city of Hondarribia, and Etxarri-Aranaz.

17. Here are found the Schools of Economics, Fine Arts (first cycle), and the Escuela de Magisterio of the University of the Basque Country. The University of the Jesuits has its campus at the entrance to the neighborhood.

18. I should point out that the official name is Plaza de España, and although the local citizens have tried to change it, they have not yet succeeded. However, reference to one name or the other is at the same time a political statement by one side or the other, as happened in Bilbo with the Plaza de España/Plaza Circular.

19. L K I stands for Liga Komunista Iraultzailea.

20. The central building of the Basque government is in the neighborhood of Lakua at the entrance to Gasteiz when traveling by highway from Bilbo. The Parliament meets in the downtown area of the city. Gasteiz was designated the seat of the Parliament and the Basque government by Law 1/1980 on May 23 (*Legislación sobre comunidades autónomas* 1982:367).

21. Name created by the PNV to identify the Basque police; however, the correct denomination is *Ertzaintza*, and in this case the correct usage would be Ertzaintzaren dirua . . .

22. Popular chant that alludes to the petition to have the Spanish police leave Euskadi. It is often heard in political demonstrations and at festivals.

23. *Ito* is an onomatopoeic sound that has no translation.

24. Referring to the policy of the French government that has caused several political exiles in Iparralde to be imprisoned by the Spanish police or to be deported to South America and Africa.

25. A slogan critical of the PSOE (Partido Socialista Obrero Español).

26. The place where the sculptor Edward Chillida, in collaboration with architect Luis Peña Gantxegi, built a monument to the traditional Basque laws (the

fueros). The plaza possesses a space dedicated to the celebration of rural games such as stone lifting and pelota and is an important place for spectacles and meetings.

1. In the nineteenth century the cantons of Aldude, Arnegi, and Etxerrenzubi in Benabarra presented the highest index of emigration of all Euskalerria (Douglass and Bilbao 1975:123).

2. The entire program defended by EEPA (Euskal Eskola Publikoaren Alde) is that of unification; that includes the ikastolas and the schools transferred from the central government to the Comunidad Autónoma Vasca.

3. The Republican flag appears frequently in political demonstrations and had its origins in the Second Republic.

4. The slogan alludes to the nuclear installation in the Bizkaian area of Lemoiz. Numerous popular movements and actions by ETA against directors of the installation have led to its paralysis.

Gladys was shot and killed by the Spanish Guardia Civil when she participated in an antinuclear demonstration in Tutera in 1979. She lived in the neighborhood of Egia, where she is remembered and where in the last few years residents have tried to change the name of the public park from Cristina Enea to Gladys Enea. A small monument in her memory has been erected in the park. The change of name has not received official approval. As a resident of the neighborhood I have followed the changes in the name on the sign over the park entrance. It is a thermometer that tells me who is in control at the moment—the popular movement or the municipal government. The last change from Cristina to Gladys took place on the occasion of the anniversary of her death, and the return to the original name occurred a few days later.

5. The word *txakurra* in the singular, or the plural *txakurrak* (dogs), is slang used by the abertzale Left to designate the Spanish police.

"You fascists are the terrorists" began to be heard in demonstrations of the Basque radical Left once the PSOE had risen to power, as a response to the campaign organized by the Spanish government that classified ETA as a terrorist group. It was shouted when two Carlists were killed at Montejurra in 1976 and at the death of Germán in 1978.

GAL stands for Grupos Antiterroristas de Liberación (Antiterrorist Groups of Liberation), a group that began to operate in Iparralde in 1983, when it was credited with the assassination of the refugee Ramón Oñaederra Bergara, known as "Kattu," on December 20 of that year while he was working in a bar in Baiona (*Egin*, December 20, 1983, p. 1). The true identity of the group is unknown, but many people believe that it belongs to the extreme Right and that it has the ear of the Spanish and French governments.

6. The first part of the banner refers to Santi Brouard since he was a native of Lekeitio and that is where he was buried.

7. Field diary, Barakaldo, June 6, 1985.

8. "Reconversion" refers to the economic policy carried out with a view to Spain's entrance into the European Community. The policy has mainly affected the industrial zones of the Spanish state, where many workers have lost their jobs, and has sparked large popular demonstrations against it.

9. "Cataluña" refers to Barcelona, Tarragona, Lérida, and Gerona. The Países Catalans are all the territories where Catalan is spoken.

10. Txantrea is a popular neighborhood on the outskirts of Iruñea that is well known for its combative spirit. Sundays bring many visitors to its market.

11. Until 1987, when the creation of a public university in Iruñea was approved, Opus University was the only one in Nafarroa. It was created during the Franco era as part of the policy to isolate Nafarroa from the rest of Euskadi. Since it is a private university with very marked ideological tendencies and an expensive tuition, the only alternative open to students was to leave Nafarroa for their higher education. They went mainly to the university districts of Zaragoza and the different campuses of the University of the Basque Country.

12. A sweet drink native to Nafarroa made with wild fruits called *patxaranes* that are marinated in crushed grape skins or anise. It has become popular in the last few years and there are several commercial brands on the market.

13. The *txistu* is a native instrument similar to an end-blown flute, generally accompanied by the rhythm of a small drum, both played by the same person.

14. The human head that appears on the poster is that of Juan Ibáñez, the oldest man in the costumed group. The figures of the cabezudos are from a photograph taken in the doorway of the Ayuntamiento (Comparsa 1984:74–75).

15. The *txalaparta* is a percussion instrument that consists of wooden boards placed over two baskets. It is associated with a primitive pastoral economy. Today it is used in popular festivals and in rituals.

16. The sound *tralaralarala* has no meaning and was inserted as a rhythmic element.

17. *Ohe* is an onomatopoeic sound that produces a rhythm suitable for marching.

18. The Gestoras pro Amnistía are organizations within the abertzale Left that support the liberation of Basque political prisoners and organize activities to that end.

19. *Euskaldunberri* is frequently used to denote a person whose first language was not Euskara but who learned it as an adolescent or an adult. In the words of writer Xabier Kintana, "This constituted a notable exception in Bilbao at the time, thirty years ago, when during a time of the most severe repression there wasn't so much as a method for beginning to study Euskara" (*Egin*, June 7, 1985, p. 3).

20. Ibid.

21. The plaza was named in honor of two ETA members shot in 1974 under the Franco dictatorship; this action generated general reproach at the time. Paredes Manot (Txiki) was the son of an emigrant, and Angel Otaegi was born in Noarbe (Azkoitia). Both passed into history as popular heroes.

22. Institutionalized competitions in which bertsolariak compete for a title. Elimination rounds begin at the local and territorial levels, then move on to the finals. The title comes from the word *txapela* (beret) for the beret that is given to the winner along with money and a trophy. These competitions are very popular.

23. Chorus of mixed voices from Gasteiz, known for the quality of their performances both inside and outside Euskadi.

24. The *blusas* are groups of men dressed in blue trousers and blue-and-white-striped shirts who encourage participation in the festivities of La Blanca in Gasteiz.

25. *Momotxorrak* are characters from the carnival of Alsasu. They wear ox horns and cowbells that clang at the slightest movement.

CHAPTER SIX. DIVERSITY AND CONTRASTS PRESENTED
BY EUSKALERRIA

1. Gómez Piñeiro's economic information (1980) concerning the valleys of Roncal and Salazar has been modified using data from informants.

2. The *Sotera* is famous for having won numerous rowing championships. The fishing boat championships are very popular and are held annually during the summer months. Vessels represent different locations with a fishing tradition. The competitions take place in Bizkaia on the Bilbo, Ciervana, Bermeo, and Lekeitio estuaries. In Gipuzkoa they take place in Donostia, Zarautz, Hondarribia, and Pasaia. Outside Euskalerria, in Cantabria, they are held in Castro-Urdiales, Santoña, and Santander; and in Galicia, in La Coruña. The fishing boats are known by name. Those with the longest tradition among Basque vessels, in addition to the *Sotera*, are the *Kaiku* from Sestao, *La Jarrillera* from Portugalete, the *Iberia* from Sestao, and the *Urkilorak* from Donostia. The championships are followed with great interest, and fans travel about to the locations where the competitions are held. (Information provided by Goio Martínez-Arteaga.)

3. Field journal from Santurtzi, June 6, 1985.

4. Leading characters in the carnivals that are celebrated annually in the Navarrese towns of Ituren and Zubieta. They are unmistakable because of their unique costumes: cone caps with colored ribbons, white skirts, and sheepskins. They march as a group with a measured rhythm that rings the two large cowbells each wears tied to his waist with a cord.

5. Field journal, Hernani, June 2, 1985, noted by Txemi Apaolaza.

6. Ibid.

7. The above quotations are from interviews conducted in Rentería on June 1, 1985, by Julio González.

8. Field journal from Ordizia, June 2, 1985, kept by Agustín Ramos.

9. Field journal from Barakaldo, kept by Ana Isabel Gandarias and Rosa María Gañán, June 6, 1985.

10. Herrera de la Mancha is a prison near Madrid where several Basque political prisoners are serving their sentences.

11. Field journal, Agurain, June 8, 1985, kept by Karmele San Pedro.

12. Field journal from Tutera, June 4, 1985, kept by Antxon Sánchez.

13. Field journal from Etxarri-Aranaz, June 9, 1985, kept by Amaia Vázquez.

Glossary

Abertzale: Patriot. The term is frequently used to refer to the radical Left; for example, to Herri Batasuna. But it is also used to refer to a person identified with the Basque cause.

AEK: Alfabetatze Euskalduntze Koordinakundea. A popular organization that has dedicated more than twenty-five years to teaching and developing Euskara.

Aguirre, José Antonio: Politician and first president of the Basque government before the Spanish Civil War.

AIZAN: A women's group within Herri Batasuna.

Aizu: A Euskara-language magazine published by AEK.

Araban euskaraz: In Araba in Euskara. Popular annual activity in Araba on behalf of Euskara in which participants walk several kilometers.

Arenaza: Prehistoric caves located in Bizkaia.

Aresti, Gabriel: A Basque poet tied to the urban world of Bilbo.

Asamblea de Mujeres: Groups belonging to the feminist movement that function locally in neighborhoods, towns, and cities.

Azurmendi, María José: Professor of sociolinguistics who teaches Euskara at the University of the Basque Country.

Barandiaran, José Miguel: Esteemed anthropologist who dedicated the greater part of his long life to the study of Basque culture. He died in December 1991 at the age of 101, a few days short of his birthday.

Barnategi: An institution that offers Euskara courses in a boarding-school atmosphere; the courses last from fifteen days to a year.

Barricada: Well-known rock group that creates and performs in Spanish.

Baserri: A typical farmhouse in the middle zone of Euskalerria.

Berezko: That which happens inevitably and under its own power.

Bertsolari: A person who improvises verses in Euskara. Although there are a few women bertsolariak, men dominate the genre.

Borda, Itxaro: A woman writer from Iparralde who creates in Euskara.

Brouard, Santi: An abertzale leader who was president of HASI when he was assassinated in November 1984.

CNT: Central Nacional de Trabajadores; now Central General de Trabajadores.

Comunidad Autónoma Vasca: Political and administrative term used to designate the territories of Araba, Gipuzkoa, and Bizkaia. It is one of the seventeen territorial divisions of the Spanish state. Each division has an autonomous government.

Deia: Newspaper whose expressed ideology is close to that of PNV.

Diario Vasco: Newspaper with conservative tendencies, widespread throughout Gipuzkoa and currently becoming popular throughout Araba.

DYA: Asociación de Ayuda en Carretera. A group that assists motorists.

EA: Eusko Alkartasuna. A party with nationalist ideology that arose out of schism in the PNV under the leadership of Carlos Garaikoetxea, former lehendakari.

EAB: Emakume Abertzale Batza (Union of Patriotic Women). An organization created in April 1922 by women members of the PNV to carry out cultural, political, and public assistance tasks.

EE: Euskadiko Ezkerra. A party that tries to reconcile nationalistic tendencies with socialistic ones. In the 1990s the party is in crisis, and two schism groups have emerged: Auñamendi and Renovación Democrática.

Egin: Newspaper whose ideology favors the abertzale Left, especially Herri Batasuna.

Ekain: Prehistoric caves located in Gipuzkoa.

Ekintza: Action.

El País: Newspaper with socialist leanings; it has the largest circulation in the Spanish state.

Enbeita, Balentin: A famous bertsolari from Bizkaia.

Ertsi: To close.

Eskualde: Region, district.

ETB: Euskal Telebista. Basque television network transmit on one channel in Euskara and on another in Spanish.

Etxeberria, Feli: A specialist in bilingualism and a professor at the University of the Basque Country. She has played a major role in the institutionalization of the ikastolas.

Euskadi: Political term that includes the four historical territories of Araba, Gipuzkoa, Bizkaia, and Nafarroa.

Euskadi Buru Batzar: The leading decision-making body within the Basque Nationalist party (PNV).

Euskaldun: A person who speaks Euskara.

Euskaldunberri: A person who learned Euskara as a second language.

Euskaldunzaharra: A person who speaks Euskara as his or her mother tongue.

Euskalerria: The geographic and cultural entity that includes the seven territories.

Euskal Herrian Euskaraz: In Euskalerria in Euskara. A social organization of the abertzale Left that proclaims Euskara as the language of Euskalerria.

Euskal rock: Music that has been developing during the 1980s and 1990s; it is principally associated with the urban ambience and social characteristics of Basque society. The groups use both Euskara and Spanish.

Euskaltegi: Academies where Euskara is taught for adults at all levels, with flexible hours throughout the day.

Euskaltzaindia: Academy of the

Basque Language; founded in 1918, it has its headquarters in Bilbo.

Eusko Gudariak: A song of the Basque soldier that is sung at ritual moments and at meetings of the abertzale Left.

Eusko Jaurlaritza: The Basque government; its headquarters are in Gasteiz.

Exeberri, Xabier: A boy who was struck and killed by a car as he was returning home from participating in Korrika 1. He is memorialized in every Korrika.

Fontán, Amaia: AEK representative in Iparralde during the fourth Korrika.

Galdeano, Xabier: Journalist with *Egin* who was assassinated by the GAL.

Ganuza, María Josefa: Wife of Telesforo Monzón.

Gau eskola: A night school where Euskara is taught to adults.

Gerriko: A sash worn about the waist.

Gestoras pro Amnistía: Organizations within the abertzale Left that favor the liberation of Basque political prisoners and organize activities to that end.

Gudari: Fighter; Basque soldier.

HABE: Helduen Alfabetatzen eta Berreuskalduntzen Erakunde. Institute dedicated to recovering and teaching Euskara to adults.

Harri: Stone.

HASI: Herriko Alderdi Sozialista Iraultzalea (Popular Socialist Revolutionary party), integrated within the Herri Batasuna coalition.

HB: Herri Batasuna. Coalition that represents the radical nationalist Left.

Hegoalde: Southern zone; a term used to denominate the four historical territories located in Spanish territory: Araba, Bizkaia, Gipuzkoa, and Nafarroa.

Herri: People.

Herrialde: Territory.

Herri Urrats: Steps of the people. Popular annual activity in Iparralde for promoting Euskara in which participants walk several kilometers.

Hitz: Word.

Ibilaldia: March. Popular annual activity for promoting Euskara in Bizkaia in which participants walk several kilometers.

Ikastola: School where primary or secondary education is conducted in Euskara.

Ikurriña: The Basque flag.

Indarra: Strength.

Iparralde: The north side. A term used to refer to the three territories located in France: Lapurdi, Nafarroa Beherea, and Zuberoa.

Irastorza, Teresita: Female writer from Iparralde who creates in Euskara.

Iriondo, Lourdes: Female writer and poet who creates in Euskara.

Irrintzi: A kind of yodeling yell with which people communicate in open country.

Jakin: A literary philosophical journal published in Euskara.

Kalzada, Julen: A key figure in the construction of the Euskara literacy and teaching movement; he is currently involved in the direction of AEK.

Kantaldi: Musical audition. The term refers to music festivals of Basque songs and music.

Kilometroak: The kilometers. A

popular annual activity in Gipuzkoa for promoting Euskara in
which participants walk several
kilometers.

Korrikalariak: Runners.

Korrika txiki: The little Korrika.

Lafitte, Pierre: An expert of Euskara
who lived and died in Iparralde and
was highly respected throughout
Euskalerria.

Lamiñak: Spirits in Basque mythology
that are generally presented as
females.

Landa, Mariasun: Female writer of
children's literature who creates
in Euskara and is a professor of
literature at the University of the
Basque Country.

Lauburu: Basque emblem; it consists
of four round intertwined elements.

Lehendakari: President of the Basque
government.

Lekuona, Manuel: Male writer who
creates in Euskara and studies
Basque oral literature.

Madariaga, Julen: Founder of ETA.

Mari: Numen of Basque mythology.

Mintegi, Laura: Female writer and
essayist who creates in Euskara; she
is also a professor at the University
of the Basque Country.

Momotxorrak: Popular characters of
the Alsasu carnival.

Monzón, Telesforo (1904–1981): Important nationalist leader. He was
linked to the PNV from before the
Spanish Civil War to the mid-1950s,
and he held several consecutive
posts, including minister in the
Second Spanish Republic. After he
left the PNV he became identified
with radical nationalism and the
pro-independence position. He

was a member and parliamentary
representative of HB.

Muga(k): Border(s).

Mugalari: An expert on the border.

Mugarri(ak): Boundary stone(s).

Nafarroa Oiñez: Nafarroa on foot.
Popular annual activity in Nafarroa for promoting Euskara in
which participants walk several
kilometers.

Oñaederra, Lourdes: Professor of
literature at the University of the
Basque Country. She writes in
Euskara.

Oñeztarri: Flash of lightning.

Oñeztu: Flash of lightning.

Orixe: Nicolas Ormaetxea, a writer
and poet who created in Euskara.

Ortzi: Pseudonym of Francisco Leta-
mendia, a famous politician at one
time involved in the direction of
EE and later in that of HB; he is
currently a professor of the history
of ideas at the University of the
Basque Country.

Oskorri: Famous musical group that
creates and performs in Euskara.

OTAN: NATO, North Atlantic
Treaty Organization.

Patxaran: A sweet drink native to
Nafarroa made with wild fruits
called *patxaranes* that are marinated
in anise and crushed grape skins.

Plaza-gizon: Literally, a man of the
plaza or town square. The term
alludes to the centrality of the figure
of the bertsolari, who improvises
verses in a central location.

PNV: Partido Nacional Vasco (Basque
Nationalist party). Founded by
Sabino Arana; at the time of this
writing it holds the parliamentary
majority in the Basque government.

PSOE: Partido Socialista Obrero Español (Spanish Workers' Socialist party). At this writing the party holds the parliamentary majority in the Spanish Parliament under the leadership of Felipe González.

Rotaetxe, Karmele: Female professor of linguistics and professor of Euskara at the University of the Basque Country.

Santimamiñe: Prehistoric caves located in Bizkaia.

Sarraonaindia, Joseba: A contemporary male writer and ex–political prisoner who creates in Euskara.

Satrustegui, José María: An anthropologist and member of Euskaltzaindia. He is also a parish priest in Urdiain, Nafarroa.

SEASKA: The ikastola association of Iparralde.

Txakurra: Dog. Used in popular slang to refer to the police.

Txalaparta: A percussion instrument associated with the pastoral economy.

Txaranga: A musical group.

Txiki: Little.

Txistu: Wind instrument with four holes resembling a flute.

Udako Euskal Unibertsitatea: Basque University Summer School; offers courses in Euskara.

Urretavizcaya, Arantza: An outstanding female writer who creates in Euskara.

Xalbador: Pseudonym of Fernando Aire, a bertsolari from Iparralde who is considered one of the best bertsolaris of all time. His life was used as the theme of a "pastoral" presented in 1991.

Xanpun: Pseudonym of Iparralde bertsolari Emmanuel Sein.

Xiberuko maskaradak: Masquerades of Zuberoa. Popular performances given in Euskara in Zuberoa.

Zazpiak Bat: Seven in one. Slogan that refers to the union of the seven territories of Euskalerria.

Ziprita, Elvira: A teacher who was extraordinarily dedicated to the development of Euskara, especially to the institutionalization of primary education in Euskara.

Zona euskaldun: The zone where Euskara is spoken.

Appendix

Basque Place-Names and

Their Spanish Equivalents

Basque	Spanish
Abaurre Gaina	Abaurre Alta
Agurain	Salvatierra
Araba	Alava
Baiona	Bayona
Bilbo	Bilbao
Donibane Lohizune	San Juan de Luz
Donostia	San Sebastián
Enkarteria	Encartaciones
Erribera	La Ribera
Erronkari	El Roncal
Gasteiz	Vitoria
Hondarribia	Fuenterrabia
Kanpezu	Campezo
Lizarra	Estella
Nafarroa	Navarra
Ondarru	Ondarroa
Ordizia	Villafranca de Ordicia
Orreaga	Roncesvalles
Otsagi	Ochagavia
Pasaia	Pasajes
Santurtzi	Santurce
Tutera	Tudela

Bibliography

A. B. 1985. "La campaña de imagen de AEK. La Korrika-4 en marcha." *Euzkadi* 184 (April 4): 24–25.

Abon, Satur. 1985. "Entrevista Remigio Mendiburu la sinceridad de una extensa obra." *Punto y Hora*, no. 383: 16–20.

"Acosado por las autoridades burgalesas Treviño Araba da." *Punto y Hora*, no. 211 (1981): 13–16.

"AEK considera vergonzosa la información que *Deia* dió de la Korrika." *Egin*, December 13, 1983.

"AEK hizo balance de la 'Korrika-2': más de once millones de beneficio." *Deia*, August 7, 1982.

Agirre, Jesús María, et al. 1985. *Euskarazko irakaskuntza Bizkaian: arazoak eta zenbait proposamen. La enseñanza en euskera en Vizcaya: problemas y algunas propuestas*. Bilbao: Colección Magisterio, Derio. Editorial Desclée de Brower.

Aguirre Franco, Rafael. 1971. *Enciclopedia general ilustrada del País Vasco*. Annex. Basque games and sports. San Sebastián: Editorial Auñamendi.

Aizu, November 1983, pp. 10–13.

Alfabetatze Euskalduntze Koordinakundea [AEK]. 1982. [Three mimeographed pages published on the occasion of the second Korrika.]

——. 1983. *La alternativa popular al euskara. Euskararen alternativa herritarra*. Newspaper published on the occasion of the second Korrika.

——. 1984. *Korrika 4. Finantziaketa aurreproiektoa*. Pamphlet published on the occasion of the fourth Korrika.

——. 1985a. *Korrika. Herriaren erantzuna euskararen alde*. Pamphlet published on the occasion of the fourth Korrika.

——. 1985b. *Korrika komikorrika*. 85/Ekaina.

——. 1985c. [Triptych with photographs and reproductions of the posters published for the fourth Korrika.]

——. 1987. *AEK: Alfabetatze Euskalduntze Koordinakundea*. Pamphlet published on the occasion of the fifth Korrika.

——. n.d. *Korrika 3. Finantziaketarako aurreproiektoa*. Undated pamphlet.

Amundarain, Dionisio. 1981. "Korrika eta euskaltzaindia." *Egin*, February 1. Translated in *Punto y Hora*, no. 222 (1981): 37–39.

Apaolaza Beraza, Txemi. 1985–87. "Zalduondo, proceso de formación de una identidad." *Kobie. Antropología cultural*. Bizkaiko Foru Aldundia-Diputación Foral de Vizcaya, no. 2, pp. 151–77.

"Apoteósico recibimiento a la Korrika en Gasteiz." *Egin*, December 9, 1983, p. 23.

Aresti, Gabriel. 1976. *Obra guztiak*. Poemak I, Poemak II. Donostia: Luis Haran-buru, Editorea Kriselu.

————. 1979. *Maldan beheran (Pendiente abajo) Harri eta herri (Piedra y pueblo)*. Bilingual edition by Javier Atienza. Madrid: Ediciones Cátedra.

Aretxaga, Santos Begoña. 1988. *Los funerales en el Nacionalismo radical vasco*. San Sebastián: La Primitiva Casa Baroja.

Arregui, Begoña. 1989. "The Evolution of Fertility in the Basque Country: 1950–1986." Ph.D. diss., University of Southampton.

Atlas de Navarra. Geográfico—económico histórico. Barcelona: Editorial Diáfora.

Aulestia, Gorka. 1981. "Poetry and Politics: Basque Poetry as an Instrument of National Revival. Part I." *World Literature Today* 55, no. 1 (Winter): 48–52.

————. 1982. "Poetry and Politics: Basque Poetry as an Instrument of National Revival. Part II." *World Literature Today* 56, no. 3 (Summer): 457–61.

"Autorizada la Korrika-2 en Navarra." *Egin*, May 22, 1982, p. 31.

Azurmendi, M. 1985. "Unas mil personas se concentraron en el paso de Biria-tou. La actitud francesa dió un relieve especial al homenaje." *Deia*, March 24, p. 10.

Bai Euskarari. [Various documents from the group's archives in Bilbao.]

Barandiaran, José Miguel de. 1972. *Obras completas*. Bilbao: Editorial la Gran Enciclopedia Vasca. Vol. 1.

Basterretxea, José "Oskillaso." 1984. *El libro negro del Euskara*. Bilbao: La Gran Enciclopedia Vasca.

B.E.L. 1971. "Balparda las Herrerias, Gregorio de." In *Enciclopedia Ilustrada del País Vasco, Diccionario*, pp. 621–22. Donostia: Auñamendi.

"Bilboko bihotzeraino sartuko da euskara gaur Korrikari esker." *Egin*, December 11, 1983, p. 3

"Bizkai mailako Korrikaren aurkezpena herenegun Bilbon." *Egin*, May 19, 1985, p. 28.

Borda, Itxaro. 1984. *Emakumea idasle*. San Sebastián: Editorial Txertoa.

Bruner, Edward M., ed. 1983. *Text, Play and Story: The Construction and Recon-struction of Self and Society*. Proceedings of the American Ethnological Society. Washington, D.C.: American Ethnological Society.

C-Núñez, Luis. 1977. *Opresión y defensa del Euskara*. San Sebastián: Editorial Txertoa.

Cabrero, Anabel. 1982. "Inicio de la campaña cultural de la Korrika." *Tribuna Vasca*, May 15.

Caja Laboral Popular. 1983. *Atlas de Euskal Herria*, dir. Francisco Javier Gómez Piñeiro. Donostia: Txertoa.

Caro Baroja, Julio. 1957. "El sociocentrismo de los pueblos españoles." In *Razas, pueblos y linajes*, 263–92. Madrid: Ediciones de la Revista de Occidente.

————. 1965. "Folklore experimental: el carnaval de Lanz (1964)." *Príncipe de Viana* 98–99: 5–22.

————. 1982. *La casa en Navarra*. 4 vols. Pamplona: Caja de Ahorros de Navarra.

————. 1985. *Los vascos y el mar*. 2d ed. San Sebastián: Editorial Txertoa.

Christian, William A., Jr. 1972. *Person and God in a Spanish Valley*. New York and London: Seminar Press.

Clark, Robert P. 1980. *The Basques: The Franco Years and Beyond*. Reno: University of Nevada Press.

———. 1984. *The Basque Insurgents. ETA, 1952–1980*. Madison: University of Wisconsin Press.

Comparsa de Gigantes y Cabezudos de Pamplona. 1984. *Los gigantes de Pamplona*. Pamplona: Excmo. Ayuntamiento de Pamplona y Caja de Ahorros Municipal de Pamplona.

"Con Bego y Carmen Galdeano. Un hombre dedicado por entero a los demás." *Punto y Hora*, no. 386 (1985): 10–12.

"Con el lema 'Euskaraz eta kitto' partirá la Korrika-3 de Baiona." *Egin*, November 19, 1983, p. 1.

Cucó, Josepa, and Joan J. Pujadas, coords. 1990. *Identidades colectivas. Etnicidad y sociabilidad en la Península Ibérica*. Valencia: Generalitat Valenciana.

Dahrendorf, Rolf. 1991. "¿Una Europa de las regiones?" *El País*, October 10, pp. 2–3.

Debray, Regis. 1991. "El desafío zoológico." *El País*, October 10, p. 5.

"Del euskara batua al AEK: PNV o el partidismo entorpecedor del Euskara." *Punto y Hora*, no. 266 (1982): 9–16.

del Valle, Teresa. 1983a. "Korrika, euskal etniaren ezangarritzat." *Egin*, December 9, p. 17.

———. 1983b. "La mujer vasca a través del análisis del espacio: utilización y significado." *Lurralde* 6: 251–69.

———. 1984. "Korrika: una acción simbólica vasca." *Langaiak* 5 (April): 93–105.

———. 1985. "Una aproximación al estudio y análisis de la etnicidad vasca." *Actas del Segundo Congreso de Antropología*, 241–45. Madrid: Centro Nacional de Información Artística Arqueología y Etnología.

———. 1988. *Korrika: rituales de la lengua en el espacio*. Barcelona: Editorial Anthropos.

del Valle, Teresa, Txemi Apaolaza, and Agustín Ramos. 1990. "Los procesos de etnicidad en Euskadi." In *Identidades colectivas. Etnicidad y sociabilidad en la Península Ibérica*, coord. Josepa Cucó and Joan J. Pujadas, 139–50. Valencia: Generalitat Valenciana.

del Valle, Teresa, et al. 1985. *Mujer vasca. Imagen y realidad*. Barcelona: Editorial Anthropos.

Departamento de Cultura, Gobierno Vasco. 1985. *Congreso de Historia de Euskal Herria*.

Descheemaeker, Jacques. n.p. "La Frontière Pyrenéenne de l'Ocean à l'Aragon." Extrait de la *Revue Générale de Droit International Public 1941–1945*. Paris: Éditions A. Pedone.

"Dibujos animados para anunciar la 'Korrika-83.'" *Egin*, November 25, 1985, p. 27.

Douglass, William A. 1978. "Influencias fronterizas en un pueblo Navarro."
    Ethnica 14: 39–52.
————. 1980. "Inventing an Ethnic Identity: The First Basque Festival." *Halcyon*
    2: 115–30.
————, ed. 1985. *Basque Politics: A Case Study in Ethnic Nationalism*. Reno:
    Associated Faculty Press and Basque Studies Program.
Douglass, William A., and Jon Bilbao. 1975. *Amerikanuak: Basques in the New*
    World. Reno: University of Nevada Press.
Echaniz, J. M. 1982. "El ayuntamiento guerniqués no colabora en la 'Korrika.' "
    El Correo Español, May 29.
Echenique Elizondo, Maria Teresa. 1984. *Historia lingüística vasco-románica*.
    Madrid: Confederación Española de Cajas de Ahorro.
"El Ayuntamiento de Donostia subvenciona la Korrika-4 con 800.000 pesetas."
    Egin, May 25, 1985.
"El Ayuntamiento de Eibar apoya y subvenciona la Korrika-2." *Egin*, May 20,
    1982.
"El Ayuntamiento pamplonés: 110.000 de subvención para la Korrika." *Deia*,
    May 27, 1982.
"El comic también corre desde ayer en la Korrika." *La Gaceta del Norte*, June 1,
    1985.
"El euskaltegi de Vitoria apoya la Korrika." *Tribuna Vasca*, May 20, 1982.
"El euskera enfrenta al PNV con la izquierda abertzale." *Tribuna Vasca*, May 14,
    1982.
"El gobernador civil Ansuátegui prohibe la Korrika-2 en Navarra." *Egin*,
    May 19, 1982, p. 1.
"El testigo, tras bordear el mar, vuelve al secano." *Egin*, June 8, 1985, p. 33.
"En Donibane Lohitzun, a pesar del cierre de la frontera un millar de personas
    dieron su último adiós a Xabier Galdeano." *Deia*, April 7, 1985, p. 2.
"Entrevista con . . . Jimeno Jurio. La búsqueda de la identidad de Navarra."
    Punto y Hora, no. 269 (1982): 19–24.
"En Ustaritze se rindió homenaje a Pierre Lafitte." *Egin*, June 2, 1985, p. 29.
"Euskadiko Ezkerra apoya la Korrika." *Egin*, May 15, 1982.
Euskal Kulturaren urtekaria (Donostia). 1984. "Alfabetatze Euskalduntze Ko-
    ordinakundea—AEK Historia laburra." *Argia* (1984): 176–77.
Euskaltzaindia. Real Academia de la Lengua Vasca. 1979. *Conflicto lingüístico*
    en Euskadi, SIADECO Report. Summary by Martin de Ugalde. Bilbao:
    Ediciones Vascas Argitaletxea.
————. 1984. *Euskaltzaindiaren historia laburra*. Bilbao: Euskaltzaindia Real
    Academia de la Lengua Vasca.
"Eusko Jaurlaritza-Kultur Saila A.E.K.-ren Eskaera Udaletan." Document from
    the HABE archive.
Fairén Guillén, Victor. 1946. "Contribución al estudio de la Facería internacional
    de los valles del Roncal y Baretons." *Príncipe de Viana* 7: 271–96.

———. 1955. "Sobre las facerías internacionales en Navarra." *Príncipe de Viana* 16: 507–24.

Fernández, James W. 1983. "Convivial Attitudes: The Ironic Play of Tropes in an International Kayak Festival in Northern Spain." In *Text, Play, and Story: The Construction and Reconstruction of Self and Society*, ed. Edward M. Bruner, 199–229. Proceedings of the American Ethnological Society.

———. 1986. "Enclosures: Boundary Maintenance and Its Representations over Time in Asturian Mountain Villages (Spain)." Paper presented at the symposium on "Symbolism Through Time," January 12–21, Fez, Morocco.

Fontán, Amaia. 1985. [Original manuscript of the message read by the author in Atharratze.]

"Gabriel Aresti y Santi Brouard fueron homenajeados in Bilbo al paso de la Korrika." *Egin*, June 7, 1985, p. 3.

García, Carmen T. 1982. "AEK en contra de las instituciones." *Euzkadi* 33: 30–33.

Garmendia Larrañaga, Juan. 1973. *Inauteria: el carnaval vasco*. San Sebastián: Sociedad Gipuzcoana de Ediciones y Publicaciones.

———. 1984. *Carnaval en Navarra*. San Sebastián: Haranburu Editor.

Gellner, Ernest. 1991. "Fuerzas liberadas." *El País*, October 10, p. 7.

Goienhetxe, Manex. 1979a. "Continúa la discriminación del euskara." *Punto y Hora*, no. 129: 34–35.

———. 1979b. "El euskara en Iparralde, un problema de supervivencia." *Punto y Hora*, no 126: 36–37.

———. 1979c. "La colonización de euskadi norte asociaciones culturales y carta cultural." *Punto y Hora*, no. 125: 36–37.

Gómez-Ibáñez, Daniel Alexander. 1975. *The Western Pyrenees: Differential Evolution of the French and Spanish Borderland*. Oxford: Clarendon Press.

Gómez Piñeiro, Francisco Javier, et al. 1980. *Geografía de Euskal Herria*. Volume 5: *Laburdi, Benabarra, Zuberoa*. San Sebastián: Luis Haranburu.

"Gran respuesta popular a la Korrika Euskal Herria." *La Gaceta del Norte*, February 25, 1980, p. 9.

Gurrutxaga, Ander. 1985. *El códico nacionalista vasco durante el franquismo*. Barcelona: Editorial Anthropos.

H. 1980. "Euskerólogos en Gernika." *Punto y Hora*, no. 189: 59–60.

"HABE Plan de Actuación, 1982–1983." Mimeo.

"HASI felicita a AEK por el enorme éxito de la Korrika." *Egin*, December 14, 1985, p. 22.

Haitzerre. 1982a. "AEK, la Korrika y el ebb." *Egin*, May 12, p. 28.

———. 1982b. "Indignadas reacciones ante la prohibición gubernativa." *Egin*, May 20, p. 3.

———. 1983. "Hirugarren 'Korrika' edonon eta beti euskaraz baliatzeko." *Egin*, December 5, p. 31.

Heiberg, Marianne. 1989. *The Making of the Basque Nation*. Cambridge: Cambridge University Press.

Henningsen, Gustav. 1980. *The Witches' Advocate: Basque Witchcraft and the Spanish Inquisition (1609–1614)*. Reno: University of Nevada Press.

Hobsbawm, Eric. 1986. "Introduction: Inventing Traditions." In *The Invention of Tradition*, ed. Eric Hobsbawm and Terence Ranger, 1–14. Cambridge: Cambridge University Press.

———. 1991. "Un futuro poco prometedor." *El País*, October 10, p. 8.

Hobsbawm, Eric, and Terence Ranger, eds. 1986. *The Invention of Tradition*. Cambridge: Cambridge University Press.

Homobono, José Ignacio. 1982. "Espacio y fiesta en País Vasco." *Lurralde, Investigación y espacio*, no. 6, pp. 91–119.

"Irakasles de AEK creen que el Gobierno vasco plantea una 'guerra abierta' a la Coordinadora." *Egin*, June 9, 1985, p. 23.

"Iruñea se convirtió en la capital del euskara." *Egin*, June 10, 1985, p. 7.

J. A. 1985. "Estudio antropológico en torno a la Korrika." *Egin*, May 19, p. 28.

J. F. 1985. "Terminó Korrika-4." *Zer Egin*, no. 194: 12–13.

Jackson, Gabriel. 1991. "El primer siglo de nacionalismo." *El País*, October 10, pp. 4–5.

Jimmi. 1985. "Hoy mismo en Iruñea: Martxa Korrikan." *Egin*, June 7, p. 18.

"Karrikan euskara korrika." *Punto y Hora*, no. 235 (1981): 44–47.

"Korrika eta euskaltzaindia." *Egin*, February 1, 1981, p. 15.

"Korrika eta euskaltzaindia." *Punto y Hora*, no. 212 (1981): 37–39.

"Korrika Euskal Herria." *Punto y Hora*, no. 205 (1980).

"Korrika Euskal Herria puede dar la campanada." *Egin*, February 25, 1980, p. 30.

"¡Korrika, Korrika! un sí al euskera." *Punto y Hora*, no. 205 (1980): 9–11.

"Korrikaren historia." *Aizu* (November 1983): [8]–9.

"Korrika 3 Más multitudinaria que nunca." *Punto y Hora*, no. 232 (1983): 22–24.

"Kuestazio Herritarra Euskararen Alde." [Full-page announcement.] *Egin*, November 26, 1983, p. 9.

Kultura Saila HABE. 1981. *Helduen euskalduntzerako programazioa*. Zarautz: Itxaropena.

"La Korrika de este año ha sido la más participativa, según AEK." *El Correo Español*, June 10, 1985.

"La Korrika de este año, llevará como lema Euskaraz eta kitto." *Egin*, November 5, 1983, p. 5.

"La Korrika de este año, llevará como lema Euskaraz eta kitto." *Egin*, December 5, 1983, p. 31.

"La Korrika despertó a los vecinos." *Navarra Hoy*, June 5, 1985, p. 11.

"La Korrika entra hoy en tierras de Vizcaya." *La Gaceta del Norte*, June 6, 1985.

"La Korrika homenajea a Santiago Brouard a su paso por las calles de Bilbao." *La Gaceta del Norte*, June 6, 1985.

"La Korrika inicia hoy desde Baiona su recorrido por Euskal Herria." *Egin*, December 3, 1983, p. 3.

"La Korrika inicia su marcha el día 31 en Zuberoa y finaliza en Pamplona el 9 de junio." *Diario Vasco*, May 8, 1985, p. 9.

"La Korrika llega hoy a Bizkaia recordando a Aresti y Brouard." *Egin*, June 6, 1985, p. 1.

"La Korrika se puso en marcha con mucha y festiva compañía." *Egin*, December 4, 1983, p. 1.

"La Korrika superó las cotas de participación de hace un año en Iparralde." *Egin*, May 25, 1982, p. 21.

"La Korrika tendrá una subvención." *Tribuna Vasca*, May 20, 1982.

"La Korrika unió a dos generaciones." *Navarra Hoy*, June 4, 1985.

"La Korrika visitará setenta pueblos de Araba, completando un recorrido de 412 kilómetros." *Egin*, May 25, 1985.

"La Ribera navarra celebró con entusiasmo la llegada de la Korrika." *Egin*, June 5, 1985, p. 22.

Lasa Apalategui, J. 1973. *Ensayos críticos sobre la unificación literaria del vascuence*. Zarauz: Itxaropena.

Legarreta, Josu. 1982. " 'Korrika-82': El pueblo no quiere engaños." *Deia*, May 22.

Legislación sobre comunidades autónomas. 1. País Vasco. Cataluña. Galicia. Andalucia. Madrid: Editorial Tecnos, 1982.

Llera Ramo, Francisco José. 1984. "La estructura política vasca en 1983." In *Revista de Sociología: Papers*, nos. 22–23, pp. 93–147. Universitat Autónoma de Barcelona.

Llobera, Josep R. 1991. "Una idea impensable." *El País*, October 10, p. 6.

"Los huelguistas de AEK desconfían de la voluntad negociadora' del Gobierno." *Egin*, May 29, 1985, p. 21.

"Los organizadores de la Korrika 2 en Navarra siguen haciendo gestiones para lograr su autorización." *Egin*, May 21, 1982, p. 20.

"Los txikis por el euskera." *Navarra Hoy*, June 8, 1985, p. 6.

Méndez, Julián. 1985. "El testigo de la Korrika 85 detuvo su marcha en las calles de Vitoria." *El Correo Español*, June 9.

"Mensaje de Pierre Lafitte." *Egin*, June 10, 1985, p. 7.

"Miles de personas recibieron el final de la Korrika 85 en Pamplona." *Diario Vasco*, June 10, 1985.

Monumentos nacionales de Euskadi Gipuzcoa. 1985. Zamudio, Vizcaya: Editorial Elexpuru. Vol. 2.

"¡Multitudinaria, más que en la edición anterior!" *Punto y Hora*, no. 268 (1982): 18–19.

1981eko Euskadiko Komunitate Autonomoko etxebizitza eta biztanlean zentsua. Biztanleriaren egitura. Censo de la población y vivienda de 1981 de la Comunidad Autónoma de Euskadi. Extructura de la población. Gasteiz: Gobierno Vasco.

"Número especial de la revista Korrok dedicado exclusivamente a la Korrika." *Egin*, May 24, 1985, p. 21.

Ormaetxea, Nicolas "Orixe." 1972. *Obras selectas Euskaldunak poema eta olerki guriak. Poema de los vascos y poesías completas.* San Sebastián: Editorial Auñamendi.

Ott, Sandra. 1981. *The Circle of Mountains: A Basque Sheepherding Community.* Oxford: Oxford University Press.

———. 1991. " 'Indarra': Some Reflections on a Basque Concept." In *Honour and Grace,* ed. J. Peristary and J. Pitt Rivers. Chicago: University of Chicago Press.

"Patxi Zabaleta: Por el número de escritores, la literature vasca en Nafarroa es floreciente." *Egin,* May 23, 1985.

Pelay Orozco, Miguel. 1978. *Oteiza su vida, su obra, su pensamiento, su palabra.* Bilbao: Editorial la Gran Enciclopedia Vasca.

Pérez-Agote, A. 1984. *La reproducción del nacionalismo. El caso vasco.* Madrid: Centro de Investigaciones Sociológicas, in collaboration with Siglo XXI.

Peristiany, J. and J. Pitt-Rivers, eds. 1990. *Honour and Grace in Anthropology.* New York: Cambridge University Press.

"Poema de Gabriel Aresti para la Korrika 3." *La Voz,* December 2–3, 1983.

Ruiz Olabuenaga, José Ignacio. 1984. *Atlas lingüístico vasco.* Gasteiz: Servicio Central de Publicaciones del Gobierno Vasco.

Ruiz Olabuenaga, J. I., and M. A. Marañon. 1983. *La lucha del euskera (Euskararen borroka).* Gasteiz: Gobierno Vasco.

Sahlins, Peter. 1989. *Boundaries: The Making of France and Spain in the Pyrenees.* Berkeley: University of California Press.

Sánchez Carrión "Txepetx," José María. 1981. *El espacio bilingüe.* Burlada: Eusko Ikaskuntza.

"Santi Brouaren oroimenezko Korrika, gaur Bilbon." *Egin,* June 6, 1985, p. 22.

"Santi Brouard eta Gabriel Aresti omenduak." *Egin,* June 7, 1985, p. 1.

Sarasola, Ibon. 1976. *Historia social de la literatura vasca.* Trans. Antonio Cid. Barcelona: AKAL.

Taldea. 1982. "La historia dirá quien tiene razón." *Deia,* May 30.

Thalamus Labandibar, Juan. 1931. "Contribución al estudio etnográfico del Pais Vasco continental." *Anuario de Eusko Folklore,* pp. 1–120.

"Treviño. Reducto del caciquismo castellano." *Punto y Hora,* no. 299 (1983): 11–13.

Turner, Victor W. 1988. *El proceso ritual: estructura y antiestructura.* 1969 (English ed.). Madrid: Taurus.

Txelu. 1982a. "El ayuntamiento de Portugalete no apoya la Korrika." *Egin,* May 20, p. 17.

———. 1982b. "El ayuntamiento de Portugalete no colaborará en los actos de la Korrika." *Tribuna Vasca,* May 19.

"Una decisión equivocada." [Editorial.] *Deia,* May 21, 1982, p. 2.

"Un refugiado de Azkoitia muerto a tiros en Baioan." *Egin,* December 20, 1983, p. 1.

Urabayen, Leoncio. 1959. *Estudios monográficos de geografía de los paises humanidos. Una geografía de Navarra.* Pamplona: Editorial LIBE.

Urbeltz Navarro, Juan Antonio. 1978. *Dantzak. Notas sobre las danzas tradicionales de los vascos*. [Mondragón]: Caja Laboral Popular.

Urrutia, Victor. 1984. "Transformaciones demográficas y organización en el País Vasco." *Revista de Sociología: Papers,* nos. 22–23, pp. 27–61. Universitat Autónoma de Barcelona.

Villán, Javier, and Felix Población. 1980. *Culturas en lucha Euskadi.* Madrid: Editorial SWAN.

"Vitoria tributa en recibimiento multitudinario a la Korrika-4 que hoy finaliza en Pamplona." *La Gaceta,* June 9, 1985.

Yrizar, Pedro de. 1981. *Contribución a la dialectología de la lengua vasca.* Dono-stia: Caja de Ahorros Provincial de Guipuzcoa/Gipuzkoako Aurreski Kutxa Probintziala.

Zubiaur Carreño, Francisco Javier. 1977. "Toponimia de San Martín de Unx (Navarra)." *Cuadernos de etnología y etnografía de Navarra* 9, no. 27: 415–62.

————. 1978. "Toponimia de San Martín de Unx según los amojonamientos de la villa en el siglo XVI." *Cuadernos de etnología y etnografía de Navarra* 10, no. 29: 255–71.

————. 1981. *Estudio etnográfico de San Martín de Unx.* Navarra: Gobierno de Navarra, Prensa, Publicaciones.

Zulaika, Joseba. 1987. *Tratado estético ritual vasco.* Donostia: La Primitiva Casa Baroja.

————. 1988. *Basque Violence: Metaphor and Sacrament.* Reno: University of Nevada Press.

"Zure atzetik nabil korika." *Enbata,* no. 873 (1985): [2].

Index

References to figures and illustrations are printed in boldface type.

211

The Basque Series

Escape via Berlin: Eluding Franco in
Hitler's Europe
  José Antonio de Aguirre
  introduction by Robert P. Clark

A Rebellious People: Basques,
Protests, and Politics
  Cyrus Ernesto Zirakzadeh

A View from the Witch's Cave:
Folktales of the Pyrenees
  edited by Luis de Barandiarán Irizar

Child of the Holy Ghost
  Robert Laxalt

Basque-English English-Basque
Dictionary
  Gorka Aulestia and Linda White

The Deep Blue Memory
  Monique Urza

Solitude: Art and Symbolism in the
National Basque Monument
  Carmelo Urza

The Circle of Mountains: A Basque
Shepherding Community
  Sandra Ott

Korrika: Basque Ritual for Ethnic
Identity
  Teresa del Valle